The Death of the Troubadour

The Late Medieval Resistance to the Renaissance

Gregory B. Stone

University of Pennsylvania Press
Philadelphia

Copyright © 1994 by the University of Pennsylvania
All rights reserved
Printed in the United States of America

Library of Congress Cataloging-in-Publication Data
Stone, Gregory B., 1961–
  The death of the troubadour : the late medieval resistance to the Renaissance / Gregory B. Stone
    p.   cm.
  Includes bibliographical references and index.
  ISBN 0-8122-3214-3
  1. Literature, Medieval—History and criticism. 2. Troubadours in literature. 3. Renaissance. I. Title.
PN682.T76S76 1994
809'.02—dc20   93-35923
                                                                          CIP

This book is dedicated to my parents,
NEIL AND AILEEN STONE

Contents

Acknowledgments ix

Introduction 1

1. Song as *Langue* 13
2. "Everyone Loves Thus..." 20
3. The *Speculum* of Song 33
4. The Burgher and the Bird 43
5. Anti-*Vida*, Anti-*Razo* 58
6. Lyric Secrecy 71
7. Four Lovers 82
8. Nameless Lovers 97
9. The Eaten Heart 101
10. Lyric Ignorance 109
11. Narrative Breakdown 134
12. Chaucer's Evening Sickness 143

Notes 199

Bibliography 221

Index 227

Acknowledgments

I wish to express my gratitude to those who have read versions of this book and offered advice and encouragement. These include R. Howard Bloch, Giuseppe Mazzotta, Alexandre Leupin, Stephen G. Nichols, and Douglas Collins.

Introduction

I

Among our various versions of the unfolding history of Western culture since Plato, one of the ideas that still looms large is the idea of the Renaissance: the idea that, somewhere in Europe at some time between the twelfth and sixteenth centuries, there took place a certain definitive rupture that parted Western cultural history into two, leaving earlier centuries on the side of the "ancient" and later ones on the side of the "modern." According to this idea of the Renaissance, the definitive rupture was not so much a *re-naissance* as a *naissance* pure and simple. What really matters about the Renaissance, for proponents of this idea, is not what seems to have mattered for the first "Renaissance men" such as Petrarch: the re-birth of philological interest in classical Roman and Greek literature; rather, it is the *unprecedented birth* of the concept and possibility of the individual, subjective self, the private, self-determining, unique, autonomous ego.

For the first time in Western history, according to this idea of the Renaissance, the driving cultural and creative force became the individual's desire to be *different*, to distinguish oneself from the crowd of others:

> The general European consensus is that the era of the Italian Renaissance created what we call individuality. By this is meant a state of inner and external liberation of the individual from the communal forms of the Middle Ages, forms which had constricted the pattern of his life, his activities, and his fundamental impulses through homogenizing groups. These had, as it were, allowed the boundaries of the individual to become blurred, suppressing the development of personal freedom, of intrinsic uniqueness, and of the sense of responsibility for one's self. I will set aside the question whether the Middle Ages lacked all traces of individuality. The conscious emphasis on individuality as a matter of principle does seem to have been the original accomplishment of the Renaissance. This took place in such a way that the will to power, to distinction, and to becoming honored and famous was diffused among men to a degree never before known. If for a time at the beginning of this period, as has been reported, there was no pervasive fashion in masculine attire, since each man wished to deport himself in a manner peculiar to himself, it was not a

matter of simple distinctiveness, of being different. The individual wanted to be *conspicuous*; he wanted to present himself more propitiously and more remarkably than was possible by means of the established forms. This is the behaviorial reality of the individualism of distinction, which is associated with the ambition of Renaissance man, with his ruthless self-aggrandizement, with his value emphasis on being unique.[1]

To be a Renaissance subject means to be distinct from and better than others; to reject public, conventional, social forms and embrace private, novel, individual inventions; to create one's own fashion, not simply accept the fashions of others. Whereas people of the Middle Ages appear content to labor within the limitations of a generalized anonymity, the primary aim of those of the Renaissance is to make a name for oneself, to forge a unique and specific identity, to be someone special.

This idea of the Renaissance, most famously articulated in the late nineteenth century by Jakob Burckhardt in *The Civilization of the Renaissance in Italy*, is a legacy of the Hegelian understanding of the history of culture as the manifestation of the dialectical development of the subject-object relation. For Burckhardt, the Middle Ages are a primitive or infantile stage of human history during which the subject, being essentially objective, does not know the difference between subject and object. In Burckhardt's Middle Ages, the individual ego is indistinguishable from the collective ego; the interior, private, or subjective individual mind is constituted by exterior, public, or objective conventional forms. Burckhardt's Renaissance is the maturation of subjectivity, as the subject becomes essentially subjective and thereby begins to recognize his or her alienation from the world "out there," begins to see a difference between self and others:

> In the Middle Ages both sides of human consciousness—that which was turned within as that which was turned without—lay dreaming or half awake beneath a common veil. The veil was woven of faith, illusion, and childish prepossession, through which the world and history were seen clad in strange hues. *Man was conscious of himself only as a member of a race, people, party, family, or corporation—only through some general category* [emphasis added]. In Italy this veil first melted into the air; an *objective* treatment of the State and of all the things in this world became possible. The *subjective* side at the same time asserted itself with corresponding emphasis; man became a spiritual *individual*, and recognized himself as such.[2]

Burckhardt's medieval subject is above all a *generalized* one, first and foremost defined as a member of a *gens*, of a "race, people, party, family, or corporation." The singular, individual medieval subject is in fact *plural*: the *I* is essentially identical to the *they*. The medieval *I* can only think what *they* think, can only say what *they* have already said. The medieval individual ego is always already absorbed by and dissolved in a collective anonymity. Only with the advent of the Renaissance is there such a thing as the individual's "self-expression"; only then can *I* say what *I* and not what others think.

Now, you may have come to anticipate that my project in this book will be to refute this idea of the Renaissance as well as the correlary idea of the Middle Ages on which it depends. Such a refutation would perhaps be worthwhile and is perfectly conceivable: one could say, for instance, that medieval subjects were much more differentiated, much less uniform than Burckhardt would have us believe.[3] Or, one could say that Renaissance subjects were much more undifferentiated, much less distinct (since, for instance, the very rejection of the fashion of others that marks the Renaissance is itself the fashion of others).[4]

Yet in fact my project is *not* to refute this idea of the Renaissance as the *naissance* of the individual ego, nor is it to refute the essential anonymity, generality, or universality of the medieval subject. I will not question that some such Renaissance "event" in the history of culture and consciousness took place; rather, I will put into question the invariably *positive valuation* ascribed to this event. Burckhardt and his disciples, influenced by the optimistic Hegelian vision that regards historical development as ultimately positive, good, beneficial for humanity, as a progress from darkness to enlightenment, must of course regard the event of the Renaissance as a beneficial maturation, as a fortunate stage in the "growth" of humanity, a move toward truth. The motive of Burckhardt's idea is to welcome the Renaissance as a *positive gain*. My motive is not simply to oppose this welcome, not simply to ascribe a *negative valuation* to the event of the Renaissance, but more precisely to demonstrate that certain literary texts in the late Middle Ages *already* ascribed such a negative valuation to this anticipated future event, *already* saw the Renaissance as a *loss*, as the destruction of a philosophy of anonymity that had been one of the great positive gains of medieval thinking. These texts have a presentiment of the idea of the Renaissance, and they do not like this idea.

For Burckhardt, the medieval subject is an infantile, primitive, or naïve one that *does not know* its own subjectivity. Medieval people—so Burckhardt would argue—must have been ignorant of the notion of the autonomous individual ego, for otherwise they would have rushed wholeheartedly into the Renaissance. For Burckhardt, to be a nameless member of the *gens* rather than a "spiritual individual," to labor in generalized anonymity, is the unfortunate lot of humanity living in a dark age in which the illuminating truth of individuality has not yet been *revealed* (indeed Burckhardt speaks of the Renaissance precisely as a *revelation*, as the lifting of a *veil*, "the veil of illusion"). Burckhardt's medieval person lives prior to the revelation of a truth that, had it been known, would have been joyously embraced.

I will contend, on the contrary, that the late Middle Ages *does know*, that, though the revelation concerning the singularity of the ego has already taken place, the "truth" of this revelation has been rejected as an un-truth, as a philosophic loss to be resisted rather than a gain to be encouraged. Late medieval anonymity, then, is not to be explained away as a symptom of immaturity, ignorance, or naïveté but rather is a deliberate, mature rejection of the new Renaissance model of the self-determining singular ego, a model with which the late Middle Ages is already quite familiar yet regards as a lie, as an untenable violation of the truth of anonymity. The Middle Ages consciously insists that *I* am *they*: that the individual subject is never singular, is always in some essential sense general, collective, objective.

This book is a collection of readings of certain "reactionary" texts, texts that react against an uncritical embrace of a false "progress" which is really a philosophical regression. They regard the Renaissance singularization of the plural or collective medieval ego not as an elevation from darkness into truth but as a "fall" into naïveté, into a dark age of individualism. The mission of these late medieval texts is to *resist* the Renaissance, to muster a last stand for the dying cause of anonymity—and thus you will, I trust, have come to understand the general sense of this book's subtitle.

But what about the title proper? What does any of this have to do with "the death of the troubadour"?

II

> Speech, it seems, was devised only for the average, medium, communicable. The speaker has already *vulgarized* himself by speaking.
>
> Nietzsche, *Twilight of the Idols*

> Grammar, which is nothing else but a kind of unchangeable identity of speech in different times and places . . . , having been settled by the common consent of many peoples, seems exposed to the arbitrary will of none in particular.
>
> Dante, *De Vulgari Eloquentia*

What these two epigraphs share in common is the insistence that language ("speech" for Nietzsche, "grammar" for Dante) necessarily entails the *vulgarization* of the individual: to speak is to identify oneself as one of the *vulgus*, one of the people, public, mass, or crowd. Speech or grammar is always the common property of the *gens*, of a general rather than a particular subject. *I* cannot express *myself*, not in a manner that is uniquely and distinctly *mine*, but rather can only express myself as *they* express *themselves*. I cannot, in speech, mark myself as being anything more than "average." I cannot bend or shape grammar into an instrument for the expression of my own "arbitrary will."

Now, the "grammar" with which Dante is concerned in *De Vulgari Eloquentia* is, strictly speaking, the language of medieval courtly lyric love poetry, the language of troubadour (Old Provençal), *trouvère* (Old French), and *dolce stil nuovo* (Italian) song. Dante identifies the "grammatical" vernacular language (the search for which is the goal of his treatise) as being, originally, the *langue d'oc* of the Provençal poets. The language of troubadour song is "grammatical" in the sense that it is *universal*: troubadour song, says Dante, "suffuses its perfume in every city, yet it has its lair in none."[5] The *locus* of song is everywhere in general and nowhere in particular, its place is no place. Grammar (which in the case of the vernacular languages is identical to the language of song), says Dante, "cannot be changed"—unlike ordinary or everyday spoken language, which is always changing and which is thus always marked as originating in a determinate locale, a specific location, a concrete historical time and place.[6] Indeed, as a matter of philological fact, troubadour song was composed in a literary rather than a spoken dialect, a "dialect" that was relatively universal and that remained current throughout much of southern Europe for at least two centuries: a twelfth-century Catalonian troubadour sounds essentially the same as a late thirteenth-century Italian one. Moreover, the troubadour himself, whose place is no place, who wanders from place to place rather than remaining fixed in a single *locus*, is a figure for the same sort of universal currency which marks his language: the troubadour, like his language, visits "every city, yet has his lair in none."[7] The language of troubadour love poetry does not permit the identification of its speaker as a certain historical and singular individual: the time and place of the *I* is no particular time and no particular place. Grammar or the language of song transcends the concrete historical situation; in Heideggerian terms, it is an ontological rather than an ontic language; it expresses Being in general rather than a certain particular being.

Courtly love lyric is "grammatical" in the sense that it is a *conventional* discourse, "settled," as Dante says concerning grammar, "by the common consent of many peoples." Troubadour song—whether in the language of the *oc*, the *oïl*, or the *sì*—expresses "the arbitrary will of none in particular": it expresses, that is, the will or desire of *everyone and no one*, and it thus always appears as an anonymous or universal language, as essentially identical to the language of others. The troubadour is always repeating the same rather than saying something different, repeating the *topoi*, the conventions of courtly love poetry.

The name "troubadour" comes from the verb *trobar*, which signifies both "to find" and the act of composing verse. To compose a courtly love song is to *find* a song, to come upon a language that is always already there. The song does not emanate from or originate within an individual subject, but rather the subject appropriates a song whose origin is elsewhere and that is not, properly speaking, the singer's own property. The individual troubadour is not a creator, not an originator of song, but rather a *trobador*, a "finder" of a song that pre-exists the act of composition. What the troubadour finds is a song that belongs to no one and whose place, whose *topos*, is no one's particular place.

Troubadour love poetry does not simply *use* an anonymous language that belongs to no one in particular; it is, more significantly, *about* the anonymity of this language. The impossibility, the inachievement of the courtly lover's desire is a *linguistic* impossibility, a failure grounded in the lover's language. The troubadour's primary aim is to make a name for himself, to distinguish himself, to convince the lady whom he loves that he is a special individual, uniquely worthy to win her love. (Throughout this book, I will use the masculine pronoun when referring to the courtly love poet, though there were female love poets in the Middle Ages; according to the conventions of the discourse of courtly love, the desiring subject is normally called "he" and the desired object called "she.") Unfortunately for the troubadour, there are always others who are and have been making precisely the same claim, a rival claim for the same thing. These others are the *lauzengers*, the "flatterers"—they who, in the eyes of the troubadour, are false lovers, liars who, using the language of seduction, distinguish themselves through mere flattery of the lady. What makes the troubadour's task impossible is that there is absolutely no objective distinction between the true and the false languages of love: the troubadour's *I* always sounds just exactly like *them*, just exactly like his rivals. In making his claim that he is not just one of the *vulgus*, not just another in the crowd of suitors, the troubadour always ends up appearing precisely as one of the *vulgus*. Saying "I love you," that is, is always a convention, a *citation*; it does not so much distinguish an individual as it makes him resemble everyone else.[8] The courtly love singer cannot appear as anything other than *they*, a subject without a name, a plural or collective rather than an individual ego. If the troubadour's love remains impossible, unfulfilled, it is because his impossible task has been to distinguish himself by using a language that does not allow individuals to distinguish themselves, to make a name for himself by using a language in which there are no names.

Even to speak, as I have been doing, of "*the* troubadour"—as if the subject who sings *I* is someone, some one certain historical individual—is already to distort the reality of courtly love lyric. The singing ego is not yet singular, remains plural, collective, purely "grammatical" in Dante's sense, everyone in general and no one in particular. The singing *I*, that is, remains a *pronoun*, a subject that—according to Priscian, the fifth-century grammarian whose work was authoritative throughout the Middle Ages—is "hollow and empty," without a determinate referent: *Pronomina . . . cassa sunt et vana . . . , nihil certum et determinatum supponerent* ("Pronouns . . . are hollow and empty . . . , they stand in for nothing definite and determined").9 The referent of the pronoun has no fixed identity, no special qualities: again according to Priscian, the pronoun *substantiam significat sine aliqua certa qualitate* ("signifies a substance without qualities fixed in some way"). The pronoun is a *pro-nomen*, a word that signifies *before* the attribution of the "name" or "noun" (both meanings are signified by the Latin *nomen*, as they still are in the Modern French *nom*). The naming of the name, the nominalization of the pronoun, the transformation from *pro-nomen* to *nomen*, is the fixing of certain particular qualities, the determination of the subject—a determination that transforms the pronominal subject from nothing or no one in particular into something or some one special, from pure Being to particular being.10 To name the name, that is, is to *historicize* the pronoun, to *localize* it, to assign it an individual referent and a particular time and place. Courtly song, being a language in which the subject remains "grammatical" or unnamed, resists this transformation from *pro-nomen* to *nomen*, resists the naming of names that determines the subject as someone with a certain *historia*, with a singular, limited, and individual "life story."

This naming of the singer's name, according to Saint Bonaventure, reduces and limits the sense of song. Bonaventure argues that Solomon, the author of the Song of Songs, intentionally presents his songs as anonymous, precisely in order to generalize and universalize their significance:

> Bonaventure claims [that] in the Song of Songs a groom is seen speaking to his bride. . . . Solomon did not want us to read the Song of Songs at the literal level, as *his* words to *his* wife, but rather as the words of Christ to the Church. Therefore, he did not give his name in the book-title, as he did in the case of

Proverbs: the Song of Songs was deliberately left without a named human *auctor*.[11]

Solomon leaves his songs anonymous so that they appear as the language of a generalized "groom" singing to a generalized "bride." If Solomon had named himself as the groom and his wife as the bride, if he had identified the singer and the lady as certain particular individuals, he would have diminished the sense of his songs; their meaning would have been determined, specified, merely literal, merely historical, for they would have referred solely to the real lived experience of Solomon and his wife. Solomon uses anonymity as a strategy meant to universalize the scope of song, so that its concern is Christ and the Church—that is, anyone and everyone, regardless of time and place. The lady sung to in the Song of Songs, being anonymous, being a *pro-nomen* rather than a *nomen*, is potentially any and all human subjects.

In the latter half of the thirteenth century, at the dawn of the Renaissance, this singing pronoun, this purely grammatical lyric ego that is the troubadour, begins to be *named*. The discursive place of this naming is not courtly lyric itself but rather prose narrative, and its geographical place is not Provence but rather Italy. I am referring to the manuscript anthologies of troubadour verse, composed in Old Provençal yet produced in Italy, that contain the *vidas* and *razos*—brief narratives recounting the "lives" or biographies of named troubadour poets (*vidas*: "lives") and the biographical, pre-textual reasons (*razos*: "reasons") that inspired a certain named individual poet to compose a certain individual verse for a certain named individual lady. Courtly lyric now begins to appear as the realistic mimesis of an extra- or pre-linguistic "life," as the "self-expression" of a unique and singular subject. The poet is now someone who has made a name for himself, and his poetry is now grounded in his own individual lived experience, in his own particular *historia*. Song becomes first and foremost the *literal* expression of an individual history, the "self-expression" of a singular subject.

Yet unlike modern literary biography, the *vidas* and *razos* themselves do not wholly pretend that the individual's "life" is the origin or source of his singing—or, if they do so pretend, this pretense is quite transparently false: the "histories" related by these narratives are clearly derived from the very verses which those "histories" are meant to explain. Dante, in the *De Vulgari Eloquentia*, recognizes this derivative or secondary status of prose narrative, its foundation, not in "life" but rather in lyric verse:

> I first declare that the illustrious . . . vernacular is suitable for use in both prose and verse. But because the prose writers mostly pick up this vernacular from those who have knit it in verse, and because *what is knit in verse seems to have remained the model for prose writers, and not the reverse (which facts would seem to confer a certain superiority on verse)*, let us first . . . etc.[12]

This "superiority" that Dante recognizes in lyric verse is its chronological priority in relation to prose narrative: song *precedes* story. For Dante, the foundation or origin of prose narrative is not "history" or "life" but rather the conventional language of courtly lyric.[13] Prose, suggests Dante, is not a realistic discourse grounded in the literal facts of lived experience or ordinary life; it is, rather, a sort of translation, imitation, or expansion of a fundamental, originary song. This is indeed the case with the narrative *vidas* and *razos*, which, beginning with a troubadour song, invent the literal sense, the historical "life" of the troubadour. The *vidas* and *razos*, like the songs upon which they are founded, represent the subject as an *effect* of language, as one who comes into being only in and through language—*not* as one who, existing within himself fully and absolutely *before* language, then *uses* language merely as the vehicle, as the instrument or tool, to "express" or externalize this extra- or pre-linguistic inner existence. Here Dante envisions and *rejects* this "reverse" possibility, this reversal of "superiority" or priority in the relation between lyric and narrative: he rejects the possibility that story precedes song, that lyric language is grounded or founded in literal *historia*, that the "histories" narrated by the *vidas* and *razos* come first, that the song is merely the imitation or expression of a chronologically prior lived experience. Dante's rejection of this "reversal" in the relation between poetic language and life indicates that he still understands the essential significance of the troubadour project, which is to represent song as the origin of the subject rather than the subject as the origin of song.[14]

Still, the *vidas* and *razos* lead inexorably toward this "reversal," toward the modern "biographical fallacy." Though they themselves derive the literal facts of *historia* ("history" or "story") from song, these narratives nonetheless help foster the novel, modern, Renaissance conception according to which song is derived from a literal *historia*. After the *vidas* and *razos*, the singing ego has a *name*, and song begins to be regarded as the after-the-fact "expression" of a certain individual's life story. Now the singer appears as "someone special" rather than "no one in particular," as a singular, distinct, determinate individual, and the song appears to originate in a specific locale, in a certain time and place. Now the singer no longer mimes the conventions of a general, universal, "courtly" or "grammatical" voice that belongs to no one, but rather he sings, deeply and sincerely, in his own voice, of his unique real-life love for a certain historically real lady—a love that comes first, an extra- or pre-textual love that can be documented: Dante's for Beatrice, whom he met in Florence in 1274; Petrarch's for Laura, whom he met in Avignon on April 6, 1327. Now song is secondary, derived from or grounded in a particular history.

Since the pro-nominal subject of courtly song is potentially anyone and everyone, the *historia* recounted by song is not the actual or literal history of a certain individual but rather the *potential* histories of a plurality of subjects. Song does not tell a story, but can possibly tell many stories: it is always about ready to disclose its secret, about ready to designate its referent, but never does. To reveal a song's secret story is to terminate its potential to signify. This, at least, seems to be the gist of the early thirteenth-century romance writer Jean Renart's explanation concerning his inclusion of the numerous songs that are interspersed or "embroidered" throughout his narrative *Roman de la Rose* (also called *Guillaume de Dole*):

> car aussi com l'en met la *graine*
> es dras por avoir los et pris,
> einsi a il *chans* et sons mis
> en cestui *Romans de la Rose*,
> qui est *une nouvele chose*
> et s'est des autres si divers
> et brodez, par lieus, de biaus vers
> que vilains nel porroit savoir.
> Ce sachiez de fi et de voir,
> bien a cist les autres passez.
> *Ja nuls n'iert de l'oï lassez,*
> car, s'en vieult, l'en i chante et lit,
> et s'est fez par si grant delit
> que tuit cil s'en esjoïront
> qui chanter et lire l'orront,
> qu'il lor sera *nouviaus toz jors*.[15]

(Just as one puts dye [*graine*, literally "seed"] in cloth to make it more praiseworthy and valuable, so has he [i.e., the author] put *songs* and melodies in this *Romance of the Rose*, which is *a new thing* and is so different from the others and embroidered, in places, with fine verses so that a *vilain* [i.e. an ill-mannered or non-aristocratic person] could not understand it. Know this surely and truly, indeed this one [i.e., this romance] surpasses the others. *No one will ever tire of hearing it*, for, if one desires, one can sing and read in it, and it's made in such a delightful way that everyone who hears it sung and read will enjoy it, because it will be *always new* to them.)

This passage implies that an ordinary romance, one that is all story and no song, quickly grows "old": to hear a story more than once is a tiring affair. Such a romance is subject to degradation and ravaged by the passage of time, for, once the literal facts of *historia* have been disclosed, those facts soon lose their interest and the romance becomes *passé*. Story is a discourse whose significance is narrowly determined, fixed, limited. This *Romance of the Rose*, on the contrary, remains *always new* (*nouviaus toz jors*), and it is precisely the element of *song* that accounts for this perpetual novelty. Because it includes song, this text resists history, will never grow old: song never becomes tiring in its repetition. The time of this text's interpretation, the time of the encounter between itself and its audience, is a perpetual Spring, a perpetual month of May (which month is called, later in the text, the *new time* [*noviaus tens*]). A song is, like the *seed* [*graine*] to which it is here compared, a *new thing* [*novele chose*]: a song is an originary entity, Being before its disclosure or unfolding, before its qualities and identity have been determined. This text remains a perpetual novelty because it is sown with seeds that never sprout, buds that never blossom, songs that never become stories. Song is, like a seed, undeveloped potential: the songs of this text are always about to bear the fruit of *historia*, yet never do so, and because they never do so one can never tire of the text. This romance remains vital for all audiences because, due to the presence of courtly language, it does not signify the actual history of certain individuals but rather the potential histories of anyone and everyone. Song is the potential to signify, language that intends to yet has not yet disclosed its meaning, language before the fixation and determination of its referent.

The "death of the troubadour" is precisely the seed's maturation into fruit or flower, the move from song to story, the transformation of the lyric singer from *pro-nomen* to *nomen*, the fixation or determination of the pronoun's referent, the triumph of the specific individual over the generalized anonymous subject. This "death" is the reverse side of that "birth" of the individual that is celebrated in the modern idea of the Renaissance.

Modern literary history celebrates this move from song to story, from nameless singer to great author, from the collective to the individual ego, as a ripening, a maturation, a positive progress for the ultimate good of Literature and Humanity. According to this version of literary history, late medieval song is a set of worn-out and tired conventions ready to be easily conquered by a novel and vigorous narration of life as it really is. Courtly lyric is seen as so entirely conventional that it cannot express that autonomous individual self that, impatiently waiting for the vehicle of its expression, requires the advent of a new realistic narrative discourse. But what if medieval song is so conventional precisely in order to combat that emergent notion of "self" that it already recognizes as a loss, a diminishment, a limitation of the potential sense of the plural subject? What if the singing ego remains "grammatical" precisely in order to resist the *nomen*, to resist that nominalization of the subject that reduces undifferentiated Being into a particular, localized, and determined being?

We shall see that the "death of the troubadour" that is the reverse side of the *naissance* of the individual is mourned and resisted in certain late medieval literary texts. We shall focus most of our attention, specifically, on certain late medieval *stories* about *singers*—certain texts in which the "grammatical" ego of troubadour lyric has been inserted into the order of *historia*, has been transformed from "everyone and no one" into "someone in particular." We shall locate the resistance to Renaissance individualism precisely in these very texts that, by naming, specifying, and historicizing the singing subject, seem to usher in the Renaissance. The very texts that are responsible for the "death of the troubadour" are also the site of a struggle to forestall or deny this "death." We shall see that at the heart of these stories about singers lurks the story of a songlike resistance to storytelling. The generalized lyric ego, that is, lingers on as a repressed or latent element of certain late medieval stories about singers. We shall come to regard story as an attempt to "repress" song, to conceal the linguistic foundation or origin of the subject. Our readings shall activate a return of this repressed song, a return by which the anonymous ego survives story's attempt to singularize it, to determine its boundaries, to give it a name.

1. Song as *Langue*

Song in the vernacular cultures of the Middle Ages is not a mere pastime, not just a decorous interlude that occasionally enlivens a world of ordinary affairs conducted in ordinary language. On the contrary, song is the vernacular equivalent of Latin grammar: language in its systematic aspect, the foundation of all speech, a regulatory code whose existence is independent of individual utterances and individual speaking subjects. In the parlance of Saussurian linguistics, courtly song is *langue* rather than *parole*, the abstract structure or grammar of language rather than its actual use. This is not to suggest that courtly lyric was in fact not actually performed, nor am I ignorant of troubadour lyric's frequent specificity, topicality, political relevance, or historicity.[1] My claim is not that actual lyric singers did not or could not refer to their actual lived experience or to their historical situation. I am suggesting, rather, that song's production by poets and its reception by audiences were ruled by a prevailing idea of lyric subjectivity. We may attempt to reconstruct this idea by investigating the question of subjectivity in courtly lyric poetry itself, and indeed such a reconstruction is one of the important achievements of recent criticism.[2] Or we may search elsewhere, outside the *corpus* of song itself, in an attempt not only to define the medieval idea of the lyric subject but also to witness that idea's operations and its effects in other discursive contexts. For the most part, it is this second tack that we shall follow in our readings. The novelty of our enterprise will be its account of the trials, transformations, and hesitations experienced by the singing subject upon its insertion into the new order of *historia*.

In the dominant lyric modes of the late Middle Ages—in, that is, the courtly love lyric, the *canso* and the *chanson*, of the troubadours and trouvères—distinctly marked, individual, historical human subjectivity is virtually absent: the singing "I" is no one in particular.[3] The song appears as the product of a general code, grammar, or regulatory system rather than a unique and localized act of original composition or performance. The courtly love lyric is quite unlike, and indeed quite the opposite of, the lyric poem as it is normally conceived in the post-Romantic age: neither the product of linguistic spontaneity nor of a distinctly-marked voice, troubadour and trouvère song is not a vehicle for self-expression nor for the manifestation of individual creative genius.[4] The voice of medieval lyric is not the voice of an autonomous ego or self-determining subject that masters language but rather that of a fragmented ego mastered by language, the site at which converge various alien and conventional voices.

The multiplicity or plurality, or, to put it another way, the impersonality or rhetoricity of the lyric "I" of the troubadours and trouvères is not an imposed invention of post-Freudian theories of subjectivity but rather is a trait recognized by the medieval lyric poet, reflected in and reflected upon by medieval narrative, and formulated in the work of medieval vernacular grammarians and theoreticians of language. The lyric "I" reflected and fostered a pervasive notion of literary subjectivity that would have gripped any and every late medieval poet.[5]

Before turning in later chapters to the idea of the lyric subject as represented in courtly song itself and in certain late medieval stories about singers, let us commence by examining the idea of this singing subject as represented by a certain late medieval vernacular "grammarian."

Medieval treatises on vernacular grammar formulate a strong kinship between lyrical and "grammatical" (here meaning general, impersonal, or universal) subjectivity, between song and *langue*. As an example of such a formulation I shall consider *Las razos de trobar*, an early thirteenth-century prose treatise on troubadour poetry and vernacular grammar written in Old Provençal by the Catalan poet Raimon Vidal.

Modern critics of the *Razos de trobar* generally stress its influence—its importance as the founding monument of the discourse of vernacular poetics and grammar, as the source of a tradition whose culmination is Dante's *De Vulgari Eloquentia*—even as they malign its quality.[6] Raimon's treatise annoys modern readers because of its anacoluthic incoherence: its end does not proceed from or logically follow its beginning. Raimon begins with a promise to teach the right manner to compose poetry—*la dreicha maniera de trobar*:

> Per so qar ieu Raimonz Vidals ai vist et conegut qe pauc d'omes sabon ni an saubuda la dreicha maniera de trobar, voill eu far aqest libre per far conoisser et saber qals dels trobadors an mielz trobat et mielz ensenhat, ad aqelz qe.l volran apenre, con devon segre la dreicha maniera de trobar.[7]
>
> (Because I, Raimon Vidal, have seen and known that few men know nor have known the right manner of composing, I want to make this book to make known and understood which of the troubadours have composed best and

taught best, and which of them he who would want to learn the right manner of composing should follow.)

After a few more paragraphs that promise a project of great scope and considerable interest, what follows is a nothing more than a catalogue of grammatical errors committed by various troubadours. As one scholar points out, the treatise has been "described derogatorily as a work which begins as an ingenious *ars poetica* but which ends up as a pedestrian grammar book."[8]

In the first paragraph Raimon anticipates his critics, foreseeing those who will say he wrote too much in some places, too little in others (for instance, too much *grammatica* and not enough *poetica*). Yet, says Raimon, there is in fact nothing wrong with the treatise, and the audience should accept the work precisely as it is written:

> Autresi vos dig qe homes prims i aura de cui enten, si tot s'estai ben, qe i sabrain bien meilhorar o mais mettre; qe greu trobares negun saber taant fort ni tan primamenz dig qe uns hom prims no i saubes melhurar o mais metre. Per qe'ieu vos dig qe en neguna ren, pos basta ni ben ista, no n deu om ren ostar ni mais metre.[9]

> (I also say that there will be clever persons who understand that all is well, although they would know how to put it better or how to say more; for you can hardly find any knowledge so strong or so excellently said that a clever person would not know how to say better or to say more. So I say that in no place, whether bad or good, should anyone take anything away or add anything.)

This claim that there is nothing wrong with the treatise suggests a way to read the gap between the work's beginning and its end, or, more precisely, a way *not* to read the gap. That is, the discrepancy between the work's beginning (*ars poetica*) and its end (*ars grammatica*) is, for Raimon Vidal, simply nonexistent. For Raimon there is no difference between an *ars poetica* and an *ars grammatica*, and thus no difference between the studied objects of those disciplines, no difference between song and grammar.

This equivalence between poetics and grammar, between song and *langue*, is invariably repeated by the inheritors of Raimon Vidal's legacy. Terramignino da Pisa, in the *Doctrina d'Acort*, and Jofre de Foixà, in the *Regles de trobar*, both found vernacular grammars upon lyric poetry, as does Dante in the *De Vulgari Eloquentia*. For these theoreticians, speculation upon language is indistinct from speculation upon song: the studied instance of language is invariably a verse or verses from a song, as if in the late

Middle Ages one could not write a vernacular *ars grammatica* without simultaneously writing an *ars poetica* whose field of concern was lyric poetry.

The highly formal quality of troubadour lyric—in particular, the pronounced emphasis upon and elaboration of rhyme—is an implicit defense of vernacular language, an attempt to endow Old Provençal with a regulatory, grammatical structure and thus with an ideal, abstract, timeless, incorruptible realm of existence. Rhyme, when present in medieval Latin poetry, is most frequently a product of grammatical inflection, and thus rhyme was regarded by vernacular poets as belonging to the general province of grammar. In other words, to the troubadour, Latin rhyme—assumed to be an element of grammar—signified, by synecdoche, everything that was grammatical about Latin. The poet's obedience to the rules of rhyme was a gesture meant to confer grammatical status—the status of the synchronic, incorruptible, atemporal, transcendent, or eternal—upon the vernacular. Since the troubadour's language lacked a codified grammatical structure, rhyme was the supplement for this lack and was transformed into an increasingly complex "pseudo-grammar."[10]

In the *Razos de trobar* Raimon Vidal asserts that Old Provençal has a regulatory code of correctness (*la dreicha maniera de trobar* ["the right manner of composing"]) every bit as stable or invariable as Latin grammar. Yet Raimon's formulation of a systematic *langue* (an ideal "grammar") is continually betrayed by the *parole* (the actual instances) of troubadour poetry. As the treatise's modern editor says,

> the grammarian's desire to formulate a clear-cut rule has led him to misrepresent the ordinary literary practice of the language. Vidal was deluded in thinking that, for any given element of the language, there must necessarily be a rule clearly separating a "correct" from an "incorrect" form.[11]

Once a grammatical structure has been posited, regardless of whether it corresponds to actual troubadour practice, there is no longer a need to defend the vernacular with the "pseudo-grammar" of rhyme. Thus a repeated object of Raimon's scorn is the practice of violating proper grammar to make a good rhyme. He says, for instance, that the poet

> deu ben garder qe neguna rima qe li mestier non la metta fora de sa proprietat ni de son cas ni de son genre ni de son mot ni de son nombre ni de sa part ni de sa persona ni de son alongamen ni de son abreuiamen.[12]
>
> (should make sure that when he needs a rhyme he does not put a word outside of its propriety either in case or in gender or in mood or in number or in part of speech or in person or in the matter of the final -s.)

The *Razos de trobar* is an implicit repudiation of the troubadours' confusion or identification of rhyme with grammar. For Raimon, the vernacular is not grammatically deficient and thus does not need to be improved or structured by a highly formal poetic practice dominated by rhyme. Instead Raimon reverses the poles of evaluation: troubadour practice (*parole*) is deficient and needs to be improved by an adherence to a theoretically posited systematic vernacular grammar (*langue*).

Perhaps this discrepancy that Raimon exposes between lyric practice and vernacular grammar seems to challenge my assertion that the *Razos de trobar* formulates an equivalence between song and *langue*. Yet it is actual poetic practice or *parole* that Raimon opposes to grammar or *langue*. The treatise posits that song itself, contrary to actually sung songs, is perfectly grammatical. In other words, grammar is equivalent not to specific lyric productions but rather to an ideal, unsung song. Thus, according to Raimon, the properly grammatical lyric language is potential rather than actual, general rather than particular, global rather than local, plural rather than singular. No troubadour has ever mastered or can ever possibly master song:

> Ni non crezas qe *neguns hom* n'aia istat maistres ni perfaig; car tant es cars et fins le sabers qe hanc *nuls homs* non se donet garda del tot: so conoissera totz homs prims et entendenz qe ben esgard aqest libre. Ni eu non dic ges qe sia maistres ni parfaitz; mas tan dirai segon mon sen en aqest libre, qe totz homs qe l'entendra ni aia bon cor de trobar poira far sos chantars ses tota vergoigna.[13]

> (Nor should you believe that anyone [*neguns hom*] has been the master of it or perfect at it; for this science is so dear and fine that *no one* [*nuls homs*] entirely encompasses it: all clever and intelligent persons who examine this book well will know this. Nor do I say that I am the master or perfect; but in this book I will say enough according to my sense that anyone who hears it and desires to compose may make songs without complete shame.)

Song is a science that no one individual can master, and the properly grammatical language of love lyric is collective rather than private property. The ideal, properly grammatical song is that which *no one* sings: the master singer is literally someone named "No one," *Nuls homs*.[14] Song cannot be mastered, is not the property of an individual subject, cannot be fixed or limited to a particular locus. The equivalence between song and grammar is founded on the fact that both elude manipulation by individual acts of will. Song, like grammar and like *langue*, is always already social and conventional rather than individual, novel, and localized.

To say, with Raimon Vidal, that song is that which no one sings is to say that song is *langue*, which remains always unvoiced, any actual utterance being an instance of *parole*. In the realm of *langue* the personal pronoun "I" is merely grammatical, impersonal, empty, meaningless, devoid of reference: "I" only has referential value in *parole*, only refers to that person who says "I" in a particular instance of discourse.[15] Thus Raimon's treatise can only be what it is, can only be an enumeration of errors, since to sing is necessarily to miss the mark: troubadour poetry is necessarily inachieved, imperfect, a violation, since the mere act of singing gives the lyric *je* a momentary referent, contaminates song with traces of individual subjectivity, transforms the singing subject from a grammatical to a human being, and transforms *langue* into *parole*. "I" in the realm of *langue*, like the "I" who masters Raimon's ideal song, is no one. As we have said, and as Raimon asserts quite literally, "No one" sings the properly grammatical song: the singer of the perfect song is no one individual or is someone called "No one."[16]

There is an obvious affinity between, on the one hand, Raimon's implied assertion of an ideal realm of song, so mysterious, so *cars* ("dear") and *fins* ("fine") that it cannot be entirely encompassed and, on the other hand, neoplatonic assertions that music is an ideal form or transcendent essence. For Augustine and Boethius, among many others, the most perfect music is unheard, ideal. Yet it would be misguided to think that Raimon similarly considers song as transcendental or as participating in the divine, since in the most famous passage of the treatise, near the very beginning, Raimon insists that song is primarily a human and a social fact:

> *Totas genz* cristianas, iusieuas et sarazinas, emperador, princeps, rei, duc, conte, vesconte, contor, valvasor, clergue, borgues, vilans, paucs et granz, meton *totz iorns* lor entendiment en trobar et en chantar, o q'en volon trobar o q'en volon entendre o q'en volon dire o q'en volon auzir; qe greu seres en loc negun tan privat ni tan sol, pos gens i a paucas o moutas, qe *ades* non auias cantar un o autre o tot ensems, qe neis li pastor de la montagna lo maior sollatz qe ill aiant de chantar. Et tuit li mal e.l ben del mont son mes en remembransa per trobabors. Et ia non trobares mot ben ni mal dig, pos troubaires l'a mes en rima, qe tot iorns non sia en remembranza, qar trobars et chantars son movemens de totas galliardias.[17]

> (*All people*—Christians, Jews, and Sarrasins, emperors, princes, kings, dukes, counts, viscounts, minor nobles, clerks, bourgeois, peasants, small and great—*every day* [or, "always"] turn their attention to composing and singing, either wanting to compose or understand or wanting to say or to hear; for you could hardly be in any place so private or solitary that you would not *always* hear people singing to one another or all together, for even the shepherds of the

most solitary mountain have singing. And all the evil and good of the world are put in remembrance by troubadours. And you will never find a word well or badly said, if a troubadour has put it in rhyme, which will not be always remembered, for which reason composing and singing are the source of all deeds.)

What is striking in this passage is the extreme universality or generality that Raimon ascribes to song, as if song were indistinct from language per se, as if song and language were utterly synonymous. For Raimon, song, occupying the role traditionally ascribed to language by classical and medieval philosophy, is the specific attribute that defines the human. Song levels all distinctions and obliterates religious and social difference. Song is the denial of the private. Song is a ubiquitous, constant, daily activity. Song is the treasury of memory and history, the motive of all human action. Song is the universal currency of communication and cannot be the exclusive property of any individual, localized group, or social class. Song in this passage counters the illusion of the singularity and autonomy of individual subjectivity. Song appears to Raimon, as it will appear to Dante, as language not marked by its manifestation in any particular locus: song, says Dante, "suffuses its perfume in every city, but has its lair in none."[18] Dante's assertion of the vaporous generality of lyric language, of song's independence from its actual, singular use or from its bodily material presence, echoes Raimon Vidal's position in the *Razos de trobar*. For Raimon, as I have demonstrated, similarly portrays the properly grammatical lyric language as universal rather than localized, general rather than particular, plural rather than singular. Yet unlike Augustine and Boethius, for whom unsung music transcends the human and participates in the divine, Raimon can say that song eludes the individual or that no one sings song not because song is supernatural but rather because *everyone always sings song*. Song for Raimon is the most basic fact of human society: everyone, everywhere, every day, is always singing.

2. "Everyone Loves Thus . . ."

I

The unsung song or song sung by someone named "No one" posited by Raimon Vidal is a limit case meant to signify the virtual disappearance, the purely discursive existence, of the subject of courtly love lyric. This disappearance is most extreme in the Old French *chanson*, in which the "I," emptied of reference, virtually never discloses the identity of the individual singer. This resistance to particular, local, historical subjectivity is witnessed and produced by the scribal exclusion or effacement of the song's *envoi* in many of the manuscript anthologies of trouvère lyric. The absence of the *envoi*—the absence of that which identifies the locus of the song's origin and initial performance as well as the locus of its destination and repeat performance—relegates to the realm of emptiness and abstraction the referential value of the "I" who sings and the "you" who listens.[1]

The suspicion that song is *langue*—language in its grammatical, conventional, social, general, and systematic aspect—profoundly affects medieval writing. Aware of its own implications, the language of courtly lyric mounts a resistance to the notion of the integrity or autonomy of the "self" (and to the concomitant notion of literary representation as the "expression" of that which is entirely prior to and uncontaminated by language) that, according to some accounts, was beginning to be forged in the twelfth century—a notion of the coherent, discrete, distinctive, autonomous ego that, in the wake of Marx, Nietzsche, Saussure, Freud, and Heidegger, has been strongly rejected in the present century.[2]

The courtly lover faces an impossibly paradoxical task: to win love he must distinguish himself in language, must sing in a manner that would set him apart for the special consideration or recognition by his lady, yet it is nothing other than language that prevents him from distinguishing himself and from being distinguished, nothing other than the extreme generality or conventionality of the language of love. The poet's incapacity to sing in his own voice, his inability to represent himself in song in a way that would prove his special worth and make manifest the distinctive nature of his "inner self," is constantly thematized in courtly love lyric. This is explicit, for example, in one of the songs of the twelfth-century trouvère Gace Brulé. Each of the song's stanzas—here I shall cite the first—closes with a refrain that laments the impossibility of distinguishing between the true and the false languages of desire—the impossibilty, that is, of distinguishing between the poet's songs and those of his rivals:

> Desconfortez, ploins de dolour et d'ire,
> M'estuet chanter, qu'aillors n'ai ou entendre.
> Tout le mont voi, fors moi, joer et rire,
> Ne je ne truis qui d'ennui me desfende.
> Cele m'ocit cui mes cuers plus desire,
> S'en sui iriez, quant ele n'en amende.
> *Chascuns dit qu'il ainme autresi,*
> *Pour ce ne conoist l'en ami.*³

> (Distressed, full of sorrow and ire, I must sing, for I have no other way to turn. I see everyone, except me, play and laugh, nor do I find anyone who defends me from torment. She kills me whom my heart most desires, and I'm irate because she doesn't help. *Everyone says that he loves thus, therefore one can't tell who is the true lover.*)

What is striking is not so much the paraphraseable content of the refrain but rather that the song itself enacts the very confusion of voices about which it complains.⁴ It is impossible to determine whether the "I" who initiates the stanza is the *fin amans* (the true-speaking courtly lover) or the *losengier* (the false-speaking rival).⁵ One cannot tell whether the singer sings in his own voice or mimes the voice of others, whether the language of the refrain is voiced by the same "I" who voices the stanza's sestet. If the sestet in fact represents the voice of a false lover or rival, then its "I" is in fact an "everyone" or a "they": the *chascuns* or "everyone" of the refrain whose language is indistinguishable from the poet's. To say that an "I" is in fact an "everyone" or a "they" is most clearly to shift subjectivity from the singular to the plural, to represent the ego as a composite of alien voices.⁶

It is the habit of modern philology to reduce the medieval text's plurality of voices by positing a consistent, coherent, psychologically unified single voice as the source of the poetic performance. Texts that resist this attempted singularization are deemed inferior or corrupt. Here I invoke the case of a strange two-stanza song by the trouvère Conon de Bethune:

22   "Everyone Loves Thus..."

> Belle doce Dame chiere,
> Vostre grans beautés entiere
>   M'a si pris
> Ke, se iere em Paradis,
> Si revenroie je arriere,
> Por convent ke ma proiere
>   M'eüst mis
> La ou fuisse vostre amis
> Ne vers moi ne fuissiés fiere,
> Car ainc ens nule maniere
>   Ne forfis
> Par coi fuissiés ma guerriere.
>
> Ne lairai ke je ne die
> De mes maus une partie
>   Come irous.
> Dehaiz ait cuers covoitos,
> Fausse, plus vaire ke pie,
> Ki m'envoia en Surie!
>   Ja por vous
> N'avrai mais les ieus plorous.
> Fous est ki en vous se fie,
> Ke vos estes l'Abeïe
>   As Soffratous,
> Si ne vous amerai mie.[7]

(Beautiful sweet dear lady, I am so taken by your entire great beauty that, if I were in Paradise, I would come back here, provided that my prayer had put me there where I were your friend and that you were not haughty toward me—for I have never done any wrong to make you my enemy.

   I cannot keep from saying a part of my grievances, as one who is angry. Cursed be the selfish heart, false, more changing than a magpie, who sent me to Syria! Never more will I have crying eyes for you. He who has faith in you is a fool, for you are the Abbey of the Suffering, and I shall never love you at all.)

The song's first stanza gives voice to elaborate praise for a beloved lady, while its second stanza gives voice to impassioned disdain for a beloved lady. There is no indication that the lady of the first stanza is the same as the lady of the second nor any indication that the "I" of the first stanza is the "I" of the second. Though it is quite easy to invent a temporal scheme and a narrative event to fill the gap between stanzas (the lady urges the lover to join the Crusade, thus incurring his wrath) in a way that would preserve the integrity of the song's "characters," and though it would then be easy to see the song as a traditional representation of the instability or mutability of passion, the stark duplicity of this particular song has prevented such a commonplace and indeed reasonable solution. That is, the song has been seen as simply too incoherent. The song's incoherence and its absolute ambivalence—an extreme instance of the courtly lover's propensity to love and hate simultaneously—has disturbed modern readers whose response is ruled by a faith in the coherence and integrity of the individual. Thus Conon's song is, according to certain modern editors, the improper and corrupt confusion of stanzas from two different songs, the monstrous progeny of scribal error. According to this view, the second stanza does not represent an alien voice that springs from a division within the selfsame subject but rather is the work of a second poet who "parodies"—in the medieval sense, meaning to imitate the metrical scheme—the first stanza, and this parody, thought by a scribe of inferior intellect to properly belong to the same poetic production as the first, was appended to the original.[8] The song's duplicity would then be attributed to its double origin in two separate acts of production. Yet such an explanation is arbitrary, founded first of all on the editor's refusal to allow a double or self-contradictory voice to a single poetic production. It is just as likely if not much more likely that the medieval poet or scribe is quite aware of the poetic effect of a song whose rhetorical technique is nothing other than the magnification of the commonplace trouvère strategy of paradoxical antithesis.[9] The single source is inherently double, and we do not need to posit a one-to-one ratio between an act of writing and a voice: a single act of writing may well yield a double and contradictory voice. That is, this song is not at all an anomaly in the trouvère *corpus* but rather is an exemplary distillation of courtly lyric's duplicitous subjectivity.

To exemplify further the fragmentation or fluidity of the singing subject, a subject whose voice can only appropriate the voice of others, I shall appropriate, by way of paraphrase, some pertinent moments of Peter Haidu's reading of Chrétien de Troyes' *D'Amors qui m'a tolu a moi*—a song whose first line ("Of Love who has stolen me from myself") tells the entire story of the devastation the language of courtly love afflicts on the ego.[10]

The following verses of Chrétien's song activate an ego, "I," or subject whose position in relation to an object, an other, or a lady is impossible to locate—a subject, that is, to which may be assigned no determinate *locus*:

> Et je, qui ne m'en puis partir
> De celi vers qui me souploi,
> Mon cuers, qui siens est, li envoi;
> Mes de noient la cuit servir
> Se ce li rent que je li doi. (ll. 14–18)

> (And I, who cannot part myself from her toward whom I incline, send to her my heart, which is hers. But I think I in no way serve her if I give her back what I owe her.)

The first two verses locate the *je* ("I") in a position simultaneously indistinct and distinct from that of the *celi* ("she"): the singer cannot part himself from his lady, yet he is parted from her by the distance across which he must incline. This oscillation of the subject's location, the possibility that the subject is in fact located at the place of the object, is repeated in the next verse: the singer claims to send his *cuers* (which signifies both "heart" and "self") to her by whom that *cuers* is already possessed. In the remaining two verses, the singer fears that he is not a proper lover, not one of Love's true servants—a fear that he is indistinct from the *losengiers* or enemies of Love in opposition to whom the true lover's value is established. And indeed the "I"'s fear that it is in fact a "they" is well founded, since the song begins as an open attack, complaint, or accusation against Love: as the song opens the singing subject *is* in fact one of Love's enemies. Thus in the space of these five lines the subject potentially occupies each of the three prominent actantial positions of courtly lyric—the positions of lover, beloved, and *losengier*.[11]

Haidu reads another stanza from the same song as the representation of a singing subject that claims to be self-determining yet reveals itself to be determined by external laws:

> Onques du buvrage ne bui
> Dont Tristan fu empoisonnez;
> Mes plus me fet amer que lui
> Fins cuers et bone volentez.
> Bien en doit estre miens li grez.
> Qu'ainz de riens efforciez n'en fui,
> For que tant que mes euz en crui,

Par cui sui en la voie entrez
Donc ja n'istrai n'ainc n'en recrui. (ll. 28–36)

(I never drank the drink with which Tristan was poisoned; but a noble heart and a good will make me love more than he. The thanks should well be mine. For I was never forced in any way, except insofar as I believed my eyes through whom I have entered the path that I shall never leave nor betray.)

Here the singer, by invoking self-determination as the criterion of judgment, contradicts a tradition in which Tristan is exemplary of the true lover: since Tristan was constrained to desire by the force of a potion, Tristan's love cannot be judged sincere. Tristan and Isolde are bound together by a spell that has the force of a law—a law that, like marriage for Andreas Cappellanus, precludes the possibility of true love. Tristan is thus exiled into the realm of the husband—a realm inhabited in courtly lyric by false lovers and *losengiers*. The singer, claiming to have freely determined his love, would attempt to locate himself in the opposite realm, the realm of the *fin amans* or true lover. Yet this claim is immediately countered by the *For que tant*—the "Except insofar as"—that obliterates the singer's distinction between himself and false lovers: he finishes the stanza by saying that he was never forced to love except when he was forced to love. The singer turns out to be indistinguishable from the *losengiers*. The singer's love is determined by the force of the external that is located within himself: on a journey to his heart or "inner self" that is initiated by passing in through his own eyes, he discovers and is compelled to follow *la voie*, the path—a figure for that which leads away from and outside the "self." To enter inside is to discover that one is outside.[12] This *voie*—which is the *voix* of others, the external voice within the subject, is inescapable and has the force of a law.[13]

This external, alien voice that haunts and inhabits the courtly poet is at once song, *langue*, the voice of the *losengier*, and courtly lyric itself. In other words, the "inner self" of the singing subject is nothing other than the locus of signifying convention: the singer has no voice and can only draw upon a conventional code or *langue* that belongs to no one in particular—a code that is just as easily and routinely appropriated by the *losengiers*, who in trouvère lyric are not merely rivals in love but also rivals in poetry. The poet's language—the language of trouvère lyric—is his own worst enemy, his own *losengier*, since it necessarily thwarts his desire to distinguish himself from his rivals, from those whose language is identical.

II

> Je suis ce malheureux comparable aux miroirs
> Qui peuvent réfléchir mais ne peuvent pas voir
> Comme eux mon oeil est vide et comme eux habité
> De l'absence de toi qui fait sa cécité
>
> (I am that wretch comparable to mirrors / That can reflect but cannot see / Like them my eye is empty and like them inhabited / by your absence which makes them blind)[14]
>
> Louis Aragon, *Contre-chant*

The singing subject's insight that exposes his own objectivity, his constitution in another's language, is starkly represented in certain troubadour songs that cleverly make explicit what is always implicit in the *canso*. Peire Rogier's *Ges non puesc en bon vers falhir* begins with five perfectly typical stanzas—of which I here cite, as exemplary, the fifth:

> Bona dòmpna, soven sospir
> E trac gran pena e gran afan
> Per vos, cui am mout e desir;
> E car no'us vei, non es mos graz;
> E si be m'estau luenh de vos,
> Lo còr e'l sen vos ai trams,
> Si qu'aissí no *sui on tu'm ves*,
> E çò que veis tot es *de liei*.[15] (ll. 33–40)

(Good lady, I often sigh and I suffer great pain and great torment for you, whom I love much and desire; and because I do not see you, it is not a pleasure to me; and because I am far from you, I have sent you my heart and my sense, so that thus *I am not where you see me*, and that which you see is entirely from her [*de liei*].)

What we find here is a stanza that would not be out of place in any *canso*. And, we find a formulation of the perpetual alienation, the permanent elsewhere-ness, of the lyric subject: "I am not where you see me" (*no sui on tu'm ves*). Such a formulation sounds strikingly like the post-Freudian relocation or dislocation of the ego and is quite literally Lacanian *avant la lettre*. This insistence that the locus of the "I" is somewhere else is followed by a similar formulation of the lack of self-presence, by a claim that what is present to the *tu* (to, that is, the audience) comes from somewhere else:

"that me which you see is all from her" or, alternately, "that me which you see is all hers" (*que veis tot es de liei*). This *de liei* may well, as we shall see in the song's closing couplet, signify *de lai*—"from there"—and thus the lady may be seen to function not so much as a certain woman desired for her physical beauty as an abstract principle of externality, of there-ness, of objectivity: "that me which you see is all from there."[16] The singing subject is marked by its lack of subjectivity, by its constitution in the place or *topos* of the object.

Yet what is so interesting about Peire Rogier's song is that, after these five commonplace stanzas that comment upon the singer's divisive self-alienation and external origin, this commentary is graphically acted out as the song loses control, loses coherence, and divides its own voice. Violating the integrity of the *canso*, another voice disrupts the song, as what began as an apparently monologic performance becomes, in stanzas 6 and 7, dialogic:

> *Ai las!* —Que plangz? —Ja tem morir.
> —Que as? —Am. —E tròp? —Ieu òc, tan
> Que'n muer. —Mòrs? —Oc. —Non pòtz guerir?
> —Ieu no. —E cum? —Tan sui iratz.
> —De que? —De lieis, don sui aissòs.
> —Sofre. —No'm val. —Clama'l mercés.
> —Si'm fatz. —No'i as pro? —Pauc. —No't pes,
> Si'n tras mal. —No? —Qu'o fas de *liei*.
>
> —*Cosselh n'ai.* —Qual? —*Vuelh m'en partir.*
> —*No far*! —*Si farai.* —Quèrs ton dan.
> —Que'n puesc als? —Vòls t'en ben jauzir?
> —Oc mout. —Crei mi. —Era digatz.
> —Sias umils, francs, larcs e pros.
> —Si'm fai mal? —Sufr'en patz. —Sui pres?
> —Tu òc, s'amar vòls; mas si'm cres,
> Aissî't poiràs jausir de *liei*. (ll. 41–56)

> (Alas! —Why are you crying? —I fear dying. —What's wrong? —I love. —Very much? —Yes, so much that I'm dying. —You're dying? —Yes. —Can't you be cured? —No. —How come? —I'm too upset. —Why? —Because of her, who makes me anxious. —Suffer. —It's no use. —Beg her for mercy. —I do so. —Doesn't it do some good? —Hardly. —Don't regret suffering pain. —No? —Since you do it for her [*liei*].

*—I have a plan. —What? —I want to separate myself from her. —Don't do it! —Yes I'll do it. —*You seek your undoing. *—*What else can I do? *—*Do you want to have joy from her? *—*Yes, much. *—*Believe me. *—*Speak now. *—*Be humble, sincere, generous and noble. *—*And what if she hurts me? *—*Suffer in peace. *—*Have I been captured? *—*Yes, if you want to love; but if you believe me, you may have your joy from her [*liei*].)

This debate of two voices within the same stanzas—the *coblas tensonadas*—may be seen as the singer's *tenso* ("debate") with himself, as a dramatization of lyric oxymoron.[17] Thus what he wants to do—*partir*—he has already done, since *partir* means not just "to leave" but also "to divide": "I want to divide myself." But this division has always already happened to one who declares in the fifth stanza that he is "not where you see me." Considered as the divided voice of a single singer, the subject of stanzas 6 and 7 cannot at any moment be pinned down. If we say that the singer is the one who says *Si farai*, we simultaneously suspect that the singer is also the one who says *No far!* The courtly singer's oxymoronic hesitation between "Yes" and "No" has here been compressed into a rapid-fire oscillatory onslaught. And this duplicitous self is furthermore insisted upon by the presence of these *two* dialogic stanzas that themselves figure an oxymoron: whereas the first of these dialogic stanzas commences on a pessimistic note (*Ai las!*), conversely the second commences on an optimistic note (*Cosselh n'ai*). If we here witness the singer subjected to a constant division, we are also told that, on the contrary, the singer cannot be divided, cannot be separated from that externality that is the place of his constitution: "I want to separate myself from her [from there]." —"Don't do it." —"Yes I'll do it." —"You seek your undoing."

Yet what is truly fascinating about Peire's song is the *envoi* that, following the two duplicitous *coblas tensonadas*, closes the song:

Mon *Tòrt-n'avètz* mant, s'a lieis platz
Qu'aprenda lo vèrs, s'il es bos;
E puòis vuelh que sia tramés
Mon *Dreit-n'avètz lai* en *Savés*:
Dieu *salv* e gart lo còrs de *lieï*. (ll. 57–61)

(I send my song to my lady "*You are Wrong*" so that she may learn it, if it pleases her and she finds it good; and then I want it to be sent to my lady "*You are Right*" *there* in la *Save*: God *save* and guard *her* person.)

Tòrt-n'avètz and *Dreit-n'avètz* are the *senhals* or nicknames of two ladies. Once again violating the latent historical fiction of song that would posit a singular desiring subject singing his desire for a singular desired object, this singer doubles and divides the destination of his discourse by sending the song twice and, by implication, by loving two ladies. This two-timing lyric transmitter—who had just doubly divided himself in the two previous stanzas—repeats this duplication by dividing his desire. Thus the beloved lady is, contrary to her usual image in the fiction of courtly love, precisely not unique, not one but two. Yet, most significantly, it is not two absolutely different ladies to whom the song is sent but rather two ladies who represent two sides of the same construct: Lady "You are Right" and Lady "You are Wrong" are the positive and negative poles, the good and evil, of the singer's divided discourse. This singer loves none other than the "Yes"/"No" or "Right"/"Wrong" that is the oxymoronic language of his own song and that signifies his self-division. The song will, according to the terms of this *envoi*, be twice performed—will, that is, have two voices; but this double performance merely repeats the song as it already is, since it already has, in the *coblas tensonadas*, two voices. And inscribed in the song's last two lines is an image of its specularity, the figure of a chiasmus that exposes these verses as mirror images of each other:

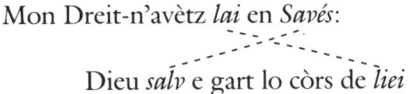

Mon Dreit-n'avètz *lai* en *Savés*:

Dieu *salv* e gart lo còrs de *liei*

Such graphic specularity signifies the song's general specular condition, according to which the singer is sending the song back to himself, back to her, back to the one who is a *liei* (the word ultimately repeated at the end of each of these stanzas), a *lieu*, a place or *topos*—back to the objectively determined realm of courtly convention that it has never left.

Another striking and illuminating counter-*canso* is Raimbaut de Vaqueiras' plurilingual *descort*.[18] The *descort*—literally, a "discord"—is typically a jumble of courtly conventions combined in a series of stanzas or *coblas* that are each formally different and thus do not properly belong together. The *descort* is a sort of parade of compositional possiblities, a discordant procession of differing discourses, a condensation of many songs under the guise of one song. This plurality of voices is meant, perhaps, to represent the discord at the heart of the singing subject.[19] The *descort* is by its nature a dis-heartened song, a song that has been *des-cor*'d, whose heart has been extracted or displaced by an onslaught of the language of those *losengiers* whose heartless stanzas display various yet similar rival poetic forms. The *descort* is a song without a core, a challenge to the fiction that the song's source is a unique centrality or interiority. For in the shuffle of stanzaic forms the center is lost, the heart cannot be located, and we cannot posit a singular singer as the source of the multiform song. The one who sings the *descort* is many singers, is in fact nothing other than the *losengiers*. "They"—who are the source of discord in the singer's world—are always singing the *descort*, and "their" singing is a discordant noise that drowns out the heartfelt song of the individual.

Now Raimbaut de Vaquieras's famous plurilingual *descort* is not, strictly speaking, a *descort*, since its *coblas* are not radically different but rather identical in form. Raimbaut's song exhibits the standard stanzaic uniformity of the *canso* and is in fact more *canso* than *descort*.[20] Thus his strategy is to show that the uniformity of the *canso* may harbor the possibility of discord, that a radical formal heterogeneity is not a requirement for representing a multiplicity of voices. The song suggests that discord is not a matter of certain technical formulae or of a studied formlessness but rather is a potential lurking within any form, any poetic production, any *canso*. If we may call Raimbaut's song a *descort*, it is not because each *cobla* is metrically different but rather because each is sung in a different romance language (respectively Old Provençal, Italian, French, Gascon, and Gallico-Portuguese) and because the singing subject explicitly regards this plurilinguism as a representation of the heart's discordant difference from itself:

> Eras quan vei verdeiar
> Pratz e vergiers e boscatges,
> Vuelh un descòrt comensar
> D'amor, per qu'ieu vauc aratges;
> Qu'una dòna'm sòl amar,
> Mas camjatz l'es sos coratges,
> Per qu'ieu fauc dezacordar
> Los motz e'ls sos e'ls lenguatges. (ll. 1–8)

> (Now that I see fields and gardens and woods turn green, I want to begin a *descort* of love, because of which I go wandering. For a lady used to love me, but her heart has changed—that's why I make discordant the words and the sounds and the languages of this song.)

What strikes us as strange about this singer's proclamation of purpose is that he intends to do nothing other than sing the language of the lady.[21] That is, he locates the site of discord not primarily as contained within the interior confines of his own heart but rather as mapped out by the shifty position of the desired object. The singer's illogical logic runs something like this: "My lady's heart is multiplicitous, *ergo* the words from my mouth must be multiplicitous." What Raimbaut has done here—almost as if he were posing a riddle—is to elide the pre-text that would make thinkable such a way of thinking. For only if the singer's heart and the lady's heart are in fact one and the same, only if "my mouth" is "her mouth," does the stanza make a semblance of sense. The song, then, does not tell us in typical troubadour fashion that the singer's heart is outside itself, dislocated onto the place of the object—but such an alienation goes without saying as the singer's tongue turns out to give expression to the lady's sliding heart. What is lodged inside the singing subject turns out to be not his own but rather his lady's heart. This song is sung by the multiplicitous tongue of the object of desire.

The song ends with a quintuple *tornada*, a final display of the five tongues of the errant singing subject, as each language returns for the duration of a couplet:

> *Belhs Cavaliers*, tant es car
> Lo vostr'onratz senhoratges
> Que cada jorno m'esglaio.
> Oi me lasso! que farò
> Si sele que j'ai plus chiere
> Me tue, ne sai por quoi?
> Ma dauna, he que dey bos
> Ni peu cap Santa Quitera,
> Mon corasso m'avetz treito
> E *mot gen favlan* furtado. (ll. 41–50)

(*Beautiful Knight*, your honorable lordship is so dear that each day I am in fear. Oh, alas! what will I do if she whom I love most kills me, I do not know why? My lady, by the faith that I owe you and by the head of Saint Quitera, you have taken my heart and, speaking very fine [*mot gen favlan*], robbed it.)

This *Belhs Cavaliers* ("Beautiful Knight")—the *senhal* or nickname by which the lover addresses the lady—is not an entirely arbitrary *senhal* but rather is one that perfectly fits this particular song: the undifferentiation of subject and object that rules this song is indistinct from a masculinization of the lady and a feminization of the man. And this collapse of the distinction between the singer and the lady—which is, as we saw, the matter of the song's opening—is most tellingly represented in the song's closing couplet. The Gallico-Portuguese *mot gen favlan* of line 50 ostensibly refers to the lady's *favlan*—to her "speaking"—which is adjectively qualified as *mot gen*—"very fine." Thus the couplet would read: the lady's "very fine speaking" has "abducted," "robbed," or "ravished" (*furtado*) and has "taken," "betrayed," or "imprisoned" (*treito*) the singer's "heart" or "self" (*corasso*). Yet the word *gen* cannot help but conjure up, especially in a text in which translation is always about to happen, the Old French *gent* or any of its Romance cognates rooted in the Latin noun *gens*, meaning "people" or "nation." Thus the *mot gen favlan* that withdraws the singer's heart from its place of interior self-presence is also the "many nations speaking," the many people singing this song. The lady is *mot gen*, perhaps "very fine" but more certainly "many people," and this exchangeable, multiplicitous identity is precisely what the singer saw in his lady at the song's outset. That is, we see again that the lady who sings the song is the *mot gen* whose *langue* is detached from a specific geographical location. The singer's heart, the possibility of his identity as a singular self centered in his *corasso*, is betrayed, robbed, and ravished by the fact that no one but rather *mot gen* are singing—and he himself is that *mot gen*. The song's final couplet reflects absolutely on the status of the song's singing subject: the tongue of the song's "I" is in fact the many tongues of the many, and in the end this generalized ego mourns its captivity in the prison-house of courtly language. For it is nothing but the international language of courtly love that has abducted and ravished the singing "I," robbing the subject of local, historical identity. A song that can slide so easily from one tongue to another, a song that can be performed anywhere but that has its "lair" (to borrow Dante's expression for the utopic homeland of lyric language) nowhere—such a song can be sung by no one or by anyone and everyone. One, however, cannot sing such a song. The singer of Raimbaut's decentered *descort* has been thoroughly *des-cor*'d.

3. The *Speculum* of Song

> a woman speaking it does not just go beyond the bounds of womanhood, but you, dear reader, might even suspect she was a man.
>
> Dante, *De Vulgari Eloquentia*

The poetic drama of courtly love, seemingly generated by the stark difference between lover and lady, by the unsurmountable distance between desiring male subject and desired female object, turns out time and again to efface and to deny whatever distance and difference may have seemed to exist. As the love poet Guillaume de Machaut writes to his lady, herself a love poet, in *Le Voir Dit*: *je ne mes nulle différence entre vous et moi* ("I do not put [i.e., 'impute'] any difference between you and me").[1] Indeed, since "she" is equally a love poet, since Machaut's singular identity has been appropriated by "her," there is no longer a clear mark of difference between them, as both speak precisely the same language, the lyric language of sameness.[2] (As our readings unfold, we shall see that the ostensible drama of courtly love song is frequently inverted, as the desiring man's song turns out to be sung by the desired woman—a woman who, meaning other than herself, represents a principle of externality, objectivity, impersonality, grammaticality, a woman who speaks the general tongue of the *gens*.) Machaut's insistence on his resemblance to his lady may be taken in two ways: on the one hand, that "her" voice is "his" signifies *her* non-existence, her status as a projection or phantasm of his imagination (Machaut, who invents a lady to put words in her mouth, is the great *auctor*, the origin, the authority entirely in charge of the text, the one and only prime Subject or Creator of the textual world); on the other hand, that "his" voice is "hers" signifies *his* non-existence, his status an an effect of her tongue (Machaut, who mimes the lady who mimes the generalized language of courtly love poetry, is perhaps not so *auctor*ial, not so original or originary, not a creator but rather a creation of the conventions of lyric language). The "author" is either all or nothing, the voice of the text either is or is not Machaut's property, and we are left unable to decide. Yet in either case—whether "she" is "he" or "he" is "she"—what matters for us is the specularity of this copulation: the subject is not a positive entity distinctly different from the object, but rather subject and object are in a mutually specular relation. This is to say that the woman is a *speculum* that not only reflects but also produces the singing ego. And, as we shall see, this *speculum* is nothing other than song itself.

Aristotle, at the opening of the early thirteenth-century Old French *Lai d'Aristote*, sternly rebukes his pupil Alexander the Great for loving a certain charming young woman and for thus neglecting the pursuit of individual heroic greatness—for, that is, languishing in the courtly lyrical rather than acting in the epic narrative world.[3] The subsequent joke of the story is that Aristotle falls slavishly in love with this very same woman, who, as payment for amorous sport, demands that the famous philosopher prance horselike on all fours while she is mounted on his back. The *Lai d'Aristote* seems at first a fairly straightforward narrative *exemplum*, an expansion of the moral proverb *amor vincit omnia*, an anti-intellectual insistence that not even the philosopher is exempt from animal desire, a fable for the triumph of the flesh or nature over the mind or culture. Yet what marks the specificity of the *Lai d'Aristote*—what distinguishes it from the multitude of versions of the "same" tale recounted throughout the Middle Ages and Renaissance—is the periodic presence of song, as passages of lyric verse are strategically inserted into the story. Not merely decorous, the moments of song become central to the fable's sense.

The four citations of song inserted into the story coincide precisely with the four occasions upon which Aristotle glimpses or encounters the desired woman. Aristotle is entirely enchanted, not so much by the wiles of a certain woman but rather by *chant* itself: he is subjected to an en-chant-ment, an in-song-ment akin to his possession by the desire of another:

> Mais, por ce que mielz le deçoive
> Et plus beau le voist *enchantant*,
> Vint vers la fenestre *chantant*
> Un vers d'une *chançon* de toile,
> Quar ne velt que cil plus se çoile
> Que tot a mis en la querele:
> > "En un *vergier*, lez une fontenele
> > Dont clere est l'onde et blanche la gravele,
> > Siet fille a foi, sa main a sa maissele.
> > En soupirant son doz ami apele:
> > > 'Hai, cuens Guis amis!

La vostre amor me tolt solaz et ris.'"
Quant ele ot ce dit, si pres passe
De la large fenestre basse
Que cil par le bliaut l'aert,
Qui cuide trop avoir soffert,
Tant par la desire a merveille. (ll. 378–394)

(And in order to deceive him [Aristotle] better and go on enchanting him better, she goes toward the window singing the verses of a *chanson de toile*, for she, who had put all her effort into the task, does not want him to hide: "In an orchard, beside a fountain / with clear water and white pebbles, / sits the King's daughter, her hand on her cheek; / sighing, she calls her sweet friend: / *'Oh! Count Guy, my friend, / your love takes comfort and laughter away from me.'*" As she sang this, she passed by the large low window. And he, who thought that he suffered too much, grabbed her by the dress, so much did he desire the young girl.)

What instigates Aristotle's desire in this passage is the thrice-repeated chant of a form of the word *chanter*, as song enchants and possesses the subject, alienates the subject from propriety and from proper self-possession.[4] Aristotle is charmed, loses possession and lacks determination of his desire—a loss and a lack that are here represented as the effect of *carmen*'s charm. Overhearing another's sung desire, he begins to desire her whom another desires, the woman desired by Alexander. Aristotle's desire, that is, is not self-generating but rather is only generated after he has been subjected to someone else's desire: he desires only after hearing her sing a desire.

Yet it is not really the desire of her whom Alexander desires that is here overheard by Aristotle—which is to say that at stake is a question of complicated citationality. For the snippet of verse that the woman sings contains within it a snippet of verse, and thus a series of screens is placed between Aristotle and the presence of the first-hand self-expression of one's proper and unique desire: authentic, autonomous, self-determined singular desire fades further and further from sight. Within the *Lai d'Aristote* is the citation of a citation, and this improper voice that triggers Aristotle's desire mimes both the voice and the desire of another. Aristotle, that is, only begins to desire after he hears her singing *someone else's* desire.

Nor is the woman whom Alexander and (subsequent to her singing) Aristotle desire merely singing a song. Rather she is singing a *chanson de toile*, a sung story that contains cited song, a lyrico-narrative text that, as such, formally mimes the *Lai d'Aristote* itself: Aristotle's desire is narcissistically fixed on a *récit/chanson spéculaire*, a song-within-a-story that is within a song-within-a-story. The text has fallen in love with itself, and indeed we are here witnessing a genuine *mise-en-abyme*, a mirror image of the text in the text, for the woman who sings of a woman singing in an orchard is herself at this very moment singing in an orchard: the singing woman, the narrator of the *Lai* has told us, *par mi le vergier se deporte* ("is strolling through the orchard") (299). When this woman commences her song by recounting her own story, the story of a woman singing *en un vergier* ("in an orchard") (384), she has become identical with the one about whom she is singing. She is simultaneously both the singing subject and the object of her song. Her song is a *speculum*, a mirror image of herself.

If we can say that the *Lai d'Aristote* recounts a history, we can equally say that the *lai* itself produces the history that it recounts: a mirror image of the *lai* (the embedded *chanson de toile*) triggers those "events" that Aristotle performs and that the *lai* subsequently narrates. The embedded song is the site of a vertiginous effect that defies our efforts to proclaim the priority of either text or history, of either present or past.

This is to say that Aristotle's desire does not exist until it has objective form, until it has been *already* formulated, until he hears it *already* expressed as song: he does not love before the composition of the song that recounts, after the fact, his love. Indeed, in his very first encounter with the woman, at the very moment of the birth of his desire, he is hearing nothing other than his own ex-propriated voice, is hearing her sing his love for her:

> Cele qui Nature avoit painte
> Nuz piez, desloiee, deschainte
> S'en vait, escorçant son bliaut,
> Chantant basset, non mie halt:
>   "C'est la jus desoz l'olive.
>   *Or la voi venir, m'amie!*
>   La fontaine i sort serie,
>   El glaioloi, desoz l'aunoi.
>   *Or la voi, la voi, la voi*
>   La bele blonde! A li m'otroi!"
> . . . .
> Levez ert, si sist a ses livres.
> *Voit la* dame aler et venir,
> El cuer li met un sovenir

Tel que ses livres li fait clorre:
"Ha! Diex, fait il, quar venist ore
Cist *mireors* plus pres de ci!
Si me metroie en sa merci." (ll. 299–328)

(She whom Nature had painted goes barefoot, loosely dressed, without a belt, shifting her dress, singing lowly, not too loudly: "There, under the olive tree. / *I see her coming, my lover!* / The fountain springs serene there, / In the gladioli beneath the alder. / *I see her, I see her, I see her,* / *The beautiful blond, I give myself to her!*" . . . [Aristotle] had risen and sits at his books. *He sees the woman* come and go, she stirs a memory in his heart that makes him close his books: "Oh God, he says, make this *mirror* come closer now! I will put myself at her mercy.")

Here the woman is singing *as a man*, and she is singing nothing other than her desire for "the beautiful blond"—nothing other, that is, than her desire for herself, which desire itself is nothing other than Aristotle's desire for her. Aristotle only begins to desire *after* this originary moment, *after* he hears her sing his desire for her. Aristotle's desire is thus instigated by this alien voice that is identical with his own, by this voice that is both "hers" and "his." And it is no longer mere speculation that powers our reading: clearly, without doubt, it is song's specularity that enchants Aristotle, as he proclaims his desire to look more closely into that self-reflecting *mireors* ("mirror") that is the singing woman.[5] The song's *la voi* ("I see her") generates its identical inversion in the guise of the story's *voit la* ("he sees her"): he later sees the woman who previously sang of his seeing the woman. She, whose tresses are, a few lines before this passage, said to be *blonde* (295), is that *blonde* whom she is singing about (308): the singing subject is herself the object of her song. And, since as the object of her song she is also the object of Aristotle's desire, Aristotle has become the subject, the singer, of the song to which he is listening—a song that fascinates him insofar as it is a mirror image of his own voice, insofar as it is the site of the originary alienation of his desire from itself. Aristotle, that is, is listening to her sing his desire for her: "*I see her, I see her, I see her,* / *The beautiful blond, I give myself to her!*" He is hearing that his own voice is elsewhere, someone else's. This makes us want to rewrite that line of the song that tells of the sighting of a singer—*la voi, la voi, la voi* ("I see her, I see her, I see her")—to make it tell of the siting, across the space of an irreducible distance, of the singer's own voice: *la voix, la voix, la voix* ("the voice, the voice, the voice"). It is this external, objective, yet specular *voix* that constitutes Aristotle's singing subjectivity, and it is his recognition that someone else possesses his voice that enchants him. She is his *speculum*, his mirror, the sign of the division and difference of his voice from itself.

The specularity of this embedded lyric *mireors* does not stop here—for the song itself displays an internal specularity, the mirror is itself structured like a mirror. The *mireors* is both the woman who has appropriated Aristotle's voice and the mirror-like song that is the objective site of Aristotle's subjectivity.[6] The voice of the cited song is not at all a unity, since the song is a *rondeau*, a song with more than one *partie*, a song sung by several. The very image of an infinitely regressive specularity, the Old French *rondeau* is a little song divided in two, each of whose two parts is itself divided in two. It is this division at the heart of the *rondeau* that prompts Aristotle to call it a *mireors*. Here, for instance, is a four-line *rondeau* inserted by Jean Renart (whom philology credits as the inventor of such a technique of insertion) into his romance *Guillaume de Dole*:[7]

First Part	Solo:	*C'est tot la gieus el glaioloi*
	Refrain:	*Tenez moi, dame, tenez moi!*
Second Part	Solo:	*Une fontaine i sordoit. A é!*
	Refrain:	*Tenez moi, dame, por les maus d'amer!*

(ll. 329–332)

Not only is the Second Part a specular image of the First, but each part is itself the site of an internal specularity: the voice of the soloist and leader of the dance bounces back to him as the refrain sung by the entire *ensemble* of dancers. Most significantly, it is the choral refrain that has become the site of the solo, that has become the place of the first-person singular imperative ("Hold me, lady, hold me!")—which means that the soloist's subjective desire can only be represented as the objective desire of the multitude: the many appropriate the voice of the singular subject. Yet if the refrain is the *mireors* of the solo, this is a special sort of *speculum* that is not ruled by a one-to-one *ratio* of reflection but rather that multiplies the image that it reflects: the solo voice is reflected back to itself as the voices of several. The *rondeau* is the denial of the solitude, the privation of the privacy, of the voice of the singing subject.

The six-line *rondeau* that Aristotle sees as the *mireors* of his own voice more precisely reflects the multiplying propensity of the *rondeau*, insofar as its Second Part is a doubling of its First:

| First Part | Solo: | *C'est la jus desoz l'olive.* |
| | Refrain: | *Or la voi venir, m'amie!* |

Second Part Solo: La fontaine i sort serie,
                       El glaioloi, desoz l'aunoi.
               Refrain: *Or la voi, la voi, la voi*
                       La bele blonde! A li m'otroi!
                                   (ll. 303–308)

The Second Part of this *rondeau* reflects, with a difference, the First: what is initially one (the one verse of the solo, the one verse of the refrain) is now two. The Second Part is the *mireors* which multiplies an original unity to reflect that unity's originary self-divided multiplicity. The Second Part of the embedded *rondeau* is, then, a mirror of that mirror which is the woman and the song. That is, the relation between First and Second Part is a mirror of the relation between Aristotle and the *mireors* which is the site of his desire: Aristotle's voice is doubled by the singing woman, a doubling which exposes its originary self-alienated multiplicity. Like Narcissus, whom the Middle Ages regards as the perfect image of the the courtly singer, *the singing subject is both multiplied and divided*. Aristotle, who at the commencement of the *lai*, in his counsel to Alexander, champions the possibility of solo self-identity, is forced face-to-face with its impossibility, as he hears the improper plurality of his voice reflected back to him from its properly objective origin.

The mere fact that her voice is his is an affront to the integrity of the proper voice—an affront which is just retribution to one who would proclaim that the subject stands before and outside the circuit of the linguistic exchange of desire. "She" can be "he" because the voice is not fixed to the body of its owner, because the voice can be appropriated by any and every one—regardless of such empirically real differences as gender and class (she sings, in the course of the *lai*, of both King's daughter and laundress, as both man and woman). Aristotle's downfall is the truth that courtly song has no fixed or necessary relation to the empirical body of the singer in the empirical world: lyric language belongs to any and everyone, duke or *jongleur*, knight or lady. The individual instrument of its utterance is always merely its temporary proprietor.

Immediately after the birth of his desire for the *mireors* of his voice, Aristotle's voice becomes a *mireors* of itself, as his speech is apprehended and suspended in a space of its own specular undoing (to which no translation can do justice):

Mal ai emploié mon estuide,
Qui onques ne finai d'*aprandre*!
Or me *desaprant* por mielz *prandre*

> Amors, qui maint preudome *a pris*,
> S'ai en *aprenant desapris*.
> *Desapris* ai en *aprenant*,
>   Puis qu'Amors me va si *prenant*. (ll. 342–348)
>
> (I, who have never stopped learning, have badly used my studies! Now Love, who has taken many good men, unlearns me, in order to take me better. I have in learning become unlearned; unlearned I have become in learning, since Love is taking me so.)

Aristotle's speech, which follows upon the sighting of the *speculum* of his desire, reflects nothing other than the specularity of his speech, which is a seemingly unstoppable series of reversals and repetitions, an alternation between positive and negative images (*aprandre/des-aprandre*) of various forms and variants of a primordial word. The essence of this speech is concentrated in verses 346–347, which, repeating each other in reverse, graphically figure the specular *X* of chiasmus:

> S'ai en *aprenant desapris*
>
> *Desapris* ai en *aprenant*

The second of these lines being entirely redundant, bearing no further information concerning the advance of the narrative, these lines tell the entire story of the story, the story of the resemblance, the undifferentiation, of Aristotle's tongue and that *mireors* that is the tongue of the singing woman who sings Aristotle's desire. If she is a mirror, what she reflects is his own mirrorlike tongue, which, turning back upon itself, repeats itself with a difference.

Since in the *Lai d'Aristote* the simultaneity of the woman's presence with the presence of her singing voice is nearly absolute, the woman's attraction is that of the Siren, more the spell of a lyric voice than the lure of physical beauty. So it appears that the proverbial sense of the *Lai d'Aristote* could equally or more properly be *cantus vincit omnia*, song conquers all. It is lyric language rather than love *per se* that is the great equalizer, that reduces the great Aristotle and Alexander the Great to the rank of all others, and that reduces all to the rank of the beasts. In the end Aristotle becomes Doctor Donkey as he is dominated by the strain of a refrain that he bears on his back:

> La damoisele fait monter
> Sor son dos, et puis si la porte.

La damoisele se deporte
En lui chevauchier et deduit;
Parmi le vergier le conduit,
Si chante cler et a voiz plaine:
"Ainsi va qui amors maine.
    Bele Doe i ghee laine.
    Maistre musart me soutient!
Ainsi va qui amors maine
Et ainsi qui les maintient!"
Alixandres ert en la tor,
Bien ot veu trestout l'ator.
"Mestre, ce dist li rois, que vaut-ce?
Je voi bien que on vos chevauche.
Comment estes vos forsenez,
Qui en tel point estes menez?
Vos me feistes l'autre foiz
De li veoir si grant desfoiz!
Et or vos a mis en tel point
Qu'il n'a en vos de *raison* point,
ainz vos metez a loi de beste." (ll. 455–477)

(The young lady mounts on his back, and then he carries her. The young lady enjoys and delights in riding him; she drives him around the orchard and sings brightly in a clear voice: "'This is how one whom love leads goes.' / *'Beautiful Doe is washing wool.'* / 'Doctor Donkey is bearing me.' / 'This is how one whom love leads goes / and also those who support them.'" Alexander was in the tower, he had seen the whole thing well. "Master," said the King, "what's this? I see very well that someone is riding you. Are you crazy, to have put yourself in such a place? The other day you made such a prohibition against my seeing her! And now she's put you in such a position that there's no reason [or, "speech"] in you at all, but rather you submit to the law of beasts.")

If Aristotle has no *raison* in him, this means not only that his philosophy has been cast aside but also that he is, like the beast that he mimes, quite speechless (the Old French *raison* possibly meaning, like the Old Provençal *razo*, "speech"). Indeed, as Alexander declares, "il n'a *en* [Aristotle] raison point" ("there is no speech at all *in* Aristotle"): the site of his speech is the singing woman, who is without and upon the exterior rather than within the interior of Aristotle. And Aristotle's speech lacks a reason insofar as the divided multiplicity of Aristotle's *raison* does not obey the one-to-one *ratio* of Aristotelian realist mimesis.

This final embedded song that signals Aristotle's ultimate subjection is the text's final insistence upon song's heteroglossia. For there is simply no way to unify this voice as it rides triumphantly over the philosophy of the solo. Verses 461 and 464–465 ("This is what happens to one whom love leads, etc.") properly belong to the register of the "moral of the story" typically tagged on the end of medieval fable and *fabliau*; these verses, that is, represent the voice of the narrator of a moral exemplum. Verse 462 (*"Beautiful Doe is washing wool"*) is another citation from a *chanson de toile*, the narrative voice of a lyrico-narrative text, a voice here appropriated by the singing woman. Verse 463 ("Doctor Donkey is bearing me") is the voice of the singing woman narrating the events of the story in which this song is embedded. Thus the song is sung by three distinct narrative voices that temporarily inhabit the body of a single performer, and song appears as a conflation of stories, as a confusion of styles voiced by a multitude of singers. Medieval lyric does not respond to a criticism grounded in the Romantic poetics of the solo singer, for in fact its essence is that very heteroglossia that recent theorists regard as properly belonging to the province of the novel.[8] To sing medieval song is to appropriate as one's own a voice that properly belongs to many, to sing as no one in particular.

Aristotle, who had counseled Alexander to stand alone and, through willful self-determination, to withdraw from the game of desire, now plays that game in which the subject is subjected to the same old song. Song is that force that collapses differential hierarchies, that reveals latent resemblances. Aristotle's defeat is the defeat of that thinking that posits a pure ego securely immune from its contamination by the impurity of others, that posits that the ego can perpetually maintain its own position. Above all, of course, the *lai* shatters the egoistic illusion that one is unique, autonomous, or extraordinary: neither king nor philosopher stand above or outside the system of linguistically determined desire. The hero's philosopher is leveled by a dominant discourse, a discourse without heroes, by the language of the *gens*, by medieval lyric's fundamentally generalized subjectivity. Or, to put it somewhat differently, Aristotle's Homeric and positively narrative concern with fame, with the preservation of Alexander's good and proper name, is defeated in its combat with song, the voice of the nameless and the champion of anonymity.

4. The Burgher and the Bird

What is an *author*? The word "author" comes from the Latin *auctor*, which means "originator," "causer," "doer." In the late Middle Ages, this *auctor* was virtually always regarded as *someone else*, someone other than the poet, someone who had, in the distant past, caused an *auctoritas* (an authoritative statement or text) to come into being. God, the "Causer" of Scripture, was regarded as the *Auctor par excellence*. The human *auctor* was a famous name from the past (Augustine, Boethius, Priscian, etc.), the value of whose text had been legitimated by its enduring for several centuries. The *auctor*, that is, was necessarily someone who had been long dead.[1] The knowledge imparted by the medieval text is not a previously unknown novelty but rather is the knowledge of the already known. In the late Middle Ages, the living writer, the one who is presently composing, represents him- or herself not as an *auctor*, not as the "originator" or "causer" of the text, but rather as a scribe, as one who is copying down or repeating a text that has already been written. Thus the late medieval narrator, for instance, does not say "*I* say that *X* happened" but rather says "*The text* says that *X* happened." The medieval writer's text, which, properly speaking, is not the *writer's*, does not originate in the present, does not say something new, but rather has already originated in the past, says what has already been said. Medieval writing is not a matter of "genius" or native intelligence but rather a matter of learning the art of the already written. The scribal writer has a *passive* relation to the already written text: the text speaks through the writer, who is merely the instrument or tool of its discourse. In brief, the medieval writer is not an "author."

At the dawn of the Renaissance, this temporal gap between the text's past origin and its present inscription, this difference between the *auctor* and the writer begins to be eliminated. The writer is no longer hesitant to regard him- or herself as the *auctor*, as the "originator" or "causer" of a text which is truly the *writer's* property. Now it is possible to be a living *auctor*. Thus Dante, for instance, needing in the *De Vulgari Eloquentia* to cite an *auctoritas* to support one of his claims, does not cite the words of a venerable *auctor* but rather cites *himself*:

> I say, then, that the *canzone* . . . is the linking together in the tragic style of equal stanzas without a "reprise" with the meaning expressed as a unity, *as I myself demonstrate where I write*: "Donne, che avete intellecto d'amore, etc. . . ."[2]

In the place where the medieval writer would customarily have inserted an *auctoritas*, Dante instead inserts a line of his own verse: his own writing has the status of an *auctoritas*.

Once the *auctor* and the living writer have become one and the same, then the nativity of the text is regarded as taking place "inside" the latter, as caused by no one other than the writer. The writer is no longer the scribe or the passive imitator of the already written, but now is the active producer of the entirely new. The origin of the text is no longer *elsewhere* and *in the past*, but now is *here and now*. This is the birth of the modern or bourgeois idea of the writer as "author"—the idea of the writer as *first cause, creator* of an original, novel, unique discourse. Now the writer's text is truly the *writer's*, bears his or her own name (and will eventually become, by the end of the Renaissance, legally and literally his or her own private property). Whereas the medieval writer appears as the scribe, as one through whom the text speaks, as merely the instrument or tool by which the text expresses itself, the modern or bourgeois "author" appears to speak through the text, which is merely the instrument or tool of the author's "self-expression."

A pair of late medieval tales, *Le vilain et l'oiselet* and the *Lai de l'oiselet* (variants of each other that I shall read as an *ensemble*), narrate the advent of the modern or bourgeois idea of the author, as well as the "death of the troubadour" that this idea precipitates.[3] These tales, which narrate the conflict between the troubadour and the bourgeois individual, suggest that courtly song no longer has a place in the new economic and ideological order. These tales recount the flight of song, its obsolescence, its disappearance from a world dominated by individuals. They represent a world in which song's essential significance is no longer understood. Yet, even while lamenting the loss of the anonymous singing subject, these tales persist in offering a glimpse of that anonymity.

These two *fabliaux* narrate the flight or disappearance of an *oiselet*, a "little bird" who represents not merely itself but also a distinct literary register: there is no more common figure for courtly song in the late Middle Ages than the voice of the *oiselet*, birdsong (time and again the troubadour *canso* commences with an analogy between avian and lyric performance). The history of the little bird recounted by these tales is nothing other than the history of the troubadour, and the little bird's fate is nothing other than the fate of courtly love lyric.

The tale's initial language is entirely lyrical, as it rehearses the typical springtime opening stanza of countless troubadour and trouvère songs:

> Un preudom ot un bel jardin,
> Entrer i selt chascun matin
> En la saison quant par delit
> Chantent oisel grant et petit.
> Une fontenele i sordoit
> Qui le liu raverdir faisoit:
> Oisel i souloient entrer,
> Et molt douce noise lever.
> Le preudom un jor i entra,
> En cel beau liu se reposa:
> Un oiselet i oit chanter . . . (Barbazan)

> (A man had a beautiful garden; he used to enter there every morning in the season when large and small birds sing with delight. A little fountain sprang up from there that made the place all green. Birds used to enter there and raise a very sweet noise. One day the man entered there; he rested in this beautiful place: he heard a little bird sing . . .)

A man goes into a garden and hears birdsong: this is precisely what is happening in the initial stanza of countless troubadour and trouvère songs. *Le vilain et l'oiselet* opens not with the promise to relate some novel adventure but rather by mimicking the most conventional of lyric conventions.

Yet, if the story opens under the guise of song, this is song with a difference: whereas the tense of true courtly love song is an ahistorical, atemporal present, this springtime opening has been set in the past ("he *used to* enter there"; "birds *used to* enter there"). At the outset of *Le vilain et l'oiselet*, atemporal lyric language has become temporal, synchrony has become diachrony, song has become story, *langue* has become *parole*, the *canso* has become *fabliau*. The tale's chief significance lies precisely in this *historicization* of birdsong, which now appears as a discourse that is historically doomed, that has been consigned to the past.

As we shall see, the adventure that follows this songlike opening tells how the perpetual present of courtly lyric is overthrown by the advent of the past tense, how the perfectly ahistorical world of birdsong is supplanted by the imperfect "used to . . ." of *historia*. Now, in the present of the storytelling, birdsong no longer graces the *locus amoenus* of literature: *Oisel i souloient entrer* ("Birds *used to* enter there"). The tale's prime purpose is to recount the historical event that precipitated this "used to . . . ," to explain song's expulsion from the garden, to narrate the *oiselet*'s flight from its perpetually unchanging *locus*. Song is gone—and the *fabliau*'s task is to disclose the reason for its disappearance. As we shall see, the reason for the fall of the bird's *régime* is bound up with the appearance of the burgher.

That courtly lyric is the language of an ahistorical synchrony, the tongue of an eternal present, is posited quite clearly by the *Lai de l'oiselet*. After describing the aviary garden as perpetually fruitful, as an Edenic *locus* not subject to seasonal change, the text tells that the secret of this resistance to *historia* is nothing other than song:

> Mais une autre mervoille y ot,
> Que li vergiers durer ne pot,
> Se tant non que li oisillons
> I venist chanter les douz sons;
> *Car de chant issent les amors*
> *Qui en vertu tienent les flors,*
> Et li arbres et toz li mez,
> Mès que li oisiax fust remez,
> Maintenant li vergiers sechast,
> Et la fontaingne restanchast,
> Qui par l'oisel sont en vertu. (Pauphilet)

(But there was another marvel: the garden could not last unless the bird came there to sing sweet songs; for *from song issue the loves that keep the flowers strong*, and the trees and all the fruits. But ever since the bird has gone, now the garden is dry, and the spring has stopped up, which the bird alone keeps alive.)

The garden is inseparable from, cannot exist without, birdsong—which means that the garden is no natural or actual place that pre-exists but rather is a *topos* or place that depends upon, is an effect of, courtly song. Song here is represented not as something produced in the world but rather as something that produces a world. Similarly, love here is not originary or natural, does not come before its expression in song, since song is itself the source of love: *de chant issent les amors / Qui en vertu tienent les flors* ("from song issue the loves / that keep the flowers strong"). Song *precedes* love: desire is not the origin of the song, but rather the song is the origin of desire (this was precisely the lesson of the *Lai d'Aristote*). Lovers do not sing as a result of loving, but rather they love as a result of singing. *Amor* is only the apparent origin of these *flors*, these flowers of rhetoric, which are in fact more deeply rooted in *chant*: the flowers of rhetoric flourish from a rhetorical, not a natural, terrain. Love stories, *les amors* that blossom into literary romance, issue not from *historia* but rather from a primordial song: from song issue the *vidas*, the life stories, which keep the garden of literature *en vertu* ("going strong").

Naturally, when the rhetorical flowers are cut off from their rhetorical source in song, the garden becomes arid: *Mès que li oisiax fust remez, / Maintenant li vergiers sechast* ("But since the bird has gone, now the garden is dry"). Without love song, there is no love—since love cannot exist independently from its linguistic expression, has no reality outside the language of love. Moreover, these lines lament the death of the troubadour, a death that is here figured as the bird's flight from the garden. Consequent upon the flight of the bird, the flowers of rhetoric have dried up, the "springs" of troubadour verse have ceased to flow.

Before its flight from the garden, the effect of song is to efface social difference, as the subject possessed by song resembles all others:

> Car ens el chant ot tel mervoille,
> Qu'ainz nus hom n'oi sa paroille;
> Quar tel vertus avoit li chanz,
> Que nus hum ne fust si dolanz,
> Pour coi l'oisel chanter oist,
> Maintenant ne s'en resjoist,
> Et obliast ses grans dolors,
> Et si represist ses amors,
> Maintenant fust d'amors *sorpris*,
> Et *cuidast estre de tel pris*
> *Com est Empereres ou Rois,*
> *Mais qu'il fust vilains ou borjois.* (Pauphilet)

(For in song there was such a magic that no one has ever heard its like; for song had such power that no one could be so unhappy that he would not rejoice because he heard the bird sing, and he would forget his great sorrows and take up his love again; now he was overtaken [*sorpris*] with love, and *he believed himself to be of such value as if he were an Emperor or King, although he was a peasant or a bourgeois*.)

The subject enchanted by song is here represented as having been *sorpris*—surprised, invaded, overtaken. Love, originating in song, is an alien force that invades and takes possession of the subject—a subject who is subjected to song, appropriated by song. The subject does not choose to love; rather love chooses its subjects, and in so doing does not discriminate between individuals. Whoever one is, in the world of song one is the same as another, one is a courtly lover like all others—the *vilain* is the Emperor, the *borjois* is the King. Song, the great equalizer, can appropriate anyone and everyone, cannot be made the private property, the special privilege, of someone in particular. Song, which makes the *borjois* into someone else, into what he is not (King), violates the bourgeois principle of the ego's self-identity, makes the burgher other than himself.

This man who goes into the garden at the tale's outset, the *vilain* of the tale's title, is a certain *borjois* who has recently acquired the title to the *locus amoenus*. This burgher has bought the garden of song—a purchase that the tale regards as a tragic fall from a feudal to a monetary system:

> Ainz fu un Chevaliers gentis,
> Après le père l'ot li fis
> Qui le vendi à cel vilain,
> Ainsi ala de main en main:
> Bien savez que par malvais hoir
> Dechiént viles et manoir. (Pauphilet)

(Before it belonged to a noble knight; after the father it belonged to the son, who sold it to this *vilain*, and thus it goes from hand to hand: you well know that through bad heirs villas and manors are destroyed.)

As a consequence of the new economic order, the *locus* of literature has shifted into the hands of the *borjois*—a shift that the rest of the tale ridicules and laments. Yet the tragedy which has befallen is not merely a matter of economics; more than the advent of buying and selling, the text laments a new ignorance of or disrespect for the power of song. Song has fallen into the possession of a new audience that has little regard for the appeal of lyric language. Whereas for the former audience song was the central source of a collective resemblance (a resemblance grounded in each one's similar self-alienated subjection to song), the latter-day audience now consists of a single individual, bent upon the acquisition of private property, who relegates song to the margins, who no longer listens to the bird's *langue* (as the bird himself laments in the following lines):

"Ci me soloient escouter
Gentis Dames et Chevalier,
Qui la fontaine avoient chier,
Qui à mon chant se delitoient,
Et par amors miex en amoient;
Si en faisoient les largesces,
Les cortoisies, les prouesces,
Maintenoient Chevalerie;
Or m'ot cil vilains plains d'envie,
Qui aime assés miex le denier
Qu'il ne face le dosnoier.
Cil me venoient escouter
Por deduire et por miex amer;
Mais *cist* i vient por miex mengier,
Por miex boire et por gloutoier." (Pauphilet)

("Here noble Ladies and Knights used to listen to me, who appreciated the fountain and who delighted in my song and loved better because of it; they performed Love's generous, courteous, and noble deeds, and they maintained the ways of chivalry. Now this lustful *vilain* has me, who loves the dollar much more than the tax collector does. *Those* used to come to listen to me for their delight and to love better; but *this one* comes here to eat better, to drink better, and to gluttonize.")

Here the voice of courtly lyric mourns its own disappearance, laments the historical turn that spelled the doom of troubadour song. Clearly, the critical turn is a change of audience from the collective to the self-centered: a undifferentiated plurality of "those" (*cil*) gives way to the singular "this one" (*cist*), to one whose prime motivation is a self-interested impulse to acquire. This change is synonymous with the silencing of birdsong. Song no longer has a place, as the burgher, ignoring its centrality, enters its place with no intent to heed its call. Whereas the aristocratic audience regarded song as the foundation upon which everything else depends, the burgher regards song—if he even regards it at all—as merely a marginal curiosity. Lyric language no longer exists as such but rather is left to lament its death, to recollect its former power. The bird, which never actually sings in this *fabliau*, narrates the history of its own obsolescence and the advent of the bourgeoisie.

There is in the tale a definitive event that precipitates the flight of the bird. The burgher begins to covet birdsong, attempts to capture it, to acquire it for himself, to make it his own private property. One day the *borjois* enters the garden of song, whereupon he attempts to snare a bird:

> Cel prist forment à desirrer.
> A un laz un oiselet prist. (Barbazan)

(He began strongly to desire. He caught a little bird with a net.)

Previously, while the garden of courtly love song still fluorished, subjects were *surprised and overtaken (sorpris) by song*. Now, after the burgher has become the proprietor of the garden, this relation between subject and song is reversed: the burgher *surprises and takes song*. Whereas previously the bird *captured* subjects, now the bird is *captured by* the subject. The difference between the courtly and the bourgeois lover, then, is the difference between a *passive* and an *active* relation to song. Whereas the courtly lover appeared as *the object upon whom song acts*, now the bourgeois lover appears as *the subject who acts upon song*, as the *auctor*, the "doer," "causer," or "originator" of an effect.

This difference between a passive and an active relation to song is clearly formulated by Dante in the *De Vulgari Eloquentia*:

> Let us look now at what a *canzone* is, and at what we mean when we say *canzone*. A *canzone* is, according to the plain signification of the name, singing itself, either in an *active* or a *passive* sense, just as an interpretation is reading in either an active or a passive sense. But let us examine what has just been said to see whether a *canzone* is so called because of the active or because of the passive sense of the term. And on this question it may be observed that the term, *canzone*, is used in two ways, in one way insofar as it is the composition of its author, and this is the active sense—used so by Virgil at the opening of the *Aeneid* where he says "Arma virumque *cano*" ["Arms and the man *I sing*"]; in another way insofar as, having been composed, it is performed either by the author or by anyone else, and either performed in time to music or not, and this is its passive sense. In the first case, the *canzone* is created—*acted upon*—while in the second it *acts upon* someone, and thus in the one case it would seem to be an action of someone, but in the other, someone's passive performance. And because it must be acted upon before it can act upon another, it is therefore more the action of someone, and should certainly seem to get its name from the one who acts upon it than from the one which it acts upon. The

evidence for this is that we never say "This is Peter's *canzone*," referring to the person who performs it, but rather to the person who composed it.⁴

Here Dante distinguishes between the *auctor*, a certain individual who can be named—Virgil, or "Peter"—and the anonymous performer ("either the author or anyone else"), no one in particular. The *auctor* is the creator, the originator, and the song is properly *his* possession. Before the *auctor* acts upon song, the song is not yet there. On the contrary, the anonymous performer, acted upon by song, is the "finder," the *trobador*, the imitator of a song that is already there and that is properly someone else's possession. The "author" is the subject who acts upon song; the troubadour is the object acted upon by song.

The burgher of our tale, who attempts actively to capture song rather than passively being caught by it, who would do something to song rather than having song do something to him, is a would-be *auctor*. He will be the "doer," the "originator" or "causer," the instigator of an effect, and, in so doing, he will make song *his* possession, will make a name for himself. This burgher's intrusion into the garden of courtly song is the advent, at the dawn of the Renaissance, of the bourgeois idea of the author.

Let us take another look at these two lines:

Cel prist forment à desirrer.
A un laz un oiselet prist.

(He began strongly to desire. He caught a little bird with a net.)

Here the burgher's desire comes first, *precedes* his possession of the little bird which is song. Moreover, rather than being *taken by desire* [*sorpris*], the burgher *takes to desiring*: *Cel prist . . . à desirrer* ["He took . . . to desiring"]. The bourgeois subject first actively determines his desire, first chooses to love, then searches for song. In brief, the bourgeois subject *precedes* his desire, which *precedes* his song. This is a precise reversal of the logic which prevailed while the bird was still master of the garden of courtly lovers. Previously, song determined desire (*de chant issent les amors* ["from song issue loves"]), then desire (*Amor*) determined (*sorpris*) its subjects. Now, the bourgeois author is the *first cause* who creates or produces a desire, then masters song in order to "express" this desire. The troubadour, on the contrary, is mastered by desire, which is created or produced by the *first cause* which is song.

While the garden of song still flourished, the bird sang for everyone in general and no one in particular. Whereas the audience was once an undifferentiated plurality, now it consists of a single individual who wants song to address him and him alone, who regards song as his own special privilege. Responding to an interrogation by the bird whom he has snared, the burgher confesses that his prime motivation is to command a private performance:

> L'oisel li demanda et dist:
> "Por qoi to vosis travailler
> Por moi deçoivre et engignier?
> Por qoi me vosis decevoir?
> Quel preu i cuides-tu avoir?"
> "*Ge vueil*," dit-il, "*que tu me chantes.*" (Barbazan)

(The bird asked him and said: "Why do you want to work to deceive and trick me? Why do you want to deceive me? What profit do you hope to gain from it?" "*I want*," he said, "*for you to sing [for] 'me.'*")

This *Ge vueil . . . que tu me chantes* ("I want you to sing 'me'") expresses the burgher's desire for a voice capable of expressing the *me*, the *moi*, the ego. He wants to have and to hold in his possession a voice that sings "me"—a "self-expressive" voice that could properly be called his own, that is his and no one else's.[5] The violence of the burgher's assault upon the bird is his attempt to transform the language of song, which addresses no one in particular, into a language that expresses the individual ego. The burgher would confine song, severely limit and reduce the range of its potential to signify.

The rest of the tale recounts the burgher's failure to confine and possess the bird, as the burgher is duped into releasing him. The bird strikes a deal with the burgher: if the latter will set him free, he will teach the burgher three items of "wisdom" or "knowledge" (*sen* or *savoir*) that no one of his "lineage" or "class" (*lignage*) has ever known. The burgher deems that this is indeed the greatest profit that he could hope to gain from song (namely, to be set apart from the rest of his *gens*, to be marked as different from and better than other burghers, to be distinguished, by his possession of a secret knowledge, as an extraordinary individual), and he thus agrees to release the bird from captivity.

Once free, the bird delivers on his promise, but what he offers the burgher is nothing special, no items of secret wisdom, but rather merely three items of proverbial wisdom (the import of which is that the burgher should never have trusted the bird, nor should he be surprised and upset at the result):

> "Ne croi pas quanque tu orras;
> Garde bien ce que tu auras,
> Par pramesse nel' perdre pas;
> Ne trop ne soies confondu
> Por nule riens qu'aies perdu:
> Ce sont li trois savoir, amis,
> Que ge à dire te pramis." (Barbazan)

> ("Don't believe everything you hear; hold on to what you have, don't lose it by trusting a promise; don't be too upset over anything you have lost: these are the three items of wisdom, friend, that I promised to tell you.")

The burgher angrily and repeatedly protests that he has been swindled, since the bird has merely told him what everyone of his lineage—and indeed everyone whomsoever—already knows:

> Le vilains fronce le nez d'ire,
> Et dist "*je le savoie bien.*" (Pauphilet)

> (The *vilain* frowned angrily and said, "*I knew that already.*")

> Li vilains ne fu mis mus,
> Ainz respondi par felonie,
> "Tu m'as ta fiance mentie:
> Trois sens me devoies aprendre,
> Si com tu me feis entendre,
> C'onques ne sot tous mes lignages;
> Mais *de ce est tous li mons sages.*" (Pauphilet)

> (The *vilain* was not silent, but responded with anger: you have broken your promise to me: You were supposed, as you led me to understand, to teach me three items of wisdom that no one of my lineage ever knew; but *everybody is wise to this.*")

> Li vilains fu moult correciez,
> Et quant il s'est téus grant pose,
> se dist, "n'estoit-ce autre chose?
> Ce sont adevinal d'enfant,
> Car je sai bien à esciant,
> Tex est poures et souffraitous,
> Qui ausi bien le set com vous,
> Menti m'avez et engignié;
> *De quanques m'avez enseignié,*
> *Estoie-je sages d'avant.* (Pauphilet)

(The *vilain* was very angry, and when after a while he had calmed down he said, "Was that all there is to it? These are the divinations of a child, for I know quite well that even the poor and the suffering know these things as well as you. You have lied to me and tricked me; *I already knew everything that you taught me.*)

Expecting the language of the bird to serve as the vehicle for novelty, the burgher is stunned to receive the repetition of the same. Desiring a secret, an extraordinary or private knowledge that will set him apart from the others, the burgher instead is taught what is already public knowledge, a knowledge that is commonplace even among children and the suffering poor. In brief, the bird says what everyone already knows.

Thus the language of the bird, which is song, is a language of proverbs, clichés, common knowledge. Song is not a language of novelty but rather a language of the already known. Song's wisdom, that is, is the wisdom of *fore-knowledge*. Song teaches only the collective knowledge of the *gens*, what the "they" already knows. Song is the patrimony of commonplaces, the already formulated discourse in which the subject finds himself always already "thrown." The subject does not precede this fore-knowledge that is song, but rather is preceded and produced by it. To be mastered by song is to be always already determined by "their" voice, by the voice of the already known. Song is the originary wisdom, the originary set of meanings, prejudices, assumptions, and pre-conceptions that shapes the subject's knowledge of the world.[6]

The bird brilliantly defends himself against the charge that he has broken his promise by demonstrating that the burgher in fact *did not know* what he already knew:

"Vilains, maintenant prouverai
Des trois sens que pas ne savoies." (Barbazan)

("*Vilain*, now I shall prove that you did not already know the three items of wisdom.")

The burgher, who has violated the three proverbs by believing everything he heard, by not holding on to what he had, and by becoming upset over what he has lost, has—thus concludes the bird—proven by his very actions that he was not already wise to that to which everyone is already wise. The bird has thus cleverly and precisely defined the bourgeoisie: what no one of the burgher's lineage knows is what he already knows. The bourgeois individual, that is, is precisely *he who is ignorant of his fore-knowledge*, he who has forgotten or repressed what he already knows, he who fails to acknowledge his position in the circular structure of knowledge, in the hermeneutic circle. The bourgeois subject regards himself as a *tabula rasa*, as one who is entirely new or original at the time of his nativity, as one who has not yet been written upon, as the *auctor*, the originator or creator of a knowledge that was in fact already created and had already originated before the subject was "thrown" into the world. The troubadour, on the contrary, is the one who acknowledges that his knowledge is founded upon an originary fore-knowledge.

The bird is now free from the burgher's grasp, and about to take flight from his world—but he does not leave before delivering a parting shot, before taking aim at another bourgeois misconception concerning the significance of song. This time, the bird plays upon the burgher's belief that the singing voice has an "inside," an interior dimension wherein resides song's true value:

"Benoit soit Diex de Maysté,
Qui t'a des elz tant avuglé
Et t'a tolu sens et savoir,
Por qu'as perdu si grant avoir.
Se *dedenz* cherchié m'éussiez,
Une jagonce i trovissiez
En un jusier, se ge ne ment,
Qui poise une once droitement." (Barbazan)

("Blessèd be Almighty God, Who has so blinded you and deprived you of sense and wisdom that you have lost such a great possession. If you would have searched *within* me, you would have found a gemstone, in my gizzard, which weighs, if I am not lying, fully an once.")

Here the bird is tempting the burgher to regard song as if it were allegory—a rhetorical surface or relatively worthless shell that harbors within it a valuable kernel. The bird dupes the burgher into considering song as the repository or container of something hidden within, something other than and more valuable than itself. The interior gemstone, that is, would be the "meaning" of song, a precious content that, being other than song, relegates song to a secondary, subservient, or marginal position with respect to itself. The burgher is he who readily denies the value, primacy, mastery, and centrality of song itself, he who would ravage, destroy, and discard song in order to get at its "inside."

Yet in fact the bird, as he himself suggests, *is* lying ("if I am not lying")—which fact he ultimately reveals to the burgher as the latter is lamenting his loss of the gemstone:

> Et quant li vileins l'entendi,
> Plora et plaint et se bati,
> Et sovent prist à regreter
> C'onques laissa l'oisel aler.
> "Musarz," dit l'oisel, "estordi,
> Or as-tu tot mis en oubli
> Les trois manieres, ce m'est vis
> Du savoir qu'orendroit te dis.
> Ge di que croire ne devroies
> Tote la riens que tu orroies:
> Por qoi crois-tu si de legier
> C'une pierre eust en mon jusier,
> Jagonce d'une once pesant,
> Quant ge toz ne poise pas tant. (Barbazan)

(And when the *vilain* heard it, he cried and lamented and beat himself, and he often regretted that he had ever let the bird go. "Moron," said the bird, "scatter-brain, now it seems to me that you have already forgotten the three manners of wisdom that I just told you. I said that you should not believe everything you hear: why do you so easily believe that there could be a stone in my gizzard, a gemstone weighing an ounce, when I myself don't even weigh so much.")

As the bird takes flight, abandoning forever what was once his garden, he admits to having nothing inside, no precious gemstone of hidden value. The value of song, that is, is its surface, nothing other than itself. Against those who, like the burgher, would readily regard song as *heavy*, *profound*, and *full*, the bird promotes a vision of song as *light*, *superficial*, and *empty*. Song's value is "outside": even when apparently internalized by the individual, song remains the language of the exterior.

5. Anti-*Vida*, Anti-*Razo*

What is questioned by postmodern poetics is the very notion of the "self" that began to be constructed and to emerge, in *narrative*, precisely when courtly lyric was at its zenith, during the late twelfth century. That is, the "renaissance" of the twelfth century is marked by the conjunction of two diametrically opposed literary models of subjectivity. The name of Chrétien de Troyes, who was both lyric poet and courtly novelist, is emblematic of this conjunction.[1] On the one hand, there is the disembodied lyric "I," nothing other than a word, a generalized subjectivity, no one in particular, a fragmented, anonymous voice that can only speak another's language, an inherited, conventional, or "found" language. On the other hand, there is the unique narrative self, the novelistic self of romance, an extraordinary, self-determining subject whose language is decidedly different. Narrative champions a hero who masters his destiny, who proves his special worth, whose quest is a frontal attack against discursive anonymity precisely insofar as it is a struggle to make a name for oneself or, more precisely, for one self. The self of story is historically, geographically, and genealogically localized. Most significantly, in narrative the triumphant hero's return to courtly society is simultaneous with the creation of a new language: the hero is he who can tell or about whom are told marvels never previously told, he who can speak or about whom are spoken novelties, he whose trials are endured for the sake of the production of a previously unheard language.[2] That is, the subject of story is not determined by an inherited and conventional language but rather determines a new language. The hero of romance is an author, a creator, a unitary and originary source of novel discourse, the very sort of individual whose existence is routinely doubted by lyric.[3]

For instance, the hero and title character of Chrétien de Troyes' *Yvain* is, as Eugene Vance suggests, a figure for the romance writer, for the *scriptor* who would be *auctor*: Yvain's victory is his ability to distinguish himself in language and to produce a discourse that courtly society recognizes as decidedly different from and better than the discourse of others (specifically, different from and better than Kay's).[4] Kay functions in the text as Yvain's *losengier*, as the exemplary type of the mass of others, and the mere fact that Yvain is able easily to defeat this *losengier* in verbal combat suggests that the victorious hero's language is unlike lyric precisely in its power to confer distinction or to generate difference. If Yvain and Kay were still in the world of lyric rather than in the world of romance, their verbal struggle would end in stalemate, since there would be no way to tell the language of one from that of the other. Yvain's quest would be, like Kay's, not achieved, and the romance would never begin.

By the late thirteenth century the outcome of the generic and ideological combat between lyric and narrative discourse is apparently clear: story, it seems, has defeated song and has replaced it as the dominant model of subjectivity. Indeed the phenomenon of late medieval lyrico-narrativity has recently been read in just this way: the text is seen as a place in which song is redeemed, transformed into an historically referential, storylike discourse that grants to the individual writer an aura of authority.[5] The consensus of recent criticism is that the inscription of individuality is invariably welcomed by the medieval lyrico-narrative text as a positive and progressive advancement. Yet we shall see that the medieval text has its own ideas concerning such discursive novelty. Still, it is easy to see why one would be led to declare the triumph of story over song in the late Middle Ages: even lyric poetry itself seems to become story, as the empty or generalized "I" of the troubadour *canso* and the trouvère *chanson* appears to be supplanted by the self of *historia*. Thus, for instance, Dante and later Petrarch organize collections of songs into autobiographical or pseudo-autobiographical narratives.[6]

This impulse toward narrativity and individualism in Italian lyric was undoubtedly influenced by the thirteenth-century Old Provençal *chansonniers* or anthologies of troubadour poetry—collections in which lyric verse is surrounded by prose narrative and that are perhaps the strongest testimony to the emergence of the individual ego in late medieval literature, to story's ostensible victory over song. Specifically, these anthologies surround song by narrative *vidas* and *razos*—stories about lyric poets that a *jongleur* would tell by way of introduction to a performance. The *vida* is a short "life" or biography of a troubadour. The *razo* (from the Latin *ratio*) or "reason" relates a specific incident in the life of a troubadour, tells a story founded upon and generated by the citation of a few lines from a given song.[7] In exegetical terms, the *razo* is a sort of gloss meant to restore the song's historical sense. The *razo* treats a given song as if it were locally referential, historically true, the undistorted mimesis of lived experience. The *razo* routinely claims that a certain historically identifiable individual lyric composer actually did love a certain lady and that the "reason" for the song's existence is accurately to report this love. The singing subject is no longer represented as an effect of the text, no longer treated as a linguistically determined ego, no longer regarded as bound by semiotic conventions, but rather is thought to express an autonomous, pre-literary, and pre-linguistic self. In short, the *razo* claims that "Someone" rather than "No one" is singing. And the same may be said about the *vida*, which is quite often indistinct from the *razo*, insofar as both narrate the "reason" behind a given poet's production of song. Together the *vidas* and *razos* stand as precursors or ancestors of the post-Romantic obsession with literary biography: the *chansonniers* give the impression that thirteenth- and fourteenth-century audiences cannot highly value a lyric poem unless the name and "personality" of its originator are positively identified.

The *razo* is exemplary of the sort of text that interests us: a hybridization of narrative and lyric in which the narrated material pretends to precede the sung material, fostering the illusion that song is simply decorous, ancillary to or commemorative of pre-literary lived experience. Yet this valorization of story and its ideology of the subject over song and its ideology of the subject—a valorization that produces texts in which song is squeezed out and all but absent or, one might say, repressed (and texts in which song *per se* is no longer present but is transformed into the "theme" or subject matter of story)—may be upset and reversed by a practice of reading that is sensitive to traces of song in story. That is, we shall show that the triumph of story is only apparent, or—where the text admits the defeat of song—that song's defeat is mourned, resisted, not felt as a positive result of progress or bourgeois advancement, not celebrated as a necessary sacrifice offered for the sake of the "self-fulfillment" of the individual. Rather, the moment of song has its revenge as we witness the return of the repressed, the reversal of story back toward its lyric origins. And this dynamic is at work, as we shall see shortly, not only in texts (such as certain *novelle* and *lais*) that are modeled upon, anticipate, or formally resemble the *vidas* and *razos* (insofar as they mingle song and story) but also in the *vidas* and *razos* themselves. That is, even the *razos* are not univocally motivated by a historical, mimetic, "serious," or rational drive, but are themselves put in question by the implicated trace of song.[8]

Before turning to *vidas* and *razos* whose power derives directly from the vengeance taken by song upon story, I cite the following delightfully obscene *razo* which, by means of its patent absurdity, irreverently mocks the notion of a pre-discursive "reason" that the song, in an after-the-fact manner, is supposed to represent. This ***anti-razo*** claims to expose the historical event that motivated the composition of one of courtly lyric's most celebrated stanzas, the opening of Bernart de Ventadorn's *Quan vei la lauseta mover*. Here is Bernart's stanza followed by its parodic gloss:

> Quan vei la *lauseta* mover
> De jòi sas alas contra'l *rai*,
> Que s'oblid' e's laissa cazer
> Per la doussor qu'al còr li vai,
> Ailas! Quals enveja me'n ve
> De cui que veja jauzion!
> Meravilhas ai, quar dessé
> Lo còrs de dezirièr no'm fon.[9] (ll. 1–8)

(When I see the lark beat its wings against the ray of the sun, then forget itself and fall, overcome by the sweetness that comes to its heart, alas, how I envy whomever I see rejoicing. I'm amazed that my heart doesn't break from desire.)

> E apelava la Bernart *Alauzeta*, per amor d'un cavalier que l'amava, e ela apelet lui *Rai*. E un jorn venc lo cavaliers a la duguessa e entret en la cambra. La dona, que'l vi, leva adonc lo pan del mantel e mes li sobra'l col e laissa si cazer el lieg. E Bernart vi tot, car una donzela de la domna li ac mostrat cubertamen; e per questa razo fes adonc la canso que dis:
> Quan vei l'alauzeta mover . . .[10]

(And Bernard called her "Lark" because of her love for a knight who loved her whom she called "Ray." And one day the knight came to the duchess and entered into her room. The lady, who saw him, raised the top of her cloak and put it over her neck and fell upon the bed. And Bernard saw everything, because one of the lady's chambermaids had hidden him there; and for this reason he then made the song that says:
When I see the lark move . . .)

What is the sense of the claim that Bernard "called her 'Lark' [*Alauzeta*] because of her love for a knight who loved her whom she called 'Ray' [*Rai*]"? That is, what natural affinity is there between a ray and a lark that would account for the motivation behind Bernard's rather obscure christening? Why does the name "Ray" so readily suggest to Bernard the name "Lark"? While it is true that birds and the sun's rays both herald the arrival of spring, this does not explain why "Ray" specifically conjures up "Lark," since it could equally have conjured up literally anything under the sun. If purely natural observation were in effect, the lady's name could perhaps be "Trout" or "Bear," since the sun's springtime rays signal and trigger the renewed activity of those creatures that have been sluggish, dormant, or absent from human perception in winter and that equally "love" those rays. If birds and sunshine seem to particularly complement each other, this is due in part to the fact that they routinely cohabit the *locus amoenus* of the typical opening springtime stanza of the typical troubadour song, an opening of which Bernard's stanza is perfectly representative. In other words, "Lark" is not naturally or even metaphorically associated with "Ray," and the motivation behind Bernard's act of naming in this story must be sought elsewhere. In fact, if in this story the name "Ray" produces or triggers in Bernard's mind the name "Lark," it is only because the two words are in metonymic proximity in the very lyric stanza that is being glossed. That is, it is only in this song and nowhere else that the two words are associated, and it is only this song that could have inspired "Lark"'s christening. Thus the plot of this story, which begins with the christening of "Lark" and ends with the composition of the stanza, depends upon the prior composition of the stanza. The song must be composed before the events of the story supposed to recount the pre-history of the song can take place. Song is not the after-the-fact representation or commemoration of the event, not secondary to *historia*, but rather is revealed as the seed from which story is generated.

To put it in a more general way, this gloss may be called an *anti-razo* simply because it seems to ridicule, by a heightened absurdity, the conventional *razo*'s claim to expose the historical and biographical reasons for the origin of lyric verse. The obscene gloss of Bernard's stanza is a verbal game that suggests that the composition of *razos* may be a literary rather than a documentary, a semiotic rather than a mimetic, endeavor.

The *razo* of Arnaut Daniel, which tells the story of an other, is among the *anti-razos* most threatening to the biographical edifice constructed by the *razos* in general. Arnaut Daniel, famous for his *caras rimas* ("intricate rhymes"), is staying at the court of King Richard Coeur-de-Lion. One day another singer, a *jongleur*, arrives at court, boasting that he can compose rhymes more *caras* than Arnaut's. A contest is proposed, which the King will judge, and the two singers are sequestered in adjoining rooms for an appointed number of days. The anonymous *jongleur* composes a song quickly and easily, while Arnaut, suffering from some sort of indeterminate *ennui*, is unable to compose. A few days before the contest the two troubadours converse:

> Lo joglars demandet a.N Arnaut si avia fag, e'N Arnautz respos que oc, passat a tres jorns; e no.n avia pessat. E.l joglars cantava tota nueg sa canso, per so que be la saubes. E.N Arnautz pessat co.l traysses isquern; tan que venc una nueg, e.l joglars la cantava, e.N Arnautz la va tota arretener, e.l so. E can foro denan lo rey, N'Arnautz dis que volia retraire sa chanso, e comenset mot be la chanso que.l joglars avia facha. E'l joglar, can l'auzic, gardet lo en la car, e dis qu'el l'avia facha. E'l reys dis co's podia far; e'l joglars pregut al rey qu'el ne saubes lo ver; e'l reys demandec a.N Arnaut com era estat. E.N Arnautz comtet li tot com era estat, e.l reys ac ne gran gaug e tenc so tot a gran esquern; e foro aquitiat li gatge, et a cascu fes donar bels dos. E fo donatz lo cantar a.N Arnaut Daniel, que di:
>   Anc yeu non l'ac, mas ela m'a.
> Et aysi trobaretz de sa obra.[11]

(The *jongleur* asked Arnaut if he had done it, and Arnaut answered "yes, three days ago," though he had not thought of it yet. And all night long the *jongleur* sang his song so that he would know it well. And Arnaut thought that he would play a trick: one night, while the *jongleur* sang his song, Arnaut memorized all the words and the melody. And when they were before the King, Arnaut said that he wanted to perform his song, and he began very beautifully the song that the *jongleur* had made. And the *jongleur*, when he heard it, looked him in the face and said that *he* had made it. And the King asked how this could be. And the *jongleur* begged the King to find out the truth. And the King asked Arnaut how it could be. And Arnaut told the King how it was, and the King was greatly amused and considered it a great joke. And the wager was dismissed, and the King gave each singer fine gifts. And the song was given to Arnaut, which says:
  I never had her, but she has me.
And here you shall find some of his work.)

In this little tale is exposed the truth that Arnaut Daniel, supposed composer of courtly songs, in fact has no language of his own and thus can only mimic another's voice. The key to reading this *razo* is to bear in mind that there was, in the tradition of Old Provençal poetics, a clear and hierarchical distinction between the *troubadour* (who composes his own songs) and the *jongleur* (who performs songs composed by others). This distinction is here deconstructed, as the great troubadour Arnaut Daniel is revealed to be one who sings a song composed by another—to be, that is, a *jongleur*. Arnaut takes possession of the song of a *jongleur*, a boaster, his poetic rival, his *losengier*. And Arnaut not only mimics this rival, this other, but rather he becomes him: Arnaut himself becomes a *jongleur*, one who does not compose his own songs but rather appropriates another's words.

The most telling moment of this *razo* is the citation of a verse from Arnaut's lyric *oeuvre*—the *jongleur*'s verse given by the King to the troubadour: *Anc yeu non l'ac, mas ela m'a* ("I never had her, but she has me"). If the *ela* ("she") is supposed to refer (as it would be supposed in a conventional or non-ironic *razo*) to an actual beloved lady for whom the song was supposedly composed, then this lady—perhaps actually loved by the *jongleur* from whom Arnaut steals the song—is certainly no woman whom Arnaut ever loved. Yet it is by no means certain that the woman was ever loved by the *jongleur*, since a *jongleur* is by definition one who sings the songs of others, who does not love women but rather sings to women beloved by others. Precisely contrary to the ordinary *razo*, which aims to assert that a certain singer's song reflects that singer's historically real love affair with a certain lady, the *razo* of Arnaut Daniel denies the possibility that Arnaut's love affair is the source of his song, denies that Arnaut even had a love affair, and denies that anyone at all in the story's represented society even had a love affair. Ironically, it turns out that the first clause of this cited verse is, in a sense, literally true, since for Arnaut to sing "I never had her" (*Anc yeu non l'ac*) would be an accurate account of his relationship with a woman whom he has never known. The troubadour here turns out to be one whose song is grounded not in his own but rather in someone else's life story.

This dismantling of the narrative edifice of *razos* in general is deepened when we consider that the *ela* may well refer to no woman, fictional or otherwise, but rather to the appropriated song, *la canso*: "I never had the song, but it has me." In this case the cited verse asserts that "she" (the beloved) is in fact "it" (the song) and that the object of the singer's concern is a linguistic rather than a human being. The cited verse, anticipating by way of paraphrase a Heideggerian proposition, tells us that Arnaut does not master but is mastered by language: the singer does not sing songs, but song sings the singer. In the verse, "I never had the song, but it has me," the "I" or subject relinquishes subjectivity and becomes a "me" or an object in the transition from the first to the second clause, and the singer is thus figured not as one who acts but rather as one who is acted upon by song.[12] In this objective position the singer cannot possess the song, and the tale thus dramatizes a critique of private property and of proprietary notions of creation as the song passes freely among those who "possess" it but momentarily: the song initially belongs to the *jongleur*, who is traditionally one to whom songs cannot belong, then belongs to Richard Coeur-de-Lion (not an arbitrarily chosen representative of the royalty, since this king was indeed a famous lyric poet) insofar as it is his to bestow, then belongs to Arnaut Daniel insofar as it is bestowed upon him by the King. The song circulates among poets of different social class (*jongleur*, troubadour, king), and thus for a moment we witness song's power to promise the sort of utopic egalitarianism, the dismantling or undifferentiation of social hierarchy, suggested by Raimon Vidal in the famous opening of the *Razos de trobar*, which we encountered earlier. Yet this egalitarianism—figured by the King's equal distribution of gifts to the two rival singers—remains merely a promise, since in the end the scales of profit incline toward Arnaut Daniel as the song is ultimately made the private property of the famous poet. The clear implication is that literary fame and canonical reputation are more the products of seigneurial patronage or authority than the products of individual poetic genius or unique merit.

The ambiguity of this cited verse is followed by another quite telling ambiguity: the *razo*'s closing comment (*Et aysi trobaretz de sa obra*) may mean either "And here you shall find some of his [i.e., Arnaut Daniel's] work" or, read as advice to aspiring poets, "And thus you shall compose from his [i.e., someone elses's] work." If one opts for the former interpretation, the sentence is quite traditional and would function as the closing of any of the *razos*. The latter interpretation, on the other hand, gives the comment a specific poetic function in this and only this *razo*, for it acts as a proverbial epilogue to the tale—as, that is, the "moral" of the story. For both the tale of Arnaut Daniel's literary larceny and the phrase "you shall compose from his work" amount to the same thing: both tell us that the troubadour shall necessarily draw upon the work of another, shall necessarily mimic "his" voice, the voice of the *jongleur*, the voice of an other who sings in a tongue or *langue* that belongs to no one.

The *vidas* and *razos* are models for the transformation of song into story, for narrative's repression of lyric, for the rise of an ideology of the individual, which began to take place in the latter half of the twelfth century. The *vidas* and *razos* defend the referential capacity of poetic language by claiming that the referent of song is local history. The price paid for this assertion of a particular, one-to-one link between text and world is, of course, the limitation of the semiotic potential of song: the narrator of a *razo*, glossing a certain verse or certain verses biographically, can tell only one among any number of possible stories. To transform song into story is to lose potential *sens*, sense, signs, seeds, or semen.[13] As we shall see, the medieval text figures this transformation from lyric to narrative as a cutting, as a castration performed upon the general and potent semiotic subjectivity of song.

The *vida* of Peire Vidal,[14] which is an *anti-vida*, tells the story of this cutting, this transformation from song to story, from *canso* to *razo*, and it mourns the semiotic loss that this transformation entails. But before turning to Vidal's *vida*, we should note that the figure of Peire Vidal is marked in the *chansonniers* by a specific sort of folly: he is repeatedly represented as one who believes in the firm conjunction of linguistic and material reality. Peire's actions are motivated by his faith in the referential capacity of language, and he thus resembles the narrator of *razos*, who treats song as if it were a referentially true language.

Let us dwell somewhat on Peire's folly, which reaches absurdly comic proportions. Peire Vidal, a singer of love songs, believes that all women love him and fancies himself the courtly lover of all women:

> E si entendia en totas las bonas dompnas que vezia e totas las pregava d'amor; e totas li dizion de far e de dir so qu'el volgues. Don el crezia esser drutz de totas e que chascuna moris per el. E totas vetz menava rics destriers e portava ricas armas e cadreilla emperial. E.l meiller cavaillier del mon crezia estre e.l plus amatz de donnas. (p. 352)

> (And he went after all the good women that he saw and asked all for their love; and all said they would do and say what he wanted. And thus he thought he was loved by all women and that they all died for him. And everywhere he led rich chargers, bearing rich armor and an imperial throne. And he fancied himself the best knight in the world and the most beloved by women.)

This folly is a direct function of Peire's vocation as lyric poet. Because he uses the language of courtly love, and because he believes that language necessarily refers to an actual material reality, Peire must believe that he is involved in an actual love affair. The referent of Peire's lyric language is in this case not a single love affair with a certain lady but rather a love affair with nothing less than the entire female sex. In his hyperbolic delusion, Peire performs the impossible project of localizing, particularizing, materializing, or historicizing the generalized subjectivity of lyric without forfeiting a lyric generality: he transforms *langue* into the collection of all possible *paroles*.

The fictional Peire Vidal's imperial pretense is a literalization of imperial metaphors present in the historical Peire Vidal's lyric poetry.[15] That is, the Peire Vidal of the *vida* is compelled to act out or actualize the language of his songs, in which he often claims to be a sort of emperor. Indeed the linguistic foundation of Peire's claim to the throne is explicitly exposed: when told that a woman whom he marries in Cyprus is the daughter of the Emperor of Constantinople, Peire declares that

> devia aver l'emperi *per rason*. (p. 352)
>
> (he should have the empire by right.)

This *per rason* may mean not only "by right" but also "by means of speech," and it is precisely by means of speech, by a self-proclamation, that Peire installs himself as emperor:

> E.n portava armas emperials e fasia se
> clamar emperaire e la muillier empararíz. (p. 352)
>
> (And he wore imperial arms and made himself proclaimed Emperor and his wife Empress.)

Peire behaves as if the speech-act is automatically felicitous, as if language necessarily entails a material referent, as if just saying something makes it so, as if, because he calls himself "Emperor" in his songs, he must also be Emperor in "life." Given the etymological kinship between *rason* and *razo* (both are rooted in the Latin *ratio*), one might say that to have the empire *per rason* is to be empowered by means of a *razo*, by means, that is, of the declaration of a stable bond or undistorted reflective reciprocity between text and world, a rational link between language and history. In other words, the fictional Peire Vidal's attempt to literalize the imperial metaphors of the actual Peire Vidal's songs represents the *razo* narrator's general

68   Anti-*Vida*, Anti-*Razo*

practice of transforming the metaphors of courtly lyric into literal narratives. Both acts insist that signs necessarily entail things, that songs necessarily entail real-world referents. Yet the empire that Peire gains *per rason* turns out to be purely and nothing other than *rason* ("speech"): he is Emperor in name only, and only because he has so named himself.

As I mentioned, this extreme cratylism (this faith that linguistic signs must entail material referents) is a reiterated trait of Peire Vidal's folly in the *chansonniers*. In one of the *razos* Peire, who loves a woman whose *senhal* (code name or nickname) is *la Loba* ("the She-wolf"), behaves as if this woman actually were a wolf, as if this *senhal* were not arbitrary, as if there were a motivated link between name and thing, between the *senhal* and the woman's body:

> La Loba si era de Carcases, e Peire Vidal si fazia apelar Lop per ela e portava armas de lop. Et en la montanha de Cabaretz si se fes cassar als pastors ab los mastis et ab los lebrers, si com hom fai lop. E vesti una pel de lop per donar az entendre als pastors et als cans qu'el fos lop. E li pastor ab lur cans lo casseron e.l bateron si en tal guiza qu'el en fo portatz per mort a l'alberc de la Loba de Pueinautier. (p. 369)

> (The "She-wolf" was from Carcassone, and Peire Vidal called himself "Wolf" because of her, and wore the raiment of a wolf. And in the mountains of Cabaretz he was chased by shepherds with their dogs and hounds, as men chase wolves. And he wore a wolf-skin to make the shepherds and dogs think that he was a wolf. And the shepherds chased him with their dogs and beat him so badly that he was carried for dead to the dwelling of the "She-wolf" of Pueinautier.)

In general terms, this passage is further testimony that the fictional Peire Vidal ignores all gaps between name and thing, language and the body, text and world. Specifically, he believes that a woman nicknamed "She-wolf," actually is a she-wolf and, acting upon this belief, hopes to become a he-wolf merely by taking on the name of one. Yet in this case the mere act of naming does not seem to satisfy, for Peire attempts to assure his transformation by cloaking himself in a wolf-skin. This cloaking is, however, another sort of naming and does not contradict the linguistic status of Peire's act, since the *pel* (which signifies in Old Provençal "skin," "hide," or, quite significantly, "parchment") is clearly a figure for the signifier, the *integumentum*, the garment of fictional language. Peire would become a wolf by covering himself with the wolf's name and the wolf's hide. This rampant cratylism seems to infect the passage itself, as the *razo*'s language begins to mime its represented world: the woman is said to come both from Carcassonne and from Pueinautier—place-names whose combination in this text conjures up the image of a *carcasse* ("carcass") with a considerable *puanteur* ("stench"), a stinking carcass that is nothing other than the dead wolf that Peire has become at the end of the passage.

The narrator of traditional or non-ironic *vidas* and *razos* is, as I suggested above, always like Peire Vidal, always exhibiting a similar cratylistic faith in the identity of text and world, in the imbrication of a poet's language and his life. The fact that Peire becomes in the *chansonniers* emblematic of the confusion between language and life is quite possibly motivated by the nature of Peire's own name: *Vidal* is a piece of language that seems to contain or give direct access to *vida*, to "life." Ironically, it is the *vida* of Vidal (which we shall read as an *anti-vida*) that recounts the story of the violence precipitated by the transformation from *canso* to *vida* and *razo*, from lyric to narrative, sign to thing, semiosis to mimesis, *langue* to *parole*, language to life:

> Peire Vidals si fo de Tolosa. Fils fo d'un pelicer. E cantava meilz c'ome del mon. E fo dels plus fols omes que mais fossen; qu'el crezia que tot fos vers so que a lui plazia ni qu'el volia. E plus leu li avenia trobars que a nuil home del mon, e fo aquels que plus rics sons fetz e majors fulias dis d'armas e d'amor e de mal dir d'autrui. E fo vers c'us cavaliers de San Zili *li tailla la lenga*, per so qu'el donava ad entendre qu'el era drutz de sa muiller. (p. 351)

> (Peire Vidal was from Toulouse. He was the son of a furrier. And he sang better than any man in the world. And he was the craziest man that ever was, for he believed that everything was true that pleased him and that he wanted. And composing songs came more easily to him than to any man in the world, and thus he made richer melodies and told more follies of arms and of love and of slander about others. And it was true that a knight from San Zili *cut off his tongue*, because Peire said that he was a lover of the knight's wife.)

In his *vida* Peire Vidal acts according to his nature, according to the dictates of his birth: son of a *pelicer* ("furrier")—one who removes the hide from the body, the wolf-skin (*pel*) from the carcass, for example—Peire follows in his father's career insofar as he attempts to remove the outer covering, the *integumentum*, the skin or coat of language in order to expose the body, the naked truth. That is, Peire reveals the historical sense of his songs, reveals the biographical secret, tells the story of his love affair. He tells that he, a lyric poet, actually loves a certain woman, and this is precisely what is typically told by the narrator of a *razo*. Thus in the course of this passage Peire relinquishes his role as lyric poet and becomes a narrator. The price paid for this transformation is the loss of *la lenga* ("the tongue," *langue*) as Peire's is cut off immediately following his act of narration. This loss signifies, first, the limitations of a narrative poetics whose *raison d'etre* is historical mimesis: such narration involves a single uniterable utterance. Once the story or the "reason/*razo*" for song has been told, there is nothing left to say and thus the narrator's tongue is expendable. The narrative (the *razo*) says what it says and nothing more. Secondly, this loss of the tongue precipitated by Peire's act of telling, by his production of *parole*, means that Peire can no longer sing, is no longer a lyric poet, is cut off from the place of the commonplace, severed from the mass multitude, from the realm of *langue*, from song. The lyric poet loses his tongue, *la lenga* or *la langue*, the very moment the woman is named. To reveal the secret of the woman's identity entails the loss of lyric subjectivity.

6. Lyric Secrecy

> A prayer sung is ten said.
> Saint Augustine

To disclose song's secret, to name the names of the lover and the lady, to transform song's pronouns into proper nouns, is, as I have argued, to reduce, determine, and limit song's *potential* to signify. To betray the secret is to fix song's referent once and for all, to destroy, by singularizing, the multiplicitous singing ego.

Perhaps the most stark representation of song's resistance to the sort of limited referential historicity fostered by the *vidas* and *razos* is a version of the *razo* of Richart de Barbezill which emerges in Italian, in the thirteenth-century collection of brief *novelle*, or stories, known as *Il Novellino*.[1] In *Novella LXIV* of *Il Novellino*, breaking the lyric secret—naming, identifying, localizing, or in any way individualizing the desired lady—is figured specifically as an act of literary narration, as the telling of *novelle*. Yet this novel discourse is not celebrated as a literary triumph. Rather, story is blamed for the death of song and is ultimately expelled from courtly society by song's full-blown and multitudinous return. That is, the movement toward the mimesis of the interiority of the individual is enacted only in order to be scorned as a failure. Such a text as *Novella LXIV* absolutely contradicts the claims of recent readers of medieval lyrico-narrativity, who would see story's emergence from song as a positively valorized shaking off of the shackles of convention, as a triumph that heralds the inauguration of a new regime of bourgeois individualism.[2]

Novella LXIV[3] opens under the rubric of an implied lyrico-narrativity:

Qui conta d'una novella che avenne in Proenza
    alla Corte del Po. (p. 269)

(Here it tells of a *novella* that happened in Provence at the Court of the Puy.)

First, the very possibilty of a story happening in Provence, of narration entering into the domain of lyric dominance, is dubious—and this rubric thus fosters suspicions of a tainted or thwarted narrativity that the text will subsequently confirm. For, though indeed there is such a thing as Old Provençal narrative, such storytelling is the exception to the rule and is indeed almost without exception a storytelling explicitly concerned with recounting the adventures of lyric singers.[4] And the dubiousness of this self-contradictory claim concerning story's arrival in Provence is heightened when we learn that the place of that arrival is supposed to be the Court of the Puy. Now, the Court of the Puy is—as a matter of historical fact—the place where the performance of song was institutionalized and turned into a sort of religious observance.[5] It is thus quite odd for this rubric to tell us that the place of narrative, the place of this "*novella* that happened," is precisely that preeminent place of lyric poetry, the Court of the Puy in Provence. Secondly, we are not told precisely that a *novella* will be told but rather that something will be told *d'una* ("about a," "concerning a") *novella*: the *novella* itself will be the object of narration, will be one of the "characters" or protagonists, one of the heroes or villains, of the tale. This rubric intimates that we will witness an encounter of adversaries, that we will witness the advent of novelty (the *novella che avvenne*) in the discourse of Provence, the intrusion of storytelling into the liturgy of courtly literature.

Yet this rubric poses as well another initial question—since does not its opening *Qui conta* ("Here it tells") ask who "it" is, *Chi conta*? or *Qui conte*? ("Who tells?"), who tells the text? This uncertainty is absolutely pertinent to *Novella LXIV*, which is not only *d'una* ("concerning a") question of the location of the authorial voice but which is dialogic on its most superficial and graphic level: as the text's editor says, the manuscript is *infarcito di francesismi* ("crammed with French-isms").[6] And it is not just that certain isolated words, here and there, of the *langue d'oc* appear in this Italian text. Rather at a certain significant point, as we shall see, Old Provençal makes a full-fledged return, and indeed the tale can only be called bilingual. Thus the bilingual *Qui conta?*, which combines the French *Qui* with the Italian *conta*, is the text's self-interrogation concerning its own identity. Indeed *Novella LXIV* is, we might say, the story of an identity crisis, and its two tongues signify its status as a straddler between France and Italy, between feudal clannishness and bourgeois individuality, between the Middle Ages and the Renaissance. We cannot locate the nationality of the voice that speaks this text nor say to which *gens* it belongs, since in fact this voice comes from more than one place.

Novella LXIV tells of a knight who is tricked by other knights into boasting of the identity of the lady whom he secretly loves. Immediately thereafter the lady breaks off the affair:

> Nel riposare, la sera, e i cavalieri si cominciaro a vantare, in sull'allegrezze loro, chi di bella giostra, chi di bello castello, chi di bello astore, chi di ricca ventura; e il cavaliere non si poteo tenere che non si vantasse ch'amava sì bella donna.
> Ora avenne ch'e' ritornò per prendere gioia di lei, sì come solea. La donna li donoe commiato. (pp. 271–272)
>
> (In the repose of the evening the knights began to boast—one of a fine joust, one of a good castle, one of a fine goshawk, one of a rich adventure; and the knight could not restrain himself from boasting that he loved such a beautiful lady.
> Now it happened that he returned to have his joy with her, as he was wont to do. The lady sent him away.)

Notice that what happens immediately after the knight's revelation of the lady's identity—after, that is, the betrayal of lyric secrecy—is happening itself, as the first verb that follows the boast is the same *avenne* which signified, in the rubric, the advent of story into the place of song. And this advent is precisely the *adventure* that is recounted in this story. For the courtly lover who localizes his own desire, who tells that he really loves a certain lady, is mimicking the narrator of *razos* and—as Peire Vidal does in his *vida*, as we saw above—is cutting off his own *langue*, severing his ties with the realm of lyric generality. The violation of the anonymity of the courtly affair must spell its end, not because the lady's shame is too great to bear but because the lady of courtly song, who is no one, cannot be rightly named by the novelistic discourse of *novelle*.

Immediately following his *razo*-like narration of his love affair and the subsequent disruption of that affair, the knight flees to the world of romance, to the wilderness of subjective singularity:

> E il cavalieri sbigottìo tutto, e *partissi* da lei e dalla compagnia de' cavalieri, et andonne in una foresta e rinchiusesi in uno romitaggio sì celatamente, che neuno il sapea. (p. 272)
>
> (And the knight was entirely dismayed, and he departed [*partissi*] from her and from the company of knights, and he went into a forest and shut himself in a hermitage so secretly that no one knew it.)

The knight separates himself from the mass life of the courtly world, parts himself (*partissi*) from the lady and the *losengiers*, from the realm of objectivity that constituted his singing subjectivity, particularizes himself.[7] Significantly, his new residence is a hermitage, and he has thus been transformed from the lyric courtly lover to the individual knight of narrative who, in the course of his quest to become an *auctor*, is initiated into the singular and private life of the hermit.[8]

Yet the courtly multitude pursues the lone knight to the place of his refuge, and there they tell a mournful story of the loss that has been occasioned by the advent of *novelle*:

> Un giorno avenne che i donzelli del Po smarriro una caccia e capitaro a romitaggio dov'era il cavaliere rinchiuso. Domandolli se fossoro del Po, et elli dissero di sì; et elli domandò di *novelle*, e i donzelli li presero a *contare* come al Po avea laide *novelle*: che per picciolo misfatto elli aveano perduto il fiore de' cavalieri, quello che pregio avea tutto, e che sua donna li avea dato commiato, e che neuno uomo non sapea che ne fosse adivenuto. (p. 272)

> (One day it happened that the young men of the Puy lost their prey in a hunt and came upon the hermitage where the knight was shut in. He asked them if they were from the Puy, and they said yes; and he asked them for news [*novelle*], and the young men began to recount [*contare*] how there was bad news [*novelle*] at the Puy: how for a small misdeed they had lost the flower of knights, he who all had prized, and that his lady had sent him away, and that no one knew what had become of him.)

The two words—*conta* and *novella*—which signified in the rubric the potentially disturbing arrival of narration into the place of song's domination (Provence and the Puy) here return to signify just that disruption of the lyric situation. For the events associated with the knight's betrayal of the lyric secret are here explicitly figured as *novelle* (and figured negatively, as *laide* or "ugly" *novelle*, as "bad news" or "ugly stories"), and thus we see that the knight is himself figured as a novelist, as the source of a novel discourse whose effects are felt by the courtly multitude as a disturbing loss. The knight's narration of his lady's identity—a narration that precipitated the present crisis—is the *novella* that Novella LXIV is *d'una* ("about," "concerning"), the ugly *novella* that *avenne in Proenza* and whose advent threatens to disintegrate the Court of the Puy.

Thus the hunt or chase in which this multitude is ostensibly engaged is a mere pretense for their real pursuit. That is, they are in fact attempting to hunt down this singular novelist, to recapture the individual, novelistic ego who has escaped their fold. The strategem upon which this chase for the return of the singing subject will turn is the announcement of a tournament (which turns out, in keeping with the tradition of the Puy, to be a literary rather than a martial contest):

> "noi pensiamo (ch'elli hae sì gentil cuore) che, in qualunque parte elli sarae, elli verrae a torneare con noi; e noi avemo guardie ordinate di gran podere e di gran conoscenza, che l'arresteranno imantenente, e così speriamo di riguadagnare nostra grande perdita." (pp. 272–273)
>
> ("we think—for he has such a gentle heart—that, wherever he might be, he will come to tourney with us; and we have marshalled guards of great power and knowledge, who will arrest him immediately, and thus we hope to regain our great loss.")

Here the knights speak strictly in a collective voice, exclusively as *noi*, "we" (and the plurality of their voice is similarly maintained in the previously cited passage, in which they speak exclusively as *i donzelli*, as "they"). Thus the encounter in the hermitage with the singular knight for whom they search is an especially stark meeting between the one and the many.

This plural subject speaks not only as if something has been lost but also as if someone has committed an offense, a crime against the state of collectivity: *noi avemo guardie ordinate . . . che l'arresteranno imantenente* ("we have marshalled guards . . . who will arrest him immediately"). The "him" has here antagonized the powerful "we." The knight who betrayed lyric anonymity is wanted for the killing of song, for the violent death of the troubadour's generalized ego.

Yet it is the multitude's desire to regain their loss that most signals *Novella LXIV*'s strangeness, its alienation from any sort of "realistic" or mimetic mode of narration: *speriamo di riguadagnare nostra grande perdita* ("we hope to regain our great loss"). In a story that begins by recounting a knight's loss of his lady, this is the very hope that we would expect, given a verisimilitudinous storytelling, to emanate from the heart and mouth of the singular knight. We expect, that is, to hear the knight say "I hope to regain my great loss." Here the collective "we" has usurped the sorrow of the autonomous "I," and *Novella LXIV*—which turns his loss into their loss—

has turned from a story about "him" to a story about "them," about their attempt to regain the lost art of singing *noi* and *nostra*. And their hope for his return, their expectation that he will come back to *ri-torneare*, to once again turn out lyric tropes, to once again take part in their collective tourney, is founded on their sense that he is, at heart, a lyric singer, one of them, one of those whose singing routinely claims to flow from his *gentil cuore* (*elli hae sì gentil cuore*) but in fact flows from the general heart of the *gens* whose tongue generates song.⁹

We suspect that the loss of plural subjectivity—*nostra grande perdita*—represented by the lone narratorial knight's flight from the multitude is indistinguishable from the loss and disappearance of song. This suspicion is strikingly confirmed by the scene that immediately follows the would-be narrator's return to the Court of the Puy. Directly contrary to the typical chivalric romance, in which the returning knight is customarily asked to tell his story, to produce a novel and *auctor*ial discourse which would set him *apart from* the crowd, this returning knight is asked *not to tell his story but to sing his song*, to perform the conventional and *actor*ial discourse which would set him *among* the crowd:¹⁰

> Le guardie l'ebbero veduto; avisarlo, et incontanente il levaro in palma di mano a gran festa. La gente, rallegrandosi, abatterli la ventaglia dell'elmo dinanzi dal viso e pregarlo per amore che cantasse; et elli rispuose: (p. 273)
>
> (The guards had seen him; they recognized him and immediately raised him in great triumph. The people, rejoicing, lowered the visor of his helmet before his face and begged him for love that he would sing; and he replied:)

The courtly multitude, previously disturbed by the advent of *novelle*, now wants as recompense song and nothing but song. What has been felt as a lack—as *nostra grande perdita*—by the plural subject is not so much the absence of a particular knight as the absence of song itself. The knight's singularization in the wilderness of romance is seen as an affront to the very institution of courtly lyric—an affront for which the only restitution would be the reconstitution of the singing subject.

Yet this reconstitution is not so easily achieved, as the returning knight is no longer a singing subject and is unable simply to deliver a command performance. For what immediately follows the *rispuose* that we left dangling at the end of the previous passage is the knight's negative response, which proclaims a lingering prohibition against the further production of lyric language:

> "Io non canteroe mai s'io non ho *pace* da mia donna." (p. 273)
>
> ("I will never sing again if I do not make peace [*pace*] with my lady.")

The advent of *novelle* in Provence, which destroyed the secrecy or non-referentiality of courtly love upon which song is founded, has brought about an impasse, an obstacle to song: the woman's identity is still no longer secret, anonymity has still been betrayed, and thus song has been, it seems, irremediably tainted and rendered permanently impure. What must take place is the return of *pace*, the reinstitution of silence, the return to the secrecy of song.

In an effort to break this impasse the courtly multitude petitions the lady, who responds with the proposal of a brilliant stratagem by which to reconstitute the plurality of both the knight and herself, of both the singing subject and the object of desire:

> I nobili cavalieri si lasciarono ire alla donna e richieserle in gran pregheria che li facesse perdono. La donna rispuose:
> "Ditelo così: ch'io non li perdonerò giamai se non mi fae gridare merzé a cento baroni et a cento cavalieri et a cento donne et a cento donzelle, che tutti gridino a una boce merzé e non sappiano a cui la si chiedere." (p. 273)
>
> (The noble knights went to the lady and asked her with great urgency to pardon him. The lady responded:
> "Tell him thus: that I will never pardon him if he does not make a hundred barons and a hundred knights and a hundred ladies and a hundred young men all cry for mercy to me, so that they all cry for mercy in a single voice not knowing from whom it is being asked.")

Just as the courtly multitude usurped the sorrow that rightly belonged to the individual knight, so too they here ask for a pardon that rightly should be asked for by him. The "they" have already begun to recapture the subjective position that the "he" had solely occupied by virtue of his *razo*-like disclosure of identity. Yet this reconstitution of the subject's plurality is most forcefully achieved when the knight fulfills—as we shall see he does—

78   Lyric Secrecy

the terms of the lady's proposition. For not only will the anonymity of the lady whose mercy is being sought be restored (*non sappiano a cui la si chiedere* ["not knowing from whom it is being asked"]), but also the courtly lover who begs for this anonymous lady's *merzé* will be hundreds and hundreds of people, women as well as men, an undifferentiated multitude whose voice is the conventional voice of those who have collectively convened. Not until what seems *una boce* ("one voice") of one singer pleading for mercy is once again a multiplicity of voices, male and female, will the radically plural subjectivity of Provence be restored to the Court of the Puy. The subject of song will then reappear as the mouth of the many, as the tongue of the *tutti*. Secrecy will be restored, since no one will know the identity of the one who loves nor of the one who is loved.

Our sense that the lady's hope for the dispersal of identity, for the reparation of secrecy, for the dissolution of singularity, depends upon the reinstitution of song is confirmed beyond doubt by the way in which the knight's subsequently fulfills the task. For, to produce the effect of a hundred-fold tongue, the errant knight returns to his role as troubadour, as one who sings before the congregration of the Puy:

> Allora il cavaliere, il quale era di grande savere, si pensò che s'aproximava la festa della candellara, che si facea gran festa al Po di Nostra Dama, là ove la buona gente venia al mostier. Si pensò:
> "Mia dama vi sarae, e saravvi tanta della buona gente quant'ella adomanda che le chieggia merzede."
> Allora trovoe una molto bella canzonetta, e la mattina per tempo salìo in sue lo pergamo. La gente si meraviglioe molto; e quelli cominciò questa sua canzonetta tanto soavemente quanto seppe il meglio, ché molto sapea bene fare. E la canzonetta dicea in cotal maniera: (pp. 273–274)

> (Then the knight, who was very clever, thought that the Feast of Candlemas was approaching and that there would be a great celebration at the Puy of Notre Dame, where the noble people would go to church. He thought:
> "My lady will be there, and there will be many noble people such as she has asked for who will cry out to her for mercy."
> Then he composed a very beautiful song, and that morning at the proper time he went up into the pulpit. The people greatly marveled at this; and then he began to sing his song so sweetly as he best knew

how—and he knew how to do it very well. And the song says in the following manner:)

Thereupon the text transcribes (in a strange manner about which we will soon have occasion to comment), like the *razo* to which it is indebted, a courtly love song of the troubadour Richart de Barbezill. In the song's closing verses, the performer relinquishes the right to beg for *mercé*, relinquishes the role of courtly lover, transfers this right to the many who are gathered in the audience, and this reoccupation of the position of singing subject by the multitude finally heals the rupture inaugurated by the advent of *novelle*:

> "Or torn' a voi doloroso e piangente
> sì come il cerbio, c'ha fatto su' lungo cors,
> torn' al morir al grido delli cacciatori:
> et io così torno alla vostra mercé;
> m'a voi non cal se d'amor no us soven."
>
> Allora *tutta la gente* gridaron mercé, e perdonolli la donna e ritornoe in sua grazia, com'era di prima. (pp. 275–276)
>
> ("Now I turn to you, sorrowful and crying, like the stag who has run his long course turns in dying amid the cry of the hunters: and thus I turn to your mercy; but I have no use for you if you do not remember love."
>
> Then all the people [*tutta la gente*] cried for mercy, and the lady pardoned him and he re-entered into her good graces, as he was at first.)

Here the singing subject, the one who pleads for mercy, becomes in *Novella LXIV*'s closing sentence *tutta la gente* ("the entire *gens*"). The song is performed precisely to reinvest the congregation with their collective and generalized singing voice. This speaking "they"—or, to return once again to the phrasing of the final line of Raimbaut de Vaiqueras' plurilingual *descort*, this *mot gen favlan* ("many people speaking")—supplants the individual knight as the courtly lover of a lady who cannot be named and who is herself *mot gen favlan*. Once again the Puy of Provence is a place wherein song is sung by everyone to no one in particular, a song sung by many to many, the language of the general tongue.

What is remarkable about the insertion of this troubadour lyric into the manuscript is that its translation is executed in a significantly half-hearted manner. For, after the first stanza and until the last (which is a hybrid of the *langue d'oc* and Italian), the song is inscribed not in Italian but in Old Provençal. Thus that very song that spells the return of the *mot gen* ("many people") reveals its own multilinguistic origins. The plural or generalized subjectivity of song is brought back by means of a text with two tongues. The song inserted into *Novella LXIV*, which is not sung in a single language, thus itself reveals that there is no singular or central place from which it can conceivably be sung, that it is not the product of a centered or unified *auctor*.

And it is no accident that this story of story's failure takes place in the Court of the Puy and that its final scene takes place inside the church. For it is not without reason that the celebration of the Christian liturgy is called "Mass"—and it is precisely at Mass that the Court of the Puy restores the dominion of mass subjectivity.

Nor is the date of this Mass that celebrates the rule of the mass merely accidental. The knight fulfills the task of reinstituting plurality on the day of the *festa della candellara*, a feast that celebrates the previous day's *Purificazione della Vergine Maria* (p. 273). And this *festa* is celebrated, as we have seen, in a place dedicated to that very same *Vergine*—namely, in the *Po di Nostra Dama*. It is difficult not to see the implication of this double insistence on the name of the Virgin: she who is purified at the Puy of Notre Dame is not just the mother of Jesus but also the lady who had been tainted or violated by the advent of *novelle* in Provence. In other words, the return of song is figured as a re-Virgination of the courtly lady. She is once again transformed into a mystery.

This exchange between the lady and the *Vergine* is repeated in another Italian text with roots in the tradition of tales about troubadours, the early fourteenth-century *La Donna del Vergiù*. This text is a *cantare*, a sung story, and a version of one of the great Old French lyrico-narrative texts, *La Châtelaine de Vergi*.[11] What interests us here about *La Donna del Vergiù* is the equivalence that it makes explicit between the courtly lady who is its heroine and *Nostra Dama*, between the Chastelaine de Vergi and the chaste Virgin. For this equivalence, which was implicit in the French text, is made explicit in the first line of the Italian text, which opens with a prayer to *Nostra Dama*:

O gloriosa, o *Vergi*ne pulzella . . . [12]

(O glorious, o Virgin maiden . . .)

This opening verse of the Italian version verifies the equivalence of the Virgin and the woman from Vergi about whom a story is told concerning the breaking of the lyric secret. The *donna del Vergiù*, whose name is also spelled *Verzù* and whose tale takes place largely in a *vergero* ("garden"), which is also spelled *verzue*, is the lady of the *vers*—which is the Old Provençal name for the courtly love song.

The fact that the lady to whom the love lyric is addressed is confused in these texts with the *Vergine* means that the lady to whom the troubadour song is sung, in the Puy of Notre Dame at the end of *Novella LXIV*, is in a very strong sense *Nostra Dama*. Thus what is told by the collective singing at Mass to an unknown lady is courtly society's recuperation of their loss, of *nostra grande perdita*—the recovery of their capacity to say *nostra*, to speak of "our" lady. This church of the Puy, which is also a court of song, is dedicated to the lady of verse every bit as much as to the Virgin. And if we can speak of the virginity or purity of the lady of verse, this is because she circulates among and is shared by all.

7. Four Lovers

A brief tale (shall we call it *Le Chaitivel* or *Les Quatre Deuls*?), composed by Marie de France in the latter half of the twelfth century, is perhaps the earliest courtly narrative entirely generated by a resistance to or a dispute over novel developments in the representation of subjectivity. Marie's tale turns around a clash between the plural and the singular—the general and the individual, *langue* and *parole*, semiosis and mimesis—and this clash is quite clearly represented as a combat between two opposed literary discourses and their respective champions: song and story. By its end the tale has formulated a stunningly acute critique of that thinking that celebrates the novel as a positively progressive sign of a discursive "renaissance."

Our hesitation concerning the proper name of Marie's tale—a hesitation pronounced by Marie herself at the very outset—signifies a choice between the two contrary models of subjectivity the tale so clearly poses:

> Talent me prist de remembrer
> Un lai dunt jo oï parler.
> L'aventure vus en dirai
> E la cité vus numerai
> U il fu nez e cum ot *nun*:
> Le Chaitivel l'apelet *hum*,
> E si i ad *plusurs* de ceus
> Ki l'apelent Les Quatre Deuls.[1] (ll. 1–8)
>
> (I have the desire to remember a *lai* that I have heard spoken. I will tell you its story and I will name the city where it was born and tell you its *name*: *one* calls it *The Prisoner* [or, *The Wretch*], and there are *many* of those who call it *The Four Sorrows*.)

Here Marie promises that she will tell the *lai*'s *name*—yet instead what she tells is its *names*: the desire to singularize the name is contradicted by the fact that the name remains plural. As our reading unfolds we shall see that Marie has, here in her formulation of the *lai*'s two names, carefully and precisely sown the seed of everything that follows: he who singularly calls (*apelet* is the singular form of the verb) the *lai* by the singular definite article (*Le*) is the one who is signified by the singular version of the indefinite pronoun (*hum*); they who plurally call (*apelent* is the plural form of the verb) the *lai* by the plural definite article (*Les*) are the many who are signified by the plural version of the pronoun (*plusurs*). As we shall discover, this dispute over the title of (or title to) the text, a dispute between singularity and plurality, is precisely what is recounted by the tale and is beyond any doubt a dispute over whether song gives voice to the interiority of individual *parole* or to the external *langue* of the *losengiers*. That is, what is eventually told as the tale is nothing but this numerical uncertainty over what to call the tale, nothing other than the question of whether the tale's concern is singular (*Le Chaitivel*) or plural (*Les Quatre Deuls*).

The tale opens by taking seriously and literally a certain commonplace *topos* of chivalric romance. A courtly lady of great beauty is loved and desired by all:

> N'ot en la tere chevalier
> Ki aukes feïst a preisier,
> Pur ceo qu'une feiz la veïst,
> Ki ne l'amast e requeïst.
> El nes pot mie *tuz* amer
> Ne el nes vot mie *tuer*. (ll. 13–18)

(There was not in the land any knight worth anything who, upon seeing her just one time, would not love and court her. She could not love them all [*tuz*], nor did she want to kill [*tuer*] them.)

Such universal appeal of the lady is commonly claimed in just this fashion in any number of courtly narratives. Yet what in romance customarily occurs immediately after the invocation of this *topos* is the nomination of the one who will be the hero, the singling out of the one who will succeed, the naming of the knight who will distinguish himself from the *tuz* ("all"). Marie's tale, on the contrary, is about the refusal to nominate the individual one who would be decidedly different from the general *tuz*. And this refusal is indistinct from a refusal to *tu-er* (*el nes vot mie tuer* ["she did not want to kill them"]), a refusal to *tutoyer* or to single out the one to address by the second-person singular pronoun *tu*: to say *tu* is to *tuer* ("kill") the *tuz* (the "all," the *gens*). The conventional *topos* is not quickly effaced by a turn to a realistic storytelling that names names but rather is retained, as if the *topos* were itself realistic. That is, when Marie tells us that "all" loved the lady she does not mean this merely as rhetorical praise. Instead, she literally means that the courtly lover of the lady really is none other than someone named "all," that *tuz* is the name of the lady's lover.

The multiplicitous courtly lover in this tale goes by another name as well, for the lady is loved by *quatre* ("four") knights who are *tuz* undifferentiated. This *quatre* is in Marie's tale the signifier of *tuz*, signifies a multiplicity or an "allness" that is the plurality of the linguistic subject. Thus *tuz*, *tuit*, and *quatre* are interchangeable nouns standing for the same thing in Marie's text—namely, for the multiplicitous subject whom she refuses to singularize. So we see that "all" repeatedly stands beside or in the place of "four":

> Tant furent *tuit* de grant valur (l. 53)
>
> (So much were they *all* of great merit)
>
> *Tuit* la teneient pur amie,
> *Tuit* portouent sa druërie (ll. 67–68)
>
> (*All* considered her their lover, *all* wore her token of love)
>
> *Tuz quatre* les ama e tint (l. 71)
>
> (She loved and retained *all four* of them)

Indeed throughout most of the tale this *tuz* is never subject to a division, never separated into its four individual parts. Until the moment of the decisive event that incites the debate over the text's title, no single one of the lady's four lovers is ever spoken of specifically, as a singular individual. None of these four, that is, is ever nominated to be the lady's one and only lover. Instead in any given scene the four are invariably signified by the selfsame linguistic unit—whether *tuz*, *tuit*, *quatre*, or *chescuns*.

Indeed, right when she introduces them into her tale, Marie quite explicitly foregrounds the impossibility of specifying these four:

> En Bretaine ot quatre baruns,
> Mes jeo ne sai *numer lur nuns* (ll. 33–34)
>
> (In Brittany there were four barons, but I don't how to *name their names*)

Marie's own storytelling here confesses a failure of mimesis, an incapacity to specify, an inability to reveal historical identity.

This incapacity or refusal to *numer* the *nun*, to name the name, to nominate the individual, to fill the pronominal emptiness of the *nun*, is the very capacity or refusal of courtly language to betray its referential secrets. Indeed, what is a name that needs further naming, that would require a further revelation, if not a pronoun? That is, Marie's *nun* that she cannot *numer* is a pro-noun, a noun that comes before or precedes the act of nomination.[2] The tale tells nothing but the resistance of the pro-noun to its entrance into the full-fledged propriety of the noun. The pro-noun resists that specifying or historicizing nomination that would limit its presently indeterminate potential. This *nun* is the negation of singularity, a *n'un*, a "not one," the no one who is the pro-nominal subject of courtly song.

In fact, as I said, the unnamed *quatre* are named repeatedly, but always they all have the same name: they are always signified generally, whether by Marie's or by their own language. Indeed the lady loved by the four is, despite an honest effort, absolutely unable to distinguish among them:

> La dame fu de mut grant sens:
> En respit mist e en purpens
> Pur saveir e pur demander
> Li queils sereit mieuz a amer.
> Tant furent tuit de grant valeur,
> Ne pot *eslire le meillur*. (ll. 49–54)
>
> (The lady was very sensible: she delayed and thought in order to know and to ask which of them would be best to love. So much were they all of such great merit that she could not *elect the best*.)

The lady's, and indeed everyone's, inability to distinguish among the four is the effect of the uniformity of their signifying practice:

> Tuit la teneient pur amie,
> Tuit portouent sa druërie,
> Anel u mance u gumfanun,
> E chescuns escriot sun nun. (ll. 67–70)
>
> (All considered her their lover, all wore her love token—ring or sleeve or insignia—and each one cried her name.)

Performing the gestures and customs always performed by courtly lovers, none of these *tuit* is different from the others. Their identical rings, sleeves, and insignia are the commonplace signifiers, appropriated by all, of a shared and freely circulating *langue*. Such accoutrements are the uniform devices that prevent the revelation of internal difference.

This is not to say by any means that the four knights are in fact the same but rather that, no matter how different they are in their hearts of hearts, such difference cannot be represented in courtly language. Yet the text attempts to foster a certain interiority effect, makes us think momentarily that we can glimpse in Marie's text if nowhere else this internal realm of individual difference. Thus we are told what each knight privately thinks—namely, that he is better than all the rest:

> Pur li e pur s'amur aveir
> I meteit chescuns sun poeir.
> Chescuns par sei la requereit
> E tute sa peine i meteit;
> N'i ot celui ki ne quidast
> Que *mieuz d'autre* n'i espleitast. (ll. 43–48)

(For her and to have her love each one did his best. Each one courted for himself and put all his effort into the task. There was not one of them who did not think that he was doing *better than the others*.)

Still, this interior discourse is itself a convention: what the courtly singer sings perhaps more often than anything else is his sense that he is *mieuz d'autre* ("better than the others"), that his love is true while the love of all others is false, that his privacy is more truly private than others' privacy, that he is the *fin amans* ("true lover") and all others are *losengiers* ("flatterers"). Yet such a claim that one stands apart is made by *chescuns*, by everyone, *losengiers* and lovers alike. Each of these four is, in the eyes of the others, merely a *losengier*. The interior or core of the self that we seem to glimpse turns out to be occupied by the tongue of the *tuz*. Marie represents, that is, the desire for singularity as a most plural desire:

> Voleit *chescuns* estre *primiers* (l. 64)

> (*Each one* wanted to be *first*)

The desire to set oneself apart does not in itself set one apart but rather indicates that one is conforming to a commonplace desire. This very desire to be first, to partake of the primacy of the number one, is itself always a second-hand desire. The lyric singer, never the first to sing, is never prime nor ever in his prime. His primary desire is never anything but the secondary effect of the desire of *chescuns*.

Now, what is interesting about the lady of Marie's tale is her ambivalence. On the one hand, she does want to *eslire le meillur*, to "elect the best," to select the superior individual, to specify and singularize. Yet on the other hand, she dreads the inevitable loss that would follow selection and nomination. Ultimately it seems that the lady's—and, as we shall see, Marie's—resistance is stronger than her desire to name the one preeminent name:

ne volt les *treis* perdre pur l'*un* (l. 55)

(she did not want to lose *three* in order to have *one*)

"Nes voil tuz *perdre* pur l'un *prendre*!" (l. 156)

("I do not want to *lose* all of them for *taking* one!")

These lines tell the entire story of this story, which is entirely composed as a representation of a critical hesitation between the plurality represented by a *treis* and the singularity represented by the *un*—a hesitation prompted by the sense that to *prendre* is to *perdre*, to take is to lose. The lady hesitates because she fears the semiotic loss simultaneous with the historical rise of an ideology of individualism. In her indecision she has already begun to mourn the dismemberment of the many.

Perhaps the lady never would have decided if the decision had not been made for her by the momentous narrative occasion of chivalric combat. Together the four fight in a tournament—the turning point of the text—from which they will not return together. In the beginning, marching toward the field of conflict, they act as one:

Li quatre dru furent armé
E eissirent de la cité. (ll. 85–86)

(The four lovers were armed and left the city.)

If this were a "normal" romance narrative, the subject here would not be "the four lovers" but rather a certain individual and (most likely) named knight. In Marie's tale, the chivalric subject is an anonymous "they," not a certain "he," and this "they" fights as if it were the "hero":

88   Four Lovers

> Si quatre dru bien le feseient,
> Si ke de tuz le pris aveient. (ll. 115–116)

(The four lovers did so well that they were considered the best of all.)

The tournament in courtly romance is meant to discern the best individual knight, to set one apart from the others—yet here the "best one" is still represented as an undifferentiated foursome.

But when the dust of battle settles the singular knight, to the great sorrow of all, has become discernible. The four will not return to the court intact, and their status as a purely grammatical unit is barbarically defeated. This moment of crisis, of the emergence of the individual, is represented precisely as the effect of a severance, a cutting off from the protective plurality of the crowd, of the *gens*:

> Tant ke ceo vint a l'avesprer
> Que il deveient *desevrer*;
> Luinz de lur *gent*, sil cumparerent,
> Kar li trei i furent ocis
> E li quarz nafrez e malmis
> Par mi la quisse e einz el cors. (ll. 123–124)

(Until evening came and they had to separate [*desevrer*]; and they paid for being far from their people [*gent*], for three were killed and the fourth wounded and maimed in the thigh and heart.)

The *quatre*'s internal severance (*il deveient desevrer* ["they had to separate"]), its separation into groups of three and one, is simultaneous with the severance of the *quatre* as a whole from its *gent* ("people"). The folly of abandoning the *folle* means that the *tuz*, which can only be situated in the place of the crowd, is no longer *tuz*. The separation of the singing subject from the place of the *gent* is the moment of the institution of discursive difference. As the wounds in the thigh and heart signify, the rupture of the integrity of the four is figured precisely as a dismemberment. Indeed the sole survivor of the violent massacre of the mass initiated by its departure from the *gent* is truly dis-membered: he is no longer a member of the gang of four whose signs were his to appropriate. The birth of the language of the individual is figured as a cutting of the *corpus* into its parts, as a violence perpetrated against the generality of the *langue* of the *gens*.

Yet strangely Marie's text and the lady and *gent* of Nantes refuse to recognize the different fate of the sole survivor. Their reaction, that is, is *reactionary*, as they resist the novelty of discursive progress. The *gent* treat the dismembered member as if he were still vitally connected, by death, to "them," to the *tuz*. And after the fatal blow has been struck the text continues to insist on the *tuit*-ness of the *quatre*:

> E *tuit quatre* furent cheü. (l. 126)
>
> (And *all four* had fallen.)

These fallen four are still placed together and are commonly mourned, as if the one presently alive were no different from and no less absent than the rest. The singularity of this sole survivor is quite simply not recognized:

> Pur la dolur des chevaliers
> I aveit iteus deus milliers
> Ki lur ventaille deslacierent,
> Chevoiz e barbes detrahierent;
> Entre eus esteit li doels communs.
> Sur sun escu fu mis chescuns;
> En la cité les unt portez
> A la dame kis ot amez. (l. 135–142)
>
> (For sorrow there were two thousand knights who unlaced their helmets and tore out their hair and beards. Among them the grief was common to all. They carried them into the city to the lady who had loved them.)

Here the crowd is grieving for the four, not yet making any distinction between the one surviving and the three slain knights. The *doels* ("grief")—a word that comes, as we shall see, to be another name for the *quatre*—is still represented as *communs*, and the singular knight is not yet seen as singular but rather as part of this community whose death is mourned by all. Sorrow is not yet the expression flowing forth from an individual heart. The discourse of the *tuz*, in which the story of one is the same as the story of another, is still dominant.

Yet the imposing edifice of this dominance begins to crack—as the lady slips, lowering her rear-guard resistance by naming names:

> Chescun regrette *par sun nun*. (l. 147)
>
> (She lamented the loss of each one *by his name*.)

Though Marie's text continues to conceal the secrets of identity (it does not actually name their names), here that text nonetheless represents the lady's betrayal of anonymity. That is, we here obliquely witness the lady, no longer unable to distinguish among the four, naming the name of each one individually. But she immediately regrets naming names, regrets this specifying, singularizing language whose possibility she has instituted: from here to the end the lady makes amends for her indiscretion, for considering each one as a discrete entity, by repeatedly refusing to recognize the survivor's singularity.

Thus the survivor's sorrow, that which gives him cause to sing, is founded on her failure to see him as autonomous, her failure to see that he is no longer represented only as an anonymous member of a collective subjectivity. Even when she visits him personally, to comfort him during his convalescence, "they" continue to be the matter of conversation, as if her language can speak only of "them":

> Ele l'alot veeir sovent
> E cunfortout mut bonement,
> Mes *les autres* treis regretot
> E grant dolur pur eus menot. (ll. 177–180)

> (She often went to see him and comforted him generously, but she lamented the other [*les autres*] three and demonstrated great sorrow for them.)

Rather than demonstrating her sorrow for "him," as would occur in a conventional romance narrative, she demonstrates her sorrow for "them"— as if, in his presence (in the presence of the "he"), she can think only of their absence (of the absence of the "they"). And what at first appears to be a dialogue between the lady and the singular knight concerning the matter of her grief turns out to be, from her perspective, a haunting conversation with *les autres*, with the dead *quatre*, for by the end of this passage she speaks to him as if he were "them":

> "Dame, vus estes en esfrei!
> Que pensez vus? Dites le mei!
> Lessiez vostre dolur ester:
> Bien vus devrïez conforter!"
> —"Amis, fet ele, jeo pensoue
> E voz cumpainuns *remembroue*.
> Jamés dame de mun parage,

Ja tant n'iert bele, pruz ne sage,
Teus quatre ensemble n'amera
Ne en un jur si nes perdra,
Fors *vus tut sul* ki nafrez fustes;
Grant poür de mort en eüstes!
Pur ceo que tant vus ai amez,
Voil que mis *doels* seit *remembrez*;
De *vus quatre* ferai un lai
E *Quatre Dols* le numerai." (ll. 189–204)

("Lady, you are upset! What are you thinking? Tell it to me! Let your sorrow be: certainly you should be comforted!" "Friend," she said, "I was thinking and *remembering* your companions. Never again shall a lady of my rank, no matter how beautiful, noble, or wise, love such four together nor lose them in a single day, except for *you all alone* who was wounded. You were nearly killed! Because I loved you so much, I want my sorrows [*doels*] to be *remembered*. I will make a song about *you four*, and I will name it *Four Sorrows*.")

Though the lady temporarily admits that the *vus* ("you") is *tut sul* ("all alone"), she immediately denies this admission by insisting on *vus*'s status as a plural rather than a singular second-person pronoun: *vus quatre* returns to challenge the primacy of the *vus tut sul*. He is in her eyes no longer the surviving "he" but rather the deceased "they."

Thus the lady has already done what she hopes to do by composing the *lai*. She has already remembered the *quatre doels*, the four sorrowful singers, by continuing to regard him as the *tuz*, as the plural *vus*. This four has already been discursively *re-membrez*, re-membered, put back together into an undifferentiated ensemble. The song or *lai* that will then be composed is thus the legacy of this return to linguistic generality. The song will sing a plural sorrow, will sing the story of not one but many. Perhaps the *lai* will lament the death of the grammatically communal subject, the passing of the *tuz*. Yet in fact that death will not have happened, since that generalized *vus* will continue to survive in song, will appear in the very song composed to regret its disappearance. Song will return to re-member its own severed subjectivity.

The sole survivor's immediate response is the proposal of a decidedly different discourse:

Li chevaliers li respundi
Hastivement, quant il l'oï:
"Dame, fetes le lai *novel*,

> Si l'apelez *Le Chaitivel*!
> E jeo vus voil mustrer *reisun*
> Que il deit issi aveir nun." (ll. 205–210)

> (The knight answered her immediately when he heard what she said: "Lady, make the song *novel*, and call it *The Prisoner*! And I want to show you the reason [*reisun*] that it should have this name.")

The singular knight champions a new sort of song, a *novel* song, a song whose novelty would be its novelistic narrativity. For the knight offers to recount a *reisun* (a word that translates into Old French the Old Provençal *razo*) that would rationalize or reveal the referential reasons for the novel *lai*, the one-to-one ratio between a text and an individual's life.[3] The sole survivor stands for the production of *novelle* and *razos*, for a discourse supposedly rooted in the local history of the individual. Marie, who apparently pre-dates by several decades the composition of the first *razos* and the *novelle* that those *razos* inspired, uses these words—*novel* and *reisun*—as if they are already institutionalized names for a mode of historically referential novelistic narrativity.

The surviving knight is thus in the position to recount his own *reisun* or *razo*, to narrate the *novella* that would tell the circumstances of his sorrow. And this is precisely what he does, as he relates the reasons—represented as prior to the song's existence—for the composition of a song that would supposedly sing, mimetically or after the fact, his and only his desire:

> "Mes jo, ki sui eschapez vifs,
> Tuz esgarez e tuz cheitifs,
> Ceo qu'el siecle puis plus amer
> Vei sovent venir e aler,
> Parler od mei matin e seir,
> Si n'en puis nule joie aveir
> Ne de baisier ne d'acoler
> Ne d'autre bien *fors de parler*.
> Teus cent maus me fetes suffrir!
> Mieuz me vaudreit la mort tenir!
> Pur c'ert li lais *de mei nomez*:
> *Le Chaitivel* iert apelez." (ll. 215–226)

> ("But I, who have escaped alive, am all lost and wretched, for she whom I love most in the world I often see come and go, she speaks

with me morning and night, but I cannot have any joy of her, either kissing or hugging or anything *except speaking*. Thus a hundred evils make me suffer! I would rather be dead! This is why the song should be *named after me*. It should be called *The Prisoner*.")

Whereas the lady proposed that a song be sung that refers to the history of the general "all" that has been dismembered, the sole survivor proposes that the song refer solely and specifically to his own history. Thus he proposes that the song be called *Le Chaitivel*—of the *lai*'s two contested names, the one that would name a singularity, that would sing the singular sorrow of the one for whom it is named, who is none other than *mei*, "me," the *moi*, the ego. What makes the *lai* proposed by the sole survivor *novel* is precisely its claim to nominate the *mei*, to name and give voice to the unitary self. So the surviving knight stands on the side of that one who at the text's inception would call the text *Le Chaitivel*, while the lady embraces the position of those many would would call the text, in remembrance of the *tuz*, *Les Quatre Deuls*.

Still, this sole surviving singular knight, who wants the song to sing *his* story alone and to be named after *himself* alone, turns out to be expressing this desire for singularity by appropriating the language of the plural subject. Thus what he calls his *reisun* or his *razo*—his story unfolding the reasons for proposing that the song concern himself alone—turns out to sound remarkably like courtly love song. That is, the passage that I just cited is meant to be the knight's *razo*, the explanation of the song's historical "reason," yet the language of this explanation in fact resembles nothing more than the song of the generalized subject:

> "But I . . . am all lost and wretched, for she whom I love most in the world I often see come and go, she speaks with me morning and night, but I cannot have any joy of her, either kissing or hugging or anything except speaking . . ."

If we had no knowledge of their context, we could not tell that these lines were not excerpted from one of the *chansons* of the *trouvères*. Attempting to set himself apart, to narrate his history, this sole survivor is forced to use the very language of courtly love that makes him sound just like all others. This would-be storyteller, founder of a *novella*- and *razo*-like discourse of novelty, cannot help but sing, even in the moment of his most critical attempt to narrate his individual difference. The *razo* of the *mei* reveals itself as a *canso*, and the story of the self shows itself to be song.

And what this *canso* laments is that which is lamented by all *cansos*—namely, the fact that the singing subject cannot have, do, or be anything *fors de parler*, "except (or outside of) speaking." The *reisun* for the sole survivor's sorrow is his recognition that he remains a purely linguistic subject, inescapably captivated and defined by a *langue* that is not properly his but rather that remains the domain of the *plusurs*. The *mei* is, despite any pretense to the contrary, unable to name itself differently from the others. Yet the *mei* pretends to have properly nominated itself, to be capable of producing the proper noun:

"Pur c'ert li lais de mei nomez;
Le Chaitivel iert apelez.
Ki *Quatre Dols* le numera
Sun *propre nun* li changera." (ll. 225–228)

("This is why the song should be named after me. It should be called *The Prisoner*. Whoever would call it *Four Sorrows* would change its proper name.")

If, as the knight proposes, the song named *Le Chaitivel* were named after him, then, consequently, he is *Le Chaitivel* as well. But this name, which The Prisoner claims is a *propre nun*, is precisely not a proper name but rather a nickname, a *senhal*—a "signal" or "sign"—that signifies without revealing specific identity. *Le Chaitivel* no more partakes of the propriety of the proper noun than does *Quatre Dols*, and both names are more properly seen as pro-nouns, as signs that signify prior to the nomination of the individual. For *Le Chaitivel* does not name anyone but rather everyone, since every lyric singer is The Prisoner, everyone is subject to captivity within the semiotic network of song. Both names are *senhals*, signifiers that cannot be steadfastly fixed to singular bodies. The *senhal* is the lyric mode of naming, a pronominal name that potentially refers to anyone whosoever, a name that is sung for the very reason that its referent is potentially more than one. Indeed, as the phrase *Quatre Dols le numera* intimates, what is at stake in Marie's tale is a question concerning names and numbers, nomination and numeration. The name in this text is always represented as one that—like the lyric *je*—stands for many, as a plural pro-noun rather than a singular proper noun. The ratio or *razo* of the correspondence between word and body, between text and world, is represented not as one-to-one but rather as one-to-several—the several being the multitude of members of that body that speaks with a single *langue*, with the tongue of the *tuz*. Still, recognizing neither the futility of his cause nor the true nature of his imprisonment, the sole survivor is the self-proclaimed champion of the *propre nun*, of the language of individual identity, of the discourse of the *mei*, of the very singularity that his own improper name negates as it returns him to the realm of the *n'un*, the no one—to, that is, the realm of the *senhal*.

In the end Marie's ambivalence toward naming names stands as the final word, and the hesitation concerning the text's title continues:

Issi fu li lais comenciez
E puis parfaiz e anunciez.
Icil kil porterent avant,
Quatre Dols l'apelent alquant;
Chescuns des nuns bien i afiert,
Kar la matire le requiert;
Le Chaitivel ad *nun en us*.
Ici finist, nen i ad plus,
Plus n'en oï ne plus n'en sai
Ne plus ne vus en cunterai. (ll. 231–240)

(Thus was the song begun and then perfected and performed. Some of those who circulated it called it *Four Sorrows*. Each of the names suits it well, for the matter requires it thus. *The Prisoner* is the *name now in use*. Here it ends, there is no more. I heard no more of it, I know no more of it, and I'll tell you no more of it.)

Though in a sense Marie admits the propriety of the two names, this very admission argues against the notion of the single proper name. If both names are proper then neither is truly proper, neither rightly "belongs" to the text to the exclusion of the other. The text may well be appropriated by either of the factions feuding over its title, and such a propensity to be appropriated by anyone and everyone is just the effect produced by the courtly *langue*. In the end Marie, like the lady of her tale, refuses to "elect the best," refuses, that is, to discern the proper name, to singularize the name, to *numer* the *nun*, to nominate the proper noun. She refuses to determine her tale's referent, to say that it is more grounded in one history than it is in another.

Yet Marie seems to know that she is on the side of a losing cause: *Le Chaitivel*, she recognizes, is the name *en us*, "in use." The specification of identity, the naming of the single proper name, the new historicism, is regarded by Marie as the current trend. Marie's songlike storytelling resists this progress toward the *ratio* of historicity by remembering the plural name. Thus she achieves her intention, announced in her text's very first two lines, to *remembrer/Un lai*: she has re-membered the *lai*, reinstituted lyric subjectivity, by recounting the return of the plural name. Marie has composed a story that, like courtly song, is unable or unwilling to reveal its specific reference, unwilling to singularize identity, to *numer* the *nun*, to nominate the noun—a story whose name is not singular, a story that refuses to elect or select the preeminent name, a story that tells nothing but its own aversion to storytelling.[4]

8. Nameless Lovers

> Di sé facea a sé stesso lucerna,
> ed eran due in uno e uno in due.
>
> (Of himself he made for himself a lantern, and they were two in one and one in two.)
>
> Dante (on the troubadour Bertran de Born), *Inferno* XXVIII

The pronoun of courtly song is truly a pro-noun, a name *before* it has been made proper, before someone has become its proprietor. A brief look at a strange, anonymous text known as *Des Deux Amans* ("Of the Two Lovers") will strengthen our sense that the pro-noun's failure or refusal to nominate signifies a resistance to the new order of novelistic narration.[1] This little text tells the story of a story that never begins precisely because the name is never named, because the plurality or impersonality of lyric subjectivity is not successfully overthrown at the outset.

At the outset of the text the narrator announces his intention to tell a story about two lovers who are, apparently, the *deux amans* of the title. This story will begin, in typical romance fashion, with the naming of the names of those whose adventures will be recounted:

> Mès ainçois que je plus vous die,
> Ne de l'ami ne de l'amie,
> Vous vueil *deviser en romanz*
> *Le nom* d'ambes .ij. les amanz. (ll. 7–10)

(But before I tell you any more, either about the lover or the lady, I want to say in romance [*deviser en romanz*] the *name* of both lovers.)

This *deviser en romanz* means, for one, to "say in the vernacular." Yet it also connotes the narrator's plan to devise a romance—to compose *en romanz*, "in the manner of romance." The narrator wants to "say, in the manner of romance, the name" (*deviser en romanz / Le nom*). As we shall see, the narrator does in fact *deviser* the *nom*, but certainly not in the manner that he here foretells. For the word *deviser* also signifies "to divide," and what the text ultimately does is to divide the name or the noun, producing two incompatible bodies of discourse whose union bears no fruit.

With great fanfare the narrator prepares to commence his story by naming names. But this nomination turns out not only to be marred by the impropriety of the *senhal* but also to be nothing other than the negation of the name:

> De l'ami premiers nommerons;
> Le nom à celui vous dirons,
> Si comme s'amie li a mis.
> Il a non: *sanz non amis*.
> Por miex entendre ma reson,
> A il à non: *amis sanz non*. (ll. 11–16)

(First we'll name the lover; we'll tell you this one's name, as his lady gave it to him. His name is: *nameless lover*. To better understand my speech, he has as his name: *lover without name*.)

It is not immediately clear how the repetition, with the variation of a specular reversal, of the nameless lover's name helps us "better understand" this somewhat puzzling passage. Yet this repetition of the non-name, code name, or *senhal* may well be the key that helps us make sense of the entire text. For the lover whose name is "nameless lover" or "lover without name" is one whose name never escapes the indeterminate generality of the pronoun. And this repetition, with variation, of the lover's name means that he is doubly named, that he has two different names (*sanz non amis* and *amis sanz non*) that are both pro-nominal, that both fail to singularize, and that are specular reflections of each other. The doubly named lover is a generalized subject divided, in a stance of specularity, from himself. The two lovers of the text's title now appear to be the divided courtly lover, the subject whose *nom* is, as the narrator promised, *devisé*, divided.

The narrator, who first appeared as the first-person singular subject in line 7, is in lines 11 and 12 the first-person plural subject: he has been transformed from "I" to "we." Thus this doubly named narrator, whose names are both pro-nominal, is the specular double of the unnamed lover. That is, the narrative voice itself appears to be the two of the text's title, and thus it may rightly call itself "we." As we shall see presently, this text is indeed spoken by two voices, and thus the narrator is truly "we."

After naming yet not naming the hero of his romance, the narrator begins to describe the lady whom this hero loves. For several lines the narrator describes the "she" whom "he"—the *sanz non amis* or the *amis sanz non*—apparently loves. Yet it soon becomes clear that the "I"—the narrator himself—is the one who truly loves this lady:

> Gorge blanche, menton bien fet
> A la bele qui tant me fet
> Chascune nuit pensser à li,
> Qu'en dormant sui avoec li.
> Chascune nuit en dormant croi,
> Qu'ele die: "Besiez-moi." (ll. 37–42)

(A white throat, a well-made chin has the beauty who each night makes me think of her so much that I think, when I am sleeping, that I am with her. Each night while sleeping I think she says: "Kiss me.")

This declaration, I repeat, is not the reported speech of a third-person, potentially nameable "he" or hero of the romance but rather the language of the "I" or narrator whose intention was to tell the story not of his own but of a third-person's love affair, a story not of "my" but rather of "his" desire. Somewhere in the course of the description of the lady the narrator has fallen in love with that description or, more likely, with the very act of singing his desire. The storyteller, that is, has become a singer. The narrator has become the lyric *je*, the "nameless lover" or the "lover without name." He ends up telling his own story, the story of a courtly singer.

This return to lyric subjectivity is, in *Des Deux Amans*, irreversible. For from here on the pretense of storytelling is completely discarded, the "he" or hero vanishes from the text, there is no story about "him" and his lady, neither can ever be named, and the abortive tale soon ends in the song of the singing narrator:

> Quant me sovient du gorgeron
> Qui tant est blanz souz le menton,
> Qui n'est jamès par moi besiez,
> Sachiez que cist gens est mult griez;
> Trestoz li cuers m'esprent et art,
> Por poi que li cuers ne me part;
> Et quant me sovient de ses iex,

> Que por moi vi plorer an .ij.,
> Sachiez que durement me grièvre,
> Par poi que li cuers ne me crièvre.
> Certes bien me devroit partir,
> Quant il me covient *départir*
> De ma très douce chière amie,
> Truis-je mult grief la *départie*. (ll. 103–116)

(When I remember the throat that is so white under the chin, that has never been kissed by me, don't you know that my grief is great. My entire heart is set afire and burns, and my heart almost leaves me. And when I remember her eyes, which I saw cry for me for two years, you know that my grief is great, so that my heart almost breaks. Certainly I must *depart*. Since I must leave my sweet dear friend, I find the *departure* very grievous.)

The text's final word is *départie*: "departure"—but also "separation," "division." What the lyric *je* laments in the end is that distance that divides the subject from the "he," from the realm of the purely objective. The text's departure follows from its recognition that the "I" cannot be that "he" about whom a story could be told.

This *départie* is the separation of the text into two discursively divided parts: a story that would objectively imitate the history of a third-person "he" and a song that subjectively sings the desire of a first-person "I." The two lovers of the text's title now appear to be not so much the male courtly lover and the beloved lady—not so much the hero and heroine—as they are two versions of the male courtly lover. The *deux amans* are two opposed representations of the troubadour: the "he" whose story can be recounted in a *vida*- and *razo*-like act of narration, and the "I" who remains the generalized, pro-nominal subject of song. In this text the "he" remains nameless, does not acquire a particular, individual, objective, or historical existence that could be properly named. Thus "he" is still subject to song's substitutive semiosis, still stands for the "no one" who is the lyric *je*. The namelessness of the hero directly causes the collapse of the narrative project, as "I" substitutes for "he" and refuses to the end to relinquish the position of discursive power. *Des Deux Amans* enacts the proposition that a romance that fails to nominate the singular subject cannot be a romance.

9. The Eaten Heart

The various versions of the widespread medieval literary legend of the Eaten Heart are united by a common concern with the limitation, particularization, and dismemberment of the singing subject. These versions are variations of the following basic plot. A courtly and adulterous love triangle issues in violence when the jealous husband murders the courtly lover. Thereupon the husband orders his cook to remove the dead lover's heart, prepare it in a casserole, and serve it to the wife, who, upon learning of the trick, takes her own life.

Significantly, the slain courtly lover in most versions of the story is not just any male member of chivalric society but is specifically a lyric poet. Thus the tale most frequently appears as a sort of *vida* or *razo*—a narrative that recounts purported events in the life (and in this case the death) of a composer of courtly love songs. The legend of the Eaten Heart mourns, in a most exemplary manner, the advent of an interpretive literalism or empiricism, the institution of a perverse delimitation of the domain of the sign to an actual, individual, phenomenal, physical body. In this and the following chapter we shall gloss three versions of the story, finishing our account of this group of self-contemplating tales about troubadours with what is perhaps the richest and most fascinating of its members, the *Lai d'Ignauré*.

The legend of the Eaten Heart appears in the *chansonniers*, where it is told as the *vida* of the troubadour Guillem de Cabestaing:

> Guillems de Capestaing si fo uns cavalliers de l'encontrada de Rossillon, que confinava com Cataloingna e com Narbones. Molt fo avinenz e prezatz d'armas e de servir e de cortesia. Et avia en la soa encontrada una domna que avia nom ma dompna Seremonda, moiller d'En Raimon de Castel Rossillon, qu'era molt rics e gentils e mals e braus e fers et orgoillos. E Guillems de Capestaing si l'amava la domna per amor e cantava de leis e fazia sas chansos d'ella. E la domna, qu'era joves e gentil e bella e plaissenz, si.l volia be major que a re del mon. E fon dit a Raimon de Castel Rossiglon; et el, com hom iratz e gelos, enqueri lo *fait*, e saup que *vers* era, e fez gardar la moiller fort.

E quant venc un dia, Raimon de Castel Rossillon troba passan Guillem senes gran compaingnia et ausis lo; e trais li lo cor del cors; e fez lo portar a un escudier a son alberc; e fez lo raustir e far peurada, e fes lo dar a manjar a la muiller. E quant la domna l'ac manjat lo cor d'En Guillem de Capestaing, En Raimon li dis o que el fo. Et ella, quant o auzi, perdet lo vezer e l'auzir. E quant ela revenc, si dis: "Seingner, ben m'avez dat si bon manjar que ja mais non manjarai d'autre." E quant el auzi so qu'ella dis, el coret a sa espaza e volc li dar sus en la testa; et ella s'en anet al balcon e se laisset cazer jos, e fo morta.[1]

(Guillem de Cabestaing was a knight from the country of Rossillon, which bordered Catalonia and Narbonnes. He was a charming man, prized for feats of arms, chivalric service, and courtesy. And there was in his country a woman whose name was Lady Seremonde, wife of Lord Rossillon, who was very rich and noble and fierce and cruel and proud. And Guillem loved the woman and sung about her and made his *cansos* about her. And the woman, who was young and noble and beautiful and pleasant, loved him more than anything in the world. And this was told to Raimon; and he, as an angry and jealous man, looked at the fact (*fait*) and knew that it was true (*vers*), and he had his wife closely guarded.

And then came a day that Raimon found Guillem passing by without companions and killed him; and he took the heart out of the body; and he had it taken to a cook at his castle; and he had it roasted and peppered, and he had it given to his wife to eat. And when the lady had eaten the heart of Lord Guillem de Cabestaing, Lord Raimon told her what it was. And she, when she heard it, lost her vision and hearing. And when she revived, she said: "Lord, you have given me such a good meal that I shall never eat another." And when he heard what she said, he ran to his sword and wanted to strike her head; and she went to the balcony and let herself fall off, and she was dead.)

The jealous husband in this *vida* generally resembles the narrator of *vidas* and *razos*, confusing the semiotic with the mimetic, the linguistic with the material, the metaphorical with the literal, the fictional with the factual. The death of the lyric singer is assured the moment he to whom the referential secret of song is disclosed becomes persuaded that *lo fait . . . vers era* ("the fact . . . was true"). The narration of Guillem's love—the telling of the hidden truth, the secret *sens* of his *cansos*—to Raimon de Castel Rossillon, which spells the death of Guillem, is another version of the narration of the courtly singer's love, another version of the sort of narration perpetrated by the *vidas* and *razos*, by the *novella* that *Novella LXIV* is *d'una*, by the *novel* or *reisun* that the singular survivor of Marie's tale attempts to tell—a historical narration that spells the dismemberment of the singing subject, the death of the troubadour.

And, up to this point, we can hardly blame the jealous husband, since his assumption that the *fait* is *vers* is perfectly reasonable: the *fait* ("fact") that he suspects, the fact of his wife's adultery, is indeed *vers* ("true"). It is only when he willfully repeats and inverts the equation of *fait* and *vers*, this time knowing that such an equation is unfounded, that Raimon commits an atrocity. The second time around Raimon acts as if *vers* were *fait*, as if *lo vers . . . fait era* ("the verse . . . were fact"). In his violent rage Raimon acts as if the metaphors of courtly verse were empirically real, literal facts, as if the signs of a linguistic system originate in and adequately represent a corresponding and prior material reality. By feeding the troubadour Guillem de Cabestaing's heart to his wife, Raimon de Castel Rossillon is literalizing or materializing, in a debased mode, the lyric commonplace according to which the courtly lover's *cor* is displaced and lodged within the breast of the beloved.[2] And this morbid meal furthermore mocks the lover's versified desire for another's "heart," as Raimon pretends to see his wife's desire as a real hunger for the anatomical organ. Yet Raimon's limited or cruelly literal reading is an inadequate misprision of the heart, which after its ingestion will not be in the lady's permanent possession, not subject to the continued domination of the desired *domna*, but rather will be subject to a speedy digestion and expelled as excrement. Raimon's naively biological and biographical reading transforms song into a reduced material of merely temporary survival whose disposal is always imminent. This excremental mode of reading that would locate the core of the desire of courtly language specifically within the heart of a specific individual is inseparable, in this *vida*, from the moment of the singer's death. Lyric language is silenced when it is definitively located within the heart of the singular singer.

It is thus no accident that the legend of the Eaten Heart is a story specifically about a lyric singer and not about just any member of courtly society, for Raimon's misprision of Guillem's heart is a figure for the violence perpetrated by all *vidas* and *razos* and indeed by all medieval stories about lyric singers. At the heart of the *vida* of Guillem de Cabestaing is embedded the materialization and particularization of a linguistic generality: *cor*, a commonplace and constantly circulating signifier in the language of courtly lyric, is transformed into a fleshly referent in a local history, a referent that is regarded as residing in the interior of the individual human breast. The physical embodiment of the linguistic heart is a figure for the narrative embodiment of the linguistic subject that *razos* and *vidas* attempt to foster.

In what may be the most famous telling of the tale of the Eaten Heart, Boccaccio's version in Day IV of the *Decameron*, the slain courtly lover is not explicitly described as a lyric singer. Yet while Boccaccio thus obscures his tale's roots in the Old Provençal *vidas* and *razos*, he conversely exposes his story's kinship to this tradition of tales about troubadours by foregrounding its setting in Provence and by alluding, at the end, to written verses:

> . . . furono i due corpi ricolti e nella chiesi del castello medesimo della donna in una medisima sepoltura fur posti, e sopr'essa scritti *versi* significanti chi fosser quegli che dentro sepolti v'erano, e il modo e la *cagione* della lor morte.[3]
>
> (. . . and the two bodies were gathered up and placed in a single sepulchre in the chapel of the lady's own castle, and upon it were written *verses* signifying who were within and the manner and cause [*cagione*] of their deaths.)

At the end, by adding to the legend this mention of *versi* ("verses") and by speaking of the *cagione* ("cause") for the composition of verses, Boccaccio situates his version firmly in the tradition of the *razo* (in Italian, the *ragione*) and the *lai*—both of which pose as accounts of the historical causes of or reasons for (*cagione* or *ragione*) the composition of surviving lyric verses.

So it is clear that Boccaccio did not elide or repress the slain lover's lyric vocation in order to distance his tale from the Old Provençal tradition and thereby to make a pretense of *auctor*ial originality. Instead Boccaccio's rewriting of the tale is the product of his profound and subtle act of reading. Boccaccio recognizes that the tale is not specifically about the lyric singer per se but rather about the lyric singer insofar as he is a figure for language in its most general and extended sense, and this very recognition is a renunciation of the limited literalism that the legend ultimately denounces. For Boccaccio what matters is not that the story is the history of a certain troubadour named Guillem de Cabestaing but rather that it stages a struggle between lyric and narrative representations of the subject. More precisely, Boccaccio reads the *vida* of Guillem de Cabestaing as a fable for the violence with which a self-fashioned autonomous, unique, or distinctive ego reacts when confronted with a glimpse of its own linguistic, generalized, and undifferentiated subjectivity.

The crucial alteration that Boccaccio performs upon the text of the *vida* of Guillem de Cabestaing is to change the jealous husband's name from *Raimon* to the Italian equivalent of *Guillem*—namely, *Guiglielmo*. The effect of this change, then, is that both husband and rival share the same name:

> Dovete adunque sapere che, secondo che raccontano i provenzali, in Provenza furon già due nobili cavalieri, de' quali ciascuno e castella e vassalli aveva sotto di sé; e aveva l'uno nome messer Guiglielmo Rossiglione e l'altro messer Guiglielmo Guardastagno. E per ciò che l'uno e l'altro era prod'uomo molto nell'arme, s'amavano assai e in costume avean d'andar sempre ad ogni torniamento o giostra o altro fatto d'arme insieme e vestita d'una assisa.[4]

> (You should know then that, according to what the Provençals tell, in Provence there were once two noble knights, each of whom had under him both castles and vassals; and one was named Guiglielmo Rossiglione and the other Guiglielmo Guardastagno. And because both were very excellent men at arms, they liked each other very much and had the custom of going to every tournament or joust together and clothed in the same heraldic device.)

By naming both knights *Guiglielmo*, Boccaccio is quite clearly foregrounding their resemblance to each other, robbing them of any singularity or uniqueness as individuals. The name *Guiglielmo*, which in this discursive world refers to both and all of the knights, thus performs the function of the plural grammatical subject and could easily be replaced in every instance by "they." As Giuseppe Mazzotta points out, they—the two Guiglielmos—are virtually identical, not only in name but in every fashion, and thus one knight's desire for another's wife follows as if automatically according to the Girardian logic of mimetic desire.[5] Specifically, Boccaccio posits that this lack of autonomous or self-standing subjectivity, this lack of difference or distinction, is the effect of a linguistic generality: the difference between two specific, discrete, distinct individuals cannot be expressed in a language that lacks differentiating names. Such is, of course, the dominant language of Provence, the *langue* of courtly love.

In the passage cited above Boccaccio furthermore alters the text of the *vida* by tailoring to suit his purpose a certain detail concerning the Guiglielmos' habit of dress. The two knights cloak their bodies in the selfsame heraldic device, signifying themselves by means of the same insignia. In this case the language of heraldry (which is normally supposed to distinguish differences) becomes, like courtly song, a language of generality, not of distinction—a language that has no way to name the difference between two concrete and discrete bodies, two fleshly entities. Just as the two knights share a single name, so they share a single insignia, and neither name nor insignia can designate singularity. Just as all lyric singers can only call themselves "I" (which is the same pronoun by which all *losengiers* call themselves), so all of the knights in Boccaccio's narrativized microcosm of the courtly discursive world can only call themselves *Guiglielmo*. The shared name and the shared insignia signify the shared language of courtly love, the linguistic generality that prevents the differentiation of lover from *losengier*, singer from husband, "I" from "they." And Boccaccio furthermore alters the *vida* by completely cutting out the lady's name, by refusing to name the lady: whereas she is known as *Seremonda* in the Old Provençal version, she is simply *donna* in the *Decameron*. This refusal to name the *donna* signifies the retreat of Boccaccio's *novella* back into the very world of purified or re-virginated courtly verse that it neglects, except obliquely, to mention. Boccaccio has re-versified the *vida*, has fashioned a world whose system of nomenclature is extremely limited or underdeveloped—nothing other than the discursive world of courtly lyric.

If lyric language may be compared to a sort of garment, it is surely most like a *uniform*—a fashion-system that does not permit the one to stand apart from the other. Like the pronoun by which the courtly singer signifies himself, the heraldic device by which the two Guiglielmos signify themselves is always the same and cannot be individually appropriated; and in both cases this sameness hides a duplicity, masks a division, since what is contained within the singularity of the outward sign is itself anything but singular. That is, the uniformity of the pronoun or the garment is the sign of an interior self-difference—the difference between one singer, between one Guiglielmo, and another. Thus we may think of Boccaccio's Guiglielmos not as two previously different characters whom he would merge into one but rather as one from which emerges the effect of a division, of a difference that is instigated by the very advent of the name. That is, the self's difference from itself is an effect of the very generality of the sign by which it would name itself—a sign that belongs properly, like the heraldic sign, not to the individual but to the *gens*.

It may seem upon a superficial reading that the surnames of the two Guiglielmos serve to distinguish them from each other. Yet if we read even more superficially, this apparent distinction collapses, as both surnames say the same thing: both name the lyric singer. In the case of Guglielmo Rossiglione this is quite manifest: he is named *Rossignol*, "Nightingale"—the *senhal* or code name routinely assigned in the courtly tradition, as we shall see later, to the lyric singer. Similarly, the other Guiglielmo's name intimates that he, too, is the troubadour. Though Boccaccio obscures the surname of that troubadour Guillem de Cabestaing whose *vida* is being recounted, the name by which Boccaccio replaces *Cabestaing* tells us to look: *Guarda-* ("Look!") is the imperative pronounced by the first half of *Guardastagno*. And what we find if we follow this imperative to look is the *stagno*—nothing other than the Italicized equivalent of the latter half of that missing Cabe-*staing*. This nominal remnant is a stain or trace of evidence that this Guiglielmo is, like the one named *Rossignol*, the troubadour. Thus the Guiglielmo's surnames do not so much serve to differentiate the two but rather to insist upon a latent resemblance—a resemblance revolving around their common identity as the troubadour.

As I said, Boccaccio obscures the fact that his tale is told about the lyric singer. Yet the tale's latent concern with and return to courtly discourse suggests that the attempted expulsion of lyric from the scene of the story follows the logic of scapegoating, the logic whereby identity is regarded as difference: narrative represents lyric as alien precisely when narrative resembles lyric most closely. And indeed this scapegoating is precisely what happens to alienate the two Guiglielmos, to trigger the event, the murder, that would construct apparent difference between them: Guiglielmo Rossiglione is outraged just when he glimpses the absolute interchangeability of himself and Guiglielmo Guardastagno. His rage is the direct effect of his resistance to his lyric generality, to his sameness in relation to the other singer of the story.[6] The moment of scandal in the legend of the Eaten Heart is when the husband—until then self-satisfied in the illusory singularity of his narrative ego—discovers that another can easily take his place, that another's desire mimicks his or that his desire mimicks another's. Guiglielmo Guardastagno, the slain courtly lover and lyric singer, is the victim of another singer's—Rossiglione's or *Rossignol*'s—positively narrative desire for difference.

Yet if it would seem that Boccaccio's tale thereby traces a trajectory from song to story, from its undifferentiated lyric opening to its narrative culmination in the violence that prompts Rossiglione to take to the wilderness in flight from courtly society, such a semblance is rendered entirely dubious by the tale's closing comments. I cite again Boccaccio's closing mention of the verses that report, after the fact, the events recounted—a mention that repeats the rationale of the *razos*:

> ... furono i due corpi ricolti e nella chiesa del castello medisimo della donna in una medesima sepoltura fur posti, e sopr'essa scritti versi significanti chi fosser quegli che dentro sepolti v'erano, e il modo e la cagione della lor morte.[7]
>
> (. . . and the two bodies were gathered up and placed in a single sepulchre in the chapel of the lady's own castle, and upon it were written verses signifying who were within and the manner and cause of their deaths.)

This last sentence is, in relation to these written verses, their *razo* or *ragione*, the historical explanation for the genesis of verse. Yet, in an anomalous departure from the model of the orthodox *razo*, the verses that are glossed are said to refer not to one but rather to two biographies. The surviving *ragione* inscribed upon the tomb gives voice to, by telling the story of, a twosome. Thus the notion of a one-to-one ratio between the *razo* and the singer, between the text and the subject, is defied. There is no singular ego whose story is told in these verses, for the verses tell the story of neither just the lover nor just the lady but rather of both the lover and the lady. The either/or distinction of narration has been thwarted by this return of the both/and of lyric, as subject and object are inextricably bound up and mingled together. Thus this inscribed sepulchre that contains in its center an undifferentiated twosome is, like the shared heraldic device that dominated the tale's beginning, a figure for the uniform semiosis of courtly *langue*, for the shared superficial generality that hides an interior doubleness, duplicity, and self-difference.[8] If there is a signified contained within such verses, this signified is more than one. Thus the ratio or rationale of story, the idea that the text is driven by a singular *causa* or *cagione*, is ultimately banished from the story that would banish song. And poetic justice is dealt to the husband whose brutality was triggered by his fear that another could take his place, as in the end the husband's place in the family sepulchre is improperly filled by another, by someone else who is equally able, in sex or in death, to fill the husband's slot.

10. Lyric Ignorance

The historical emergence of story and the concomitant diminishment of song is richly recounted—and, as in the *vida* of Peire Vidal, figured as a sort of cutting or castration that limits the dispersal of seeds or signs—in the early thirteenth-century *Lai d'Ignauré*, composed, according to a signature inscribed at the end, by a certain Renaus de Beaujeu. But before we initiate a reading of this remarkable *lai*, we must stress that the analogy between signification and dissemination, between sense and semen, is entirely medieval, not post-Freudian, and is explicitly formulated by the tale's prologue. For the *Lai d'Ignauré* opens with a traditional *topos* of medieval romance prologue—namely, with the narrator's claim that producing linguistic signs is akin to sowing seeds:

> *Sens* est perdus, ki est couvers;
> Cis k'est moustrés et descouvers
> Puet en auchun liu *semen*chier.
> Pour chou, voel roumans coumenchier,
> Une aventure molt estraingne
> Que, jadis, avint en Bretaigne
> D'un chevalier de grant *poissanche*,
> Ki bien doit estre en ramenbranche.[1] (ll. 11–18)

(Sense [*Sens*] that is covered is lost; that which is shown and uncovered may in some place inseminate [*semen-chier*]. This is why I want to commence a romance—a very strange adventure that once happened in Brittany to a very *potent* knight who well should be in remembrance.)

An entire cluster of signifiers, including the Old French *sens* and the Old Provençal *senhal*, stems from the Greek *semeion*: sense, seed, semen, sign, semiosis. So, in a sense, we may say that the *Lai d'Ignauré* opens under the sign of the seed, with the narrator's claim that he shall expose himself, shall sow seeds in an act of authorial ejaculation, that he shall exercise the penis-pen.² Here in the prologue is sown the seed, in the form of *sens*, of the tale's later concern with signs and semen. The opening of the *Lai d'Ignauré*—declaring this imperative to make the sign public, not to hoard, hide, or keep it private—suggests that what is at stake in the tale is a question concerning Ignauré's semiotic *poissanche*, his potency, his power to signify.

The tale commences, in a manner that seems perfectly consonant with the conventions of romance narrative, by naming the name of its hero:

> *Ignaures* ot li chevaliers non;
> Molt par estoit de grant renon. (ll. 19–20)

(This knight was named *Ignauré*, and he enjoyed a great renown.)

Then we learn of this hero's habitual observation of the rites of song:

> Si tos com entrés estoit mais,
> A l'ajornee se levoit;
> Cinq jougleres od lui menoit,
> Flahutieles et calimiaus:
> Au bos s'en aloit li dansiaus.
> Le mai aportoit a grant bruit.
> Molt par estoit de grant deduit;
> Chascun jour l'avoit a coustume.
> Fine amors l'esprent et alume,
> Femmes l'apielent *Lousignol*. (ll. 28–37)

(As soon as the month of May arrived, he rose early in the morning, taking with him five *jongleurs*, some flutes and pipes. The young man went into the woods, and he brought back the May-tree with great fanfare. His company was very agreeable, and pleasure was his daily habit. Love burned and inflamed him, and the women called him *Rossignol* [*Lousignol*].)

Though it would surely seem that this hero's single proper name is revealed from the outset, there is good reason to challenge the propriety of the name *Ignauré*. Still, at first sight we presume that *Ignauré* is, within the frame of the fiction, the historically "real" name, the true identity, of the one to whom the courtly ladies refer by the *senhal* or nickname *Rossignol* ("Nightingale"). In this scheme, which seems quite reasonable, *Rossignol* would be the signifier of the signified "Ignauré," would be the *senhal* that masks the hero's true identity or *propre nun*.

Now, before we pursue our interrogation of the name *Ignauré*, let us expound very briefly on *Rossignol*'s significance as a *senhal*. From the outset of troubadour poetry, the analogy between the bird—most often the *rossignol*—and the lyric singer is commonplace. Jaufré Rudel, for instance, compares his vocal production with that of the nightingale:

> Quan lo rius de la fontana
> S'esclarzís, si com far sòl,
> E par la flors aiglentina,
> E'l *rossinholetz* el ram
> Vòlf e refranh et aplana
> Son dous chantar et afina,
> Dreitz es qu'ieu lo mieu refranha.³

(When the brook from the spring becomes clear, as it happens, and the eglantine appears, and the nightingale [*rossinholetz*] on the branch turns and repeats and planes and polishes his sweet song, it is right that I repeat mine.)

When the singing subject or lyric voice itself is "personified"—transformed into a narrative character, such as the *jongleur* who serves as a messenger by transmitting the song to the beloved lady—this voice goes by the name *Rossignol*.

In the brief lyrico-narrative tale *Le Sort des Dames* (which, virtually devoid of narrativity, recounts nothing more than a messenger's delivery of a love lyric to a lady) the messenger identifies himself to the lady in the following manner:

> Je vous vueil dire qui je sui:
> *Roxignolet* m'apele l'on.⁴

(I want to tell you who I am: they call me *Rossignol*.)

Rossignol seems to be the name given to a voice that, despite its appearance in narrative, remains the voice of the singing subject. Thus, although this messenger claims immediately upon appearing to the lady that he intends to deliver *une novele* (line 8), what he in fact delivers is not a novel discourse but rather more of the same, as *Le Sort des Dames* quickly ends with his performance of a commonplace *trouvère* stanza. *Rossignol* is the *senhal* given to the lyric voice that resists transformation into narrative, the voice that cannot simply be inserted into a story and be expected thereupon to produce novelistic discourse. *Rossignol* is the name of the one who resists being named.

Rossignol is also the *senhal* assigned to the *jongleur* who, according to the *vida* of Raimbaut d'Aurenga, stands in for that troubadour and sings his songs:

> . . . et Rambauz, senes veser leis, per lo gran ben que n'ausia dire, si enamoret d'ella et ella de lui. E si fez sas chansos d'ella; e si.l manda sas chansos per un joglar que avia nom *Rossignol*, si con dis en una chanson:[5]

> (. . . and Raimbaut, without seeing her, for the great good that he had heard said of her, fell in love with her and she with him. And he made his *cansos* about her; and he sent his songs through a *jongleur* whose name was *Rossignol*, as he tells in one of his songs:)

In short, *Rossignol* is the name appropriated by the lyric *je* upon its transformation into narrative. It is not, however, a proper, specifying name, since it retains its status as a *senhal*, as a signifier that can potentially refer to anyone and everyone, that keeps hidden the secret of historical identity. Like the lyric *je*, *Rossignol* does not signify individual singularity or difference. All courtly singers may call themselves *Rossignol*.

There is no question that the mere appearance in the text of Ignauré's nickname, *Rossignol*, raises certain suspicions that initiate and will guide our reading of the *Lai d'Ignauré*. That is, we cannot forget that the adventure of Ignauré does not so much happen to a certain character or individual person as it happens to courtly song itself. Above all the story recounts a discursive crisis precipitated by song's insertion into or apprehension by a progressive historical order. The nickname *Rossignol* is there to trigger and to confirm our recognition of song's insistence in this story.

What is in question is the scheme that would posit *Rossignol* as the *senhal* or signifier of the *signified* "Ignauré." Instead we shall see the pertinence of a new scheme describing the relation between the hero's two names: *Rossignol* as the *senhal* or signifier of the *signifier Ignauré*. The name *Ignauré*, in other words, is not the hero's real or proper name but rather is itself a *senhal*, not a signified but rather itself a signifier. We say this not merely because *Ignauré* signifies a certain "ignorance"—a connotation that makes his name the possible site of interpretive speculation—but rather because *Ignauré* quite simply is, as a matter of literary historical fact, a *senhal*. *Ignauré* is, according to philologists, the *langue d'oïl* version of the Old Provençal *senhal* appropriated by the troubadour Raimbaut d'Aurenga—namely, *Linhaura*.[6]

Indeed this Raimbaut d'Aurenga whose *senhal* is *Ignauré* is the same Raimbaut d'Aurenga whose *vida* names his voice *Rossignol*. And he who is named *Ignauré* and *Rossignol* is, of course, none other than the hero of our *lai*. Our text tempts us, teases us, to perform the act of proper naming, to reveal the hidden referential secret, to announce to the world that this tale is in fact told about the troubadour Raimbaut d'Aurenga.[7]

Yet such an indiscretion would betray the text by questioning its ignorance. For what we mean by considering *Ignauré* a signifier rather than a signified, a *senhal* rather than a *propre nun*, is that the tale from the outset refuses to name names and thereby maintains its lyric secrecy. The historical identity of the hero—Raimbaut d'Aurenga—remains utterly unspoken. The text makes us ignore, and seems itself to ignore, the singular proper name (Raimbaut d'Aurenga) signified by the sign *Ignauré*. Despite appearances, the hero's name remains at the outset a generalized element of *langue* rather than a particular instance of *parole*. The hero is not truly nominated at the beginning of this tale: his name is still a site of potential semiotic substitution, still a sign prior to its dismemberment or particularization, prior to its bondage to one particular body.

Ignauré's other name, *Rossignol*—or, as it happens not by chance to be spelled in our text, *Lousignol*—is nothing if not a speculation on the semiotic status of the hero. *Lousignol* is what we might call a meta-*senhal*, a *senhal* that reflects on the *senhal*. For *Lousignol* most clearly signifies *lo signol* or *lo signal*: the *signum*, the "sign," the "signifier," the *senhal*. *Rossignol* or *Lousignol* is the *senhal* of the lyric voice not only because of the nightingale's famous talent but because it signifies itself, like courtly song, in a most specular manner. Ignauré's other name is *Lo signol*—a name which describes the semiotic status of the name *Ignauré*, a name which tells us that the hero is not to be taken as such-and-such empirical individual but rather as the signifier of the signifier. That is, our *lai* is more properly named the *Lai du Signol*, the "Song/Story of the Sign." In following the adventures of *Lousignol* we witness the fate of the lyric sign in its encounter with and insertion into the order of story.

The lyric sign *par excellence* is the grammatical *je*, the "I" of *langue*, which refers to no one in particular and may be appropriated by all. This *je* is the *senhal* behind which the singing subject's historical heart is hidden. The language of the sign *je* is identical to the language of the *losengier*, of *chescuns*, of all the others. And this should not come as a surprise, since the *losengier* and the *je* are one and the same—the one simply another name for the other. For *losengier* harbors within itself, not very secretly, the signs *sen* ("sign") and *gié* (*je*, "I"): *losengier* is *lo sen gié*, is another way to say "the sign

'I.'" Thus we see that *Lousignol*, the *senhal* of the lyric *je*, is also the *senhal* of the *losengier*—and indeed both of these *senhals* commence by pronouncing "the sign." *Ignauré*, it would appear, is equated by a chain of semiotic substitutions to the *losengier*. The hero of our tale is this generalized lyric subject, this semiotic *je* who is undifferentiated from the *losengiers*, from all the other *je*'s, from the multitude of "the signs 'I.'" And indeed Ignauré is quite properly named, for *lo signol* or the sign that he is—namely, *lo sen gié*, the sign "I"—is by its nature ignorant, unknowing, indifferent to its appropriation by anyone whosoever. Ignauré is, as we shall see, he who ignores difference, he to whom one is as good as another, he to whom being the *losengier* is as good as being the *je*. Ignauré is the *senhal*, the sign of the general subject, the unnamed name, the pro-noun, lyric language, song itself. The crisis that will eventually cut short, by cutting off, Ignauré's semiotic freedom to fulfill a vast variety of assignations will be simultaneous with the institution of differential hierarchy, with the establishment of knowledge conceived as reason, *ratio*, or *razo*.

If the *Lai d'Ignauré* is a version of the legend of the Eaten Heart, it is a version composed under the influence of another *lai*—namely, Marie de France's *Le Chaitivel* or *Les Quatre Doels*. For, like Marie's tale, the *Lai d'Ignauré* is inaugurated under the sign of the *tuz* or the *chescuns*. What is narrated at the outset is a pluralized courtly love situation: Ignauré is the courtly lover of not one but rather *twelve* ladies. This "twelve" is, like the "four" of Marie's tale, the sign of a collective subjectivity. Like the lady of Marie's tale who could not bear to *tu-er* or *tutoyer* the *tuz*—who could not bear to address her love to a singular individual, thereby killing the others—Ignauré is the lover of no one in particular but rather addresses his songs to the multitude:

> Dedens le chastiel, a Riol,
> Avoit douse pers a estage.
> Chevalier erent de terre et de rente;
> Chascuns ot femme biele et gente,
> De haut linage, de grant gent.
> A toutes douse s'acointa;
> Et tant chascune l'en creanta
> S'amour trestout a son voloir,
> Et, s'el de li voloit avoir,
> K'il seroit servis comme quens,
> *Chascune cuide k'il soit siens*. (ll. 38–50)

(Twelve peers resided in the Castle of Riol. They were knights rich in land and income. Each had a beautiful and elegant wife, of high lineage, of great nobility. Ignauré became close to all twelve. And he swore to each one that he loved her with all his heart and said that, if she wanted to have it, that he would consider himself royally served. *Each one imagined that he was hers.*)

Such an account of an adulterous courtly affair is routinely furnished by the *razos*, but here of course this account resists *razo*-like specificity. The particulars of a love affair are recounted without the loss of lyric generality. The story does not disclose the identity of the unique lady supposed to be the singular object of the singer's desire, and thus the story remains songlike at its outset. Ignauré, the one who is shared, circulates freely among all, while each thinks that Ignauré is uniquely hers. Ignauré is that which is common to all, that which is on the tip of every tongue. The object of Ignauré's desire is "them," and "they" are that which his songs celebrate.

If we consider this set of ladies while recalling the passage cited above that told of Ignauré's springtime excursions, accompanied by five other *jongleurs*, into the woods to sing as *Rossignol*, then we see that Ignauré's voice is represented as the voice of six singers singing to twelve ladies. A certain lyric ratio is thereby established: the singer is to the lady as 1:2. Perhaps the lesson of this ratio is that the lady is site of a duplicity insofar as she is the specular double of the singer: the lady is plural, both subject and object, both herself and the one who sings. For the lady is, as Raimbaut de Vaquieras' plurilingual *descort* dramatizes, the tongue of the *tuz* who sings the song. Yet whatever else this ratio signifies, its foremost effect is to defy the 1:1 mimetic narrative ratio propagated by the *razo*, which normally posits a one-to-one correspondence between the singer and the lady and, more generally, a one-to-one correspondence between text and historical event. And perhaps the ratio is meant in our tale to be irreducible, to be taken as not 1:2 but rather 6:12. This latter possibility confirms our sense that courtly song, sung by no one, is sung by many to many.

At any rate, and no matter the ratio, Ignauré, the lover of everyone, is at the outset of his tale no one. To make someone of Ignauré, the possibility for the advent of narrative singularity must be established. And this is precisely what comes to pass just after we learn of Ignauré's involvement with the entire *gens* of courtly society:

Toutes les ama plus d'un an,
Tant c'une feste saint Jehan,

> K'esjoïst toute creature,
> S'en alerent, par aventure,
> Les grans dames esbanoier,
> *Toutes douse*, en un vregier.
> Ains plus n'i ot que eles douse.
> *Une* en i ot, molt tres jalouse
> A *dire chou ke elle pense.* (ll. 65–73)

(His love for them all lasted more than a year, until it happened that—during the feast of Saint John when all creatures are joyful—*all twelve* of the noble ladies went to amuse themselves in a garden. There were no more there but they twelve. There was *one* among them who was very eager to *say what she was thinking*.)

This passage distills the transformation from generalized to individual subjectivity that is allegorized and resisted by the sort of lyrico-narrative text that draws our attention. For we here witness the severance or division of the *toutes douse* ("all twelve"), the emergence of the *une* from among the *tuz*, the one from among the many. This is the critical point at which one is singled out, as one of the twelve ladies begins to stake a claim for preeminence. And, as we shall see, this one who speaks her mind continues to act differently, to appear foregrounded as a sort of heroine, right until the reinstitution of song that we have come to expect at the tale's end.

Significantly, what apparently singles this one out is nothing other than her desire to say what she thinks. That is, the emergence of the individual in this passage is simultaneous with the formulation of a conception of discourse as a disclosure of interiority, as an expression of that which resides inside, in the heart and mind. And what she then reveals as the special thought that she harbors inside is the desire to institute a discursive practice that would accomplish nothing other than this sort of revelation of interiority. For she proposes to institute that which, following Augustine, is in the Middle Ages virtually synonymous with autobiographical narration—namely, confession:

> "Dames sommes, et renvoisies,
> Cointes, et nobles, et prisies,
> Femmes as pers de cest chastiel;
> Plainnes sommes de grant reviel.
> N'i a cheli n'aint par amours,
> Et molt est envoisiés cis jours.

D'*une* de nous fasons no prestre;
Seoir en voist en mi cel estre,
Lés cele ente ki est flourie.
Chascune i voist, et se li die
Cui ele aimme, en *confiession*,
Ne a cui elle a fait le don:
Ensi sarons certainnement
Li quele aimme plus hautement." (ll. 81–94)

("We are charming, elegant, noble and worthy women. We are the wives of the peers of this castle and we are bursting with joy. There is not one among us who is not amorous, and this is a day of pleasure. Let us make *one* of us the priest; let her go sit in this place there beside that blossoming branch. Let each one visit her and *confess* to her the name of him whom she loves and to whom she has given the gift. Thus we will know, in all certainty, which one loves the most noble one.")

Indeed the institution of private confession belongs to the constellation of discursive practices that reflected and propagated the rise of the autonomous individual self in the late Middle Ages.[8] And this one lady who has singled herself out, in a passage that moves from "we" to "one," proposes that one be singled out to preside over the singling out of the one preeminent courtly lover. She would establish, by fostering a sense of private interiority, a discourse able to designate both singularity and differential hierarchy. She would institute a discourse that transforms the present situation of collective resemblance into one of individual distinction. In short, she would do just what the lady of Marie's tale resisted—namely, *eslire le meilleur*, "elect the best."

In accordance with her preeminence among the twelve, this one is elected confessor, is selected to play the unique role of the priest who will hear the ladies' *razo*-like revelations of their love affairs. The confessions that follow are, as demanded by the lady/priest, nominations of the name, revelations of the true identity of the singing subject:

"Séés vous dont, si me contés—
Et gardés que ne me mentés—
Comment a vos amis a non." (ll. 107–109)

("Then sit down, and recount to me—and watch that you don't lie to me—what your lover's name is.")

What is sought is a truthful account, a *conte*, a storytelling that tells the true name and that betrays lyric secrecy. Each lady is asked to disclose that name that is uniquely bound up with hers and which defines her as unique.

Of course there is an ensuing scandal when the ladies learn that naming the name does not inaugurate singularity, that their private speech makes absolutely no difference. Twelve times the same name is spoken, and each time—as in the following instance—the would-be preeminent one is stunned by the commonplace quality of her desire:

> "Ignaures, li prus, l'ensaigniés,
> C'est cil a cui je suis donnee."
> Li prestre a la coulour muee
> Quant ele ot que son dru nomma
> (C'ert cele ki le mius l'ama). (ll. 114–118)

> ("Ignauré, the noble, the well-bred—it is he to whom I have given myself." The priest changed color when she heard her lover named [it was she who loved him the most.]")

(Does she really love him most, or does she merely think, like all courtly lovers do, that she loves better than the others?) This generality of the lover's name triggers an angry mutation in the one who privately thinks that she is, more than the others, most properly addressed by the sign: she thinks that the name *Ignauré* can only be her private property, no one else's. And this violent reaction to the demystification of the self's private relation to language is itself a general reaction, as all twelve, upon learning of their shared appropriation of the same name, cry out for vengeance:

> "Dame, or nous dites ki vous sanle?
> Li quele a plus vaillant ami?"
> "Certes, chascune a dit a mi
> Le non d'un tout seul chevalier;
> Molt nous a faites avillier.
> Et jou meïsmes l'ainc aussi,
> Et vous trestoutes autressi!
> Par le carbiu! mar i fut fait.
> Ignaures a esmut tel plait,
> Il le comperra sans targier."
> "Comment nous em porons vengier?" (ll. 202–211)

("My lady, tell us how it seems to you? Which one of us has the most worthy lover?"

"Surely, each one has told me the name of a single knight. He has shamed us greatly. And I myself also love him, and you all love him as well. Egads! how unfortunate! Ignauré has caused such a wound, he will pay for it without delay."

"How shall we avenge ourselves?")

The game meant to foster selection and nomination by probing the private realm of the self has backfired, producing instead equivalence and the reassertion of the anonymous, collective voice of the *tuz* ("How shall *we* avenge *ourselves*?"). The great scandal that prompts the violent reaction is the disclosure that the language of the heart is conventional, that private interiority is located in and regulated by the realm of the public. What each one privately thinks to be her individual desire originating in her own heart is exposed as a desire dictated by courtly *langue*, by Ignauré. Each one thinks herself to be different and thinks that the name of her lover is the special sign of that difference—whereas in fact that name turns out to be the sign of their undifferentiation. The violent impulse, as in the legend of the Eaten Heart, follows immediately upon the recognition that one's place could easily be filled by another, that one is captivated by a *langue* ignorant of and indifferent to the individual.

After the naming of the name that fails to singularize, a plan for vengeance is pronounced:

> "Li une a l'autre creantera
> A cheli u premiers venra,
> K'en cel vergié terme li mete
> Et nous toutes, sans ademetre.
> Et si faisons savoir le jour,
> Toutes i serons sans sejour.
> S'aport chascune coutiel a pointe!
> De fol outrecuidier et cointe
> Ki vers nous toutes a mespris
> Soit cruele venganche pris." (ll. 213–222)

("Let's promise that the first one who finds him will arrange a date with him in this garden, and also with all the others, without exception: we will make known to each other the day, and we will all be here on time. Each of us will bring a sharp knife! A cruel vengeance will be wreaked for the sly and deceptive presumption that has hurt us all!")

In the *Lai d'Ignauré* the wives are the ones who first brandish knives, thereby occuping that position of violent avenger occupied by the husband in standard versions of the legend of the Eaten Heart. The twelve husbands are virtually absent from this tale—appearing in the end, as we shall see, as a sort of afterthought that merely ratifies what has come before. The tale exhibits, that is, a certain indifference to gender, as the women play the role of men and the man, Ignauré, functions as the desired lady. If the tale is in many respects a version of Marie's *Le Chaitivel* or *Les Quatre Doels*, its twelve women perform the function of Marie's four men (insofar as both groups signify the *tuz*), while Ignauré is like the lady of Marie's tale who hesitates to choose.

Indeed there is throughout a certain hermaphroditic insistence in the *Lai d'Ignauré*. We have already witnessed, for instance, the spectacle of a woman representing herself as the male priest who hears confession. Yet such a representation is already an allegory, already a second-order hermaphrodism, since the priest is already a sort of not-man, a man who is supposed to wield nothing underneath his vestments. The woman's role-playing only makes explicit the originary sexual ambiguity that divides the the figure of the priest. And as the women gather at the fatal rendezvous to enforce their revenge, they turn out to resemble once more their husbands, to resemble the knight whose *puissance*, contrary to the priest's, stems precisely from that something that he possesses under his cloak:

Le dyëmenche, sans dangier,
Se repusent en cel vregier,
Bien garnies de bons coutiaus
K'eles orent sous les mantiaus. (ll. 245–248)

(That Sunday, without hesitation, they hid themselves in the garden, well armed with sharp knives hidden underneath their dresses.)

They are clearly playing here the role of the jealous husband who ambushes the courtly singer in the legend of the Eaten Heart. But these knives are not simply the self-identical or positivistic objects of the sort posited by an outmoded Freudianism. These knives, on the contrary, signify both the phallus and its absence, because the knives are precisely that which will eventually and literally cut off Ignauré's penis by the end of his tale. So the women who brandish phallic knives in a display of power are at the same time figuring forth the moment of castration, the moment of the member's severance. The knife-wielding women signify, like the priest whom one of them temporarily represents, both man and not-man—and what matters is not the man-ness but rather the both/and-ness of this signification. For the *Lai d'Ignauré* is nothing if not a fable about the both/and's replacement by the either/or (*Ignauré*, who loves both one and the others, is forced to love either one or another).

The troubadour Raimbaut d'Aurenga—that *Ignauré* and *Rossignol* whom our Ignauré may or may not represent—represents himself in one of his songs as a eunuch, as a man who is not one, a man who lacks that thing that makes one a man:

D'aisso vos fatz ben totz certz:
Qu'aicels don hom es plus gais
Ai perdutz, don ai vergoigna[9]

(Of this you may well be certain: I have lost that thing that gives man the most pleasure, and thus I am ashamed.)

And, to repeat, the Ignauré of the *Lai d'Ignauré* is similarly hermaphroditic: he simultaneously occupies both the position of male courtly lover and (insofar as he, desired by the multitude, resembles the lady of courtly romance) the position of desired lady.

So, in general, the *Lai d'Ignauré* suggests, subtly and not so subtly, that the man may be womanly and the woman may be manly. Like the identity of the singing subject, gender is represented in this text as radically and vertiginously unstable: one's gender is not a positive essence nor is it determined by empirical bodily fact, but rather it is a product of the structural position that one happens to be occupying at a given moment.

The hermaphroditic Ignauré is one who simultaneously occupies two positions, who is both singing subject and desired object. Ignauré is both courtly lover and lady, both signifying subject and signified object. He is the semiotic principle of a *langue* that is ignorant of and indifferent to gender. Yet the castration that we will soon witness spells the death of Ignauré's capacity to function as both subject and object. This dismemberment inaugurates the rule of differential hierarchy: knives will be permanently returned to husbands, men will be men and women women, and

Ignauré's ignorance will be replaced by a knowledge of either/or. Ignauré will no longer freely and indifferently disseminate his seeds and signs.

Let us return to the scene in the garden, a locus whose obviously Edenic connotations contribute to our sense that what is taking place is a story about the institution of the knowledge of difference. The women successfully ambush our hero, surround him, and begin to interrogate him:

> La prestresse parla premiers:
> "Souffrés, je vous en voel proier,
> Me laissiés dire mon samblant;
> Puis die chascune son talent.
> Ignaures, or ne mentés mie
> Maint jour ai esté vostre amie,
> En vous avoie mon cuer mis."
> "Dame, je suis li vostre amis,
> Et vos hom, et vos chevaliers,
> Et de vrai cuer fins et entiers."
> Une s'en lieve, desdaigneuse,
> Si a parlé comme orgilleuse:
> "Ignaures, trop estes drufeüs!
> Comment? En'estes vous me drus?"
> "Oïl, dame, se Dex me saut,
> Mes cuers ne m'amours ne vous faut;
> Je ne faurai ja en ma vie."
> Une autre en ot molt grande envie,
> Sel regarda a cruel chiere:
> "A!" fait ele, "malvais trechiere,
> Ceste raisons n'est pas a moi!
> Tous estes miens par sairement."
> "Dame, je vous ainc voirement
> Et amerai sans contredit."
> "Coi?" dist une autre, "c'avés dit?
> Enne m'amés vous par fianche?"
> "Oïl, de toute ma *poissanche*,
> Et vous, et les autres *trestoutes*
> Ain ge bien: *trestoutes*, sans doutes." (ll. 285–314)

(The priestess spoke first:
"Please permit me to say what I think. Then everyone can say what

she wants to say. Ignauré, now don't lie. I have been your lover for a long time, I had given my heart to you."

"My lady, I am your lover, your vassal and your knight, with an entire and perfect heart!"

Another one stood up, full of hatred, and she spoke with pride:

"Ignauré, you are a miserable wretch! How can this be? Are you not my lover?"

"Yes, my lady, and may God protect me! My heart and my love do not betray you. Never in my life would I hurt you."

Another one felt extremely jealous, and she looked at him with an angry face.

"Ah," she said, "infamous deceiver, is it not me to whom these words are addressed? Do you then love someone else? You have sworn that you were entirely mine!"

"My lady, I love you in all sincerity and I will love you faithfully!"

"What—" said another, "what have you said? Do you not love me as you have sworn?"

"Yes, with all my power [*poissanche*], both you and *all* the others, I love them: *all*, without any doubt.")

Clearly, without any doubt, Ignauré is the lover of *tuz*, and this capacity to love *trestoutes* is his semiotic *poissanche*. Yet the twelve fail to grasp the generality of their own desire. Nor is Ignauré, as they believe, a liar. On the contrary, he is constantly telling the truth of his sincere indifference. The twelve, failing to recognize that what pours forth from Ignauré's mouth is a mass of courtly conventions, treat him as if he were some one individual speaking from the heart—a heart capable of lying. He is, however, not the in-divisible individual but rather one who is infinitely divisible. They do not see that Ignauré's claim to love sincerely is the claim made by innumerable *losengiers*, by innumerable courtly singers. They do not see that Ignauré is speaking song and nothing but song. In short, they believe in the stability of the *moi* whom they think they are and to whom they think the language of Ignauré is addressed: "is it not *me* to whom these words are addressed?" But he does not address anyone personally, since she whom he always addresses is *Dame*, a courtly commonplace, a *lieu* that is the locus of his language. They are the deluded advocates of the sort of ego psychology whose inadequacy his heartless indifference threatens to expose. And their failure to see that he is the sign of no one in particular means that the subsequent castration of the generalized subject has already begun.

124   Lyric Ignorance

We are ready to read the moment around which the entire tale turns, the moment of crisis, the cut-off point between conceptions of subjectivity. The scene of dismemberment begins, as the women expose those knives with which they threaten to exact their revenge:

> Les coutiaus ont avant sachiés
> Que eles avoient muciés:
>   "Ignaures, vous avés tant mesfait
> Que mors estes tout entresait." (ll. 319–322)

(They pulled out the knives that they had hidden: "Ignauré, you have committed such a great crime that you shall die immediately.")

But the twelve are diverted from their course of violence in the nick of time, and the physical body of Ignauré is left, for the time being, without a nick. For instead of actually carving up the flesh of Ignauré, the women settle on a more subtle mode of linguistic dismemberment, deciding to make Ignauré decide:

> "Ignaures, tu nous as bien dechutes
> Tant con en sommes aperchutes;
> Ne t'amerons plus en tel guise.
> Car il nous ramembre et avise
> Que cele ki mius te plaira
> Ert toie, et si te remanra.
> Chascune velt son dru avoir." (ll. 341–347)

("Ignauré, you greatly deceived us, until the moment when we discovered the truth. We will no longer love you in the same manner. It seems to us that she who pleases you the most should be yours and stay with you. Each one wants her lover for herself.")

Ignauré still dares to resist this singularization of desire, but his force has diminished and he is fighting a losing cause:

> "Nel feroie pour nul avoir,
> Ains amerai toutes encore
> Si que j'ai fait desci a ore."
>   "Fai mon commant," che dist li prestre,
> "U morras ja, par ma teste.

Prent la quele que veus de nous."
"Dame," dist il, "chou estes vous.
De ma perte sui molt dolans
Qu'eles sont toutes molt vaillans,
Mais li vostre amors m'atalente."
"Grans merchis," chou a dit la gente.
Les autres molt dolantes erent.
Namporquant toutes afierent
Qu'eles ja mais ne l'ameront,
Tout em pais cuite li lairont.
Quant devisé ont or afaire,
Chascune a on ostel repaire,
Et Ignaures el bourch revint. (ll. 348–365)

("I won't do it for anything in the world, but rather I will continue to love all of you, as I have done up until now."

"Do what I command," said the priest, "or you will die, I swear! Choose from among us the one whom you desire!"

"My lady," he said, "it's you! I am sad about the loss of the others, because they are all very worthy, but your love attracts me."

"Great thanks," said the noble lady.

The others were very sad. Nonetheless they all swore that they would never love him, that they would abandon him without a fight and in peace. Since they had settled their affair, each one went home, and Ignauré returned to town.)

Thus while the physical, literal castration does not yet occur, it has in fact already taken place symbolically or metaphorically. Indeed the moment of decision is simultaneous with the moment of dismemberment, since to single out one member of the *tuz* is to sever the part from the body of the twelve. The *Lai d'Ignauré* is, it seems, entirely generated by a certain etymological joke that links selection and severance: "to decide," from the Latin *decidere*, means "to cut off." Ignauré's decision to sing his desire to one and only one lady is the moment of his cutting off. The tale's seed is this semiotic kinship between choosing and cutting, and we must appeal to this seed to make sense of the tale's anomalous departures from the standard version of the legend of the Eaten Heart. For two oddities set this *lai* apart from the other various versions of the legend: Ignauré is the lover of twelve, not one woman, and the twelve jealous husbands not only cut out Ignauré's heart but also cut off his penis. These two anomalous aspects of the tale are intimately connected, insofar as castration is the singularization of an originary plurality. The tale tells not just the dismemberment of one Ignauré but more significantly the dismemberment of the multitude, the reduction of the twelve to the one, of the *plusurs* to the *hum*. Ignauré's castration is their castration, insofar as Ignauré is the *tuz* that they are as well. So, in short, the violent cutting that is literally performed later by the husbands already happens here in the garden when the twelve make the decision to decide, cutting off themselves and Ignauré from the realm of courtly *langue*.

In fact it is much more likely that the women do not symbolically castrate Ignauré so much as they castrate themselves. For we cannot tell if Ignauré has really decided, while it seems clear that they have decided for themselves. Let us recall the critical moment:

"Prent la quele que veus de nous."
"Dame," dist il, "chou estes vous.
De ma perte sui molt dolans
Qu'eles sont toutes molt vaillans,
Mais li vostre amors m'atalente."
"Grans merchis," chou a dit la gente. (ll. 353–358)

("Choose from among us the one whom you desire!"
"My lady," he said, "it's you! I am sad about the loss of the others, because they are all very worthy, but your love attracts me."
"I am grateful to you," said the noble lady.")

Ignauré's response commences with that very word *Dame* that signaled the commonplace status of his generalized speech to the women before the threatening knives were exposed. Ignauré tells the very one who addresses him precisely what she wants to hear, and this is just what he has done all along, as each one has thought that his words were addressed to her. We suspect that whichever *dame* had posed the question would have been gratified by Ignauré's response: he would have answered positively to whomever had first asked. So Ignauré may well have survived this threatening encounter, may still speak nothing but song. And indeed Ignauré's remembered reappearance at the end of his *lai* suggests that his death has not taken place. Yet the twelve, believing that they have witnessed the singularization of song, choose to abandon Ignauré and decide to disband or to cut off a member of the *tuz*.

After this decisive scene of differentiation in the garden, in which the women gain knowledge of that which they had previously ignored—namely, which one of them stands to be nominated as singularly preeminent—the tale turns to the narration of Ignauré's actual, physical death and dismemberment. And this death is represented as the immediate consequence of the singularization of his desire:

Soris ki n'a c'*un trau* poi dure. (l. 373)

(A mouse that has but a *single hole* does not have a very long life.)

Ignauré, left with but one place to direct his desire, forced to unload all of his *sens*—his sense, seeds, or semen—in a "single hole" (the crude obscenity should not go unremarked), cannot survive. Furthermore, a troubadour who has but a single *trou* or *trau* ("hole"), who is forced to fill a single slot in an historical or narrative scheme, does not live long.[10] Ignauré's bondage to one particular body spells his death, as the text most clearly states:

S'a toutes fust, n'i alast mie,
Mais or n'a c'*une seule voie*. (ll. 368–369)

(If he had still belonged to all of them, this would not have happened, but now he was left with but *a single path*.)

When we consider that the road or *voie* is perhaps the most frequently traveled figure for narrative in the Middle Ages, we see that the single path or *seule voie* that Ignauré is now compelled to follow is the straight line of story. Ignauré can no longer freely choose his assignations, but rather he is now someone who has a definite end in sight. Significantly, following the critical turning point in the garden the *Lai d'Ignauré* is itself transformed, as it begins to follow very closely and almost automatically the path marked by the legend of the Eaten Heart that had come before. The text itself begins to follow a narrow, circumscribed narrative logic. After the crisis of decision, the text decides to fit itself into the *trou* already dug by previous versions of the legend. The text cuts off other, less straightforward, narrative possibilities, begins to pursue the direction of singularity.

Indeed this singularization of the pathway is the cause of Ignauré's demise, since it allows him to be—in fact ensures that he will be—easily located. Ignauré is caught occupying, and caught because he is occupying, a single place. He who was invisible because he was so divisible is now seen, is no longer dispersed or scattered but now concentrated. His whereabouts can be narrowed down because he now predictably traverses a central field of activity:

> Mais or n'a c'une seule voie.
> Souvent i va, ki ke le voie.
> Par le trop aler fu dechus
> Et engigniés et percheüs. (ll. 369–372)

> (Now he was left with but a single path. He went there often at the risk of being seen. It was because he went there too often that he was deceived, betrayed, and cut apart.)

This singularization of the path, the selection of one *trou* into which to plant his seeds and signs, is nothing other than the breaking of the lyric secret. And the one who, upon seeing Ignauré pursue his singular route, tells the story of adultery to the twelve husbands is represented as a storyteller, a speaker of *contes* and *razos*:

> Ains k'il isse de la maison,
> Lor *contera* tele *raison*. (l. 388)

> (Before he would leave the house, he would *recount* to them such a *razo*.)

Identity is revealed, the name is named, as he who sees Ignauré recounts his knowledge to the husbands in the form of a story:

> Toute lor *conte* l'*aventure*. (l. 422)

> (He *recounted* the entire *adventure* to them.)

After this decision to name the name, this advent of story, the husbands behave narratively, following the course mapped out by the legend of the Eaten Heart. The knives are returned to the husbands, and they do with these knives just what we expect them to do. Like the jealous husband of the legend, their violence is the literalization of the metaphorical, the confusion of the linguistic with the material, of the symbolic with the empirically real. The husband of the legend treats the *cor* of courtly language as the actual fleshly organ lodged within the human breast. Similarly, the husbands of the *Lai d'Ignauré* tranform the symbolic, linguistic castration that had been performed by and upon their wives into an actual dismemberment: they cut off Ignauré's penis after cutting out his heart. In the husbands' hands the symbolic knife of decision has become the actual thing, an instrument of incision. In this newly instituted narrative world of phenomenal or empirical fact, husbands have knives and wives do not. The knife is no longer something freely circulated that determines the structural position of whoever happens to be holding it at a given time but rather is placed in the permanent physical possession of a single proprietor. The sort of referential, biological realism enacted by the husbands' narrative goes hand in hand with the sort of hierarchical difference according to which men are men and women are women. Subjectivity is now seen as essential, determinate, naturally fixed. By cutting off Ignauré the husbands affirm the rigidity of their own positions, affirm their own standing as autonomous subjects, free from the grasp of the objective.

So the organs are cut and cooked in an organic casserole, which is fed to the women, who, upon learning the morbid truth of their last meal, swear that they will starve themselves to death. And this is indeed what they do, but not without collectively composing a decidedly lyric discourse, a mournful lament for the death of Ignauré:

> En lor vivant complainte en fisent:
> Li une plaignoit sa biauté,
> Tant membres biaus et bien molé
> Que lait erent tout li plus biel;
> Ensi disent dou damoisel.
> L'autre plaignoit son grant barnage,
> Et son gent cors, et sa largeche;
> Et la quarte, les iex, les flans
> K'il ot si vairs et si rians;
> Et l'autre plaignoit son douch cuer:
> Ja mais nul n'en ert de tel fuer.
> —"Lasse! que vous avons cangié
> Trop se sont cruelment vengié
> Li jalous! Mais ne mangerons;
> En tel guise nous vengerons."
> Et l'autre plaignoit ses biaus piés
> Si bien seans en ses estriers.
> Sor tous hommes ert couvignables

De ciens, d'osiaus—et delitables.
Toutes plaignoient son delit:
Ki de lui ert si bons eslit?
Pour la dolour d'eles plouroient
Tout cil ki les regrès ooient. (ll. 588–610)

(While they were still alive they made a complaint: one lamented his beauty, his members so fine and well made that the finest in the world seemed ugly next to them. In this manner they spoke of the young man. Another mourned his great merit, his elegant body and his generousity. And another lamented the lively and laughing spark in his eyes. And another missed his sweet heart; never more would there be one of such worth.

"Alas! Ignauré, how we have changed you! The jealous have too cruelly avenged themselves. We will never eat again, and thus we too will avenge ourselves!"

Yet another lamented his fine feet, so elegantly poised in the stirrups. More than all others, he was so skillful at hunting with dogs and birds—and charming. *All lamented* the pleasure that he brought. Who would ever be as good as he? Moved by the sorrow that they expressed, all who heard their lament cried.)

This collective lament, composed in remembrance of Ignauré, collects in verse his various parts. Ignauré is truly re-membered, put back together, by this songlike language of praise. And this reappearance of song coincides with the return of the twelve to plural subjectivity: "All lamented (*toutes plaignoient*) the pleasure that he brought." While the death of the singing subject is mourned, singing subjectivity survives in that very act of mourning. Thus the one lady who had been singled out as the tale's heroine—who had instituted individualism by presuming to reveal her private thoughts, who had been nominated to play the priest, who had been selected as the unique object of Ignauré's desire—is no longer in sight, can no longer be distinguished from the rest, is no longer the preeminent member, is consumed by the multiplicitous and anonymous voice of this *lai* they collectively compose as a reversal of the dismemberment.

After singing their *lai* for Ignauré, the twelve die by starvation. This death of the *tuz* inspires another collectively and anonymously composed *lai* of remembrance:

> D'eles douse fu li deus fais,
> Et douse vers plains a li lais
> C'on doit bien tenir en memoire. (ll. 617–619)
>
> (The people grieved for them twelve, and the *lai* that one must hold in remembrance has twelve even verses.)

The length of the *lai* that survives the death of the *tuz* is exactly equivalent to their number. The twelve ladies are ultimately represented as having a purely discursive existence, as they are transformed into twelve lines of verse. And this twelve-line song re-members the *tuz*, as no one stands out from the rest but rather an order of linguistic egalitarianism is established: the twelve, sharing equally in the language of the song, are each given a verse.

The *lai* whose composition is recounted—in the manner of Marie de France—is, it turns out, not so much *d'Ignauré* as *de douze*. The text could easily be called *Les Douze Doels*. That is, the story gives the *razo*-like reasons for the composition of this *lai de douze vers*, a *lai* composed in remembrance not of Ignauré but of the twelve ladies. But then again, there really is no difference between Ignauré and the twelve ladies: both are the generalized subject, both figure the *tuz*. The twelve are re-membered in song, as if they had been castrated, and indeed they have been insofar as Ignauré signifies nothing other than "them." Thus, difference—between Ignauré and the twelve, between subject and object—is once more ignored as song returns to dominate the end of this text.

Still, the *lai* has not quite run its course. For in the end this substitution at the site of the subject runs rampant. The narrator's voice returns to conclude the tale:

> Ensi con tiesmoigne *Renaus*,
> Morut Ignaures, li bons vassaus. (ll. 621–622)
>
> (As *Renaus* testifies, Ignauré the good vassal died.)

Yet nothing about Renaus' testimony proves this case, as Ignauré seems to survive, linguistically, quite well in these very lines that tell of his passing. He survives, for one, in the name of RENAUs, which anagrammatically names *igNAURE*.[11] And this *Renaus* may or may not call to mind that troubadour—d'AURENga—who is also known as *Ignauré*. In short, there is every reason to believe that the narrator Renaus is indeed that Renaus de Beaujeu whom he is believed to be by literary historians, since the inscription of his name in the text is truly followed by a *beau jeu*, by a good game, by a fine play of the signifier. And what this *beau jeu* tells us is that he—the voice that speaks this text—is linguistically akin to Ignauré, which is to say that the story is spoken by the language of song.

But is not Renaus a storyteller rather than a singer? No, ultimately he is not, as the text that began with the narrator's advocation of the dissemination of signs ends with the narrator's transformation into the lyric *je*. The *Lai d'Ignauré* ends as the narrator sings a song to an unnamed lady, a song in whose closing lines Renaus' voice is the voice of no one in particular:

> Molt sui en tres douche *prison*,
> Issir n'en quier par raenchon. (ll. 655–656)

(I am in a very sweet *prison* and I do not seek to leave it by ransom.)

Renaus is in the end the lyric *je*, Ignauré, the tongue of the *tuz*. The narrator has returned to his troubadour roots, and thus Ignauré survives in the guise of this Renaus. The *Lai d'Ignauré* or the *Lai du Signol* ends where it began, in the radically undifferentiated world of song.

And at the very end this courtly lover who sings of his imprisonment calls further attention to the resemblance between himself and Ignauré:

> C'est la matere de cel lay
> Ichi le vous definerai.
> Franchois, Poitevin et Breton
> L'apielent le *Lay de Prison*.
> Ichi faut li *lays del Prison*
> Je n'en sai plus ne o ne non.
> Si fu por Ignaure trouvés
> Ki por amours fu desmembrés. (ll. 657–664)

(This is the matter of this *lai* which I will here bring to an end. Those from France, Poitiers, and Brittany call it the *Lai of the Prisoner*. Here ends the *Lai of the Prisoner*, I do not know another word more. It was composed in remembrance of Ignauré, who through love was castrated.)

This *Lay de Prison* that ends here and that is here twice-named (though both names are the same) is both the story of Ignauré's capture, imprisonment, and subsequent execution and the song that has just been sung by one who says that he is in a *tres douche prison*. The singing storyteller here voluntarily commits himself to occupying that position occupied in the tale by Ignauré. And, since the Old French *prison* may mean either the place of captivity or the captive, we suspect that this text is most properly named the *Song/Story of the Prison*, that it is more concerned with an anonymous institutional structure than with distinguishing the identities of individuals. Ignauré and Renaus are one and the same insofar as both are inmates in the *Prison* or prison-house of courtly language.

11. Narrative Breakdown

Let us now listen to a scene from a much longer text, a full-scale romance narrative, the anonymous Old French *Joufroi de Poitiers*.[1] My aim here is not primarily to propose a way of reading the entire romance—though perhaps the scene in question could be the starting-point for such a proposal—but rather to bring to light a remarkable moment in which the text formulates a theory of the battle between song and story, a theory that accounts quite nicely for the impulses behind the production of the *corpus* of texts that have drawn our attention.

First, one should know that *Joufroi de Poitiers* participates, albeit most ironically, in a popular thirteenth-century literary trend—namely, the composition of narrative romances with periodic lyric insertions. Typically, as in Jean Renart's *Le Roman de la Rose ou de Guillaume de Dole*, the inserted songs are in some manner appropriate to or in accordance with the narrated episode in which they appear. The songs are not, however, to be taken as simply decorous, secondary, or after-the-fact embellishments to a primary and mimetic discourse of realist narrative. Rather, Jean Renart quite clearly begins with previously composed and indeed quite famous songs, then invents an appropriate story by which to string those songs together. Despite the very historically accurate qualities of Renart's romances (he names the names of real people and places, and he completely ignores the "fantastic" so often thought essential to medieval romance), his strategy is nothing other than the deconstruction of the naïve, *razo*-like mimetic assumption according to which literary discourse reflects prior historical events. Thus characters and events are seen not to pre-exist but rather to flourish from the linguistic, discursive seed of song. Renart exposes romance's lyric roots, shows the primacy of language in the invention of narrative.[2]

Joufroi de Poitiers has something in common with the compositional practice instituted by Jean Renart. Yet unlike the songs in the typical romance with lyric insertions, the songs scattered throughout *Joufroi de Poitiers* have absolutely nothing to do with the story that is being recounted, but rather they are disruptions or interruptions that break into the text. Nor are they really songs, but rather they are passages of songlike language that suddenly and sporadically (and for no apparent reason) interrupt the story. The text has occasional lyric fits or attacks, during which song simply takes over discursive command without apparent cause or motivation. In Jean Renart's romances, the songs are performed by certain "characters" who exist within the world of the story; in *Joufroi de Poitiers*, the story is halted while songlike language, uttered by no one in particular (except, perhaps, the "narrator"), takes over for a spell. Reading *Joufroi de Poitiers* is a strange experience, as one comes to realize that the narrative voice is struggling to keep down or repress a lyric voice that is always ready to break out and that comes to regard the story with disdain.

The singing storyteller of *Joufroi de Poitiers* makes explicit that his two discourses have no significant or necessary relation, that there is no proper accord between the story and the songs, that sometimes he simply prefers singing to storytelling. Thus, after a lengthy stint of storytelling, he introduces several lines of lyric language in the following manner:

> Or ai trop segui ceste voie,
> Si ai trop *ma lengue laissee.*
> Or voil qu'ele soit sojornee
> En parler de ma douce dame.[3] (ll. 2390–2933)

(Now I have followed this path for too long, and I have made my tongue too weary [*trop ma lengue laissee*]. Now I want to rest it by speaking about my sweet lady.)

This transition resembles the common romance narrative technique of "interlacing," in which the text leaves off speaking of one knight or group of knights to speak of another. Yet this resemblance is parodic, since in this case the text leaves off speaking one *genre* of literature to speak another. The *voie* or path that the narrator ("I") says he has followed "for too long" is the sequential path of narrative, the road of romance, and the narrator here seeks respite for his "weary tongue" by temporarily returning to lyric. Storytelling is figured as a laborious, wearisome journey.

These lines are also significantly paradoxical: the narrator will rest his tongue by speaking ("Now I want to rest it by speaking about my sweet lady"). If we care to resolve this paradox, we see that what is restful in "speaking about my sweet lady," in speaking lyric language, is that such language does not join in the wearisome journey. Song's resistance to temporality is here figured as a freedom from the burden of travel: the *langue* that speaks of *ma douce dame* does not go anywhere, has no end in sight.

The phrase that signifies the fatigue of the narratorial tongue—*ma lengue laissee*—may in fact signify something else. Let us reconsider those lines that speak of too much story:

> Or ai trop segui ceste voie,
> Si ai trop ma *lengue laissee*. (ll. 2930–2931)
>
> (Now I have followed for too long this path [of narrative sequence], and for too long I have *bound/leashed/neglected* my *langue*.)

Story is that *laisse* or leash that has bound or tied up the tongue of he who would sing "I." Story is a constraint that curbs the lyric voice. The occasional deposits of song spread throughout *Joufroi de Poitiers* are violations of a narrative leash-law that is supposed to bind language to its owner. The occasional lyric moment in this text may be likened to a rest area along the highway of story where song is unleashed and encouraged to unburden itself. Or, alternately, the word *laissee* may mean not that the narrator, in following the straight way of story, has "bound" or "leashed" his *langue*, but rather that he has "neglected" it, that he has left it behind or aside. But this amounts to the same thing, for either way these lines formulate a miniature allegory of resistance to the path of literary historical progress. The thirteenth-century trend in which *vida*- and *razo*-like historical narrative appears to become dominant spells the neglect and the restraint of courtly *langue*. The "I" in these lines stands for thirteenth-century courtly literature: "I have been following for too long a progressive narrative path, I have been neglecting to speak of *ma douce dame*, and through this neglect I have bound up the semiotic power of my *langue*." The singer is here beginning to glimpse the limitations of the narrator's repressive regime.

Now, it is quite appropriate to compare the narrative episodes of *Joufroi de Poitiers* to a *vida*- and *razo*-like narrative discourse. For philologists contend that the hero of this romance is meant to be Guillaume, Comte de Poitiers—the first of the troubadours. Indeed the story—among whose cast of characters figures another historically identifiable troubadour, Marcabru—has been regarded as an expanded *vida* of Guillaume de Poitiers.[4] *Joufroi de Poitiers* is marked, like the romances of Jean Renart, by a certain historicity or "realism."[5] It is thus no accident that this particular romance is punctuated by disruptive lyric moments: the generalized voice of the troubadour returns to mock that very story meant to embody

Narrative Breakdown 137

the troubadour as a historical individual. The lyric outbursts struggle to overthrow that story that would grant the singing subject a historical existence. The two discourses that fight for attention in *Joufroi de Poitiers* are two opposed modes of representing the troubadour.

Throughout most of this text, story maintains its dominance, continues to contain song despite occasional lapses or relaxations of control. That is, songlike language is relatively infrequent until the time of a truly stunning lyric eruption very near the end of *Joufroi de Poitiers*. Near the end there is an explosion of song, as the story is violently disrupted by a lyric discourse of extreme ignorance and undifferentiation:

>   Or pais! seignors, si m'escoutez,
> S'orrez con ge sui bestornez:
> Ne sai si muer o si ge vi,
> Ne sai que faz ne que ge di,
> Ne sai quant chant ne quant ge plor,
> Ne sai si je ai joie o dolor,
> Ne sai quant je dorm ne quant veil,
> Ne sai quant ge cri ne conseil,
> Ne sai quant ge voi ne quant vien,
> Ne sai quant ge ai o mal o bien,
> Ne sai quant ge ai o fain o seis,
> O si sui vilains o corteis,
> Ne sai don sui ne de quel terre,
> Ne quant ge ai ne pais ne guerre,
> Ne sai si ge ai pere ne mere,
> Ne sai si ge ai soror ne frere,
> Ne sai si ge sui ome o beste,
> Ne sai si ge ai cors ne teste.
> Mi braz me resenblent dous maces,
> Et li doi de mes mains limaces;
> Mi pié me resenblent chasteus,
> Et li ortels i sunt creneus.
> Quant ge oi fame ne ome chanter,
> Si cuit oïr les lou usler;
> Chant d'estornel et d'oriol
> Et de merle et de roisinol,
> De quinçon, d'aloe et d'aurés
> Me sanblent raines en marés.

> Li pre me resenblent livieres,
> Et li bois et li puis riveres.
> Ne sai que soit flors ne verdure,
> Que del jor cuit soit noit oscure.
> Quant ge oi ome que vïele,
> Ne sai s'il corne o chalemele:
> Tuit estrument m'i sunt sauvage.
> Si m'a bestorné lo corage
> Une amor que ge ai servie;
> Avoir cuidai leial amie
> Et qui m'amasst de cuer verai,
> Quant ge cest romanz comenchai.
> Or si m'a tot changiez l'afaire
> Que ne sai que g'en doie faire. (ll. 4345–4386)

(Now silence, lords, and listen to me, and you will hear how I'm overthrown: I don't know if I'm dead or alive, I don't know what I'm doing or saying, I don't know when I'm singing or when I'm crying, I don't know if I'm joyful or sad, I don't know when I'm asleep or when I'm awake, I don't know when I'm crying or giving comfort, I don't know when I'm going or when I'm coming, I don't know when I'm sick or well, I don't know when I'm hungry or thirsty, or if I'm a peasant or a noble, I don't know where I'm from nor what country, nor when I'm at peace or at war, I don't know if I have a father or mother, I don't know if I have a sister or brother, I don't know if I'm man or beast, I don't know if I have a body or a head. My arms resemble two maces, and the fingers of my hands snails; my feet resemble castles, and the toes are battlements. When I hear a woman or a man sing I think I'm hearing wolves howl; the songs of the oriole and the blackbird and the nightingale and the finch and the lark and the yellow songbird seem to me like the sounds of frogs in the swamp. The fields seem to me to be ditches, and the woods and the hills streams. I don't know the flowers from the grass, and I think the day is the darkest night. When I hear a man play the fiddle, I don't know if he's playing the horn or pipe: all instruments are foreign to me. Thus has a love that I have served overturned my heart; when I began this romance I thought I had a loyal love who loved me with a true heart. Now the affair has completely changed me so that I don't know what I should do.)

Who is this singer who can say little more than *Ne sai* ("I don't know"), who cannot tell the one from the other, who can only pronounce his own ignorance, if not that Ignauré whom we have come to know as the undifferentiated singing subject? Ignauré has survived his death to have his say at the end of this romance narrative, and what he says—an ignorant, irrational, anti-mimetic language in which fingers are snails and toes battlements—is an affront to the notions of knowledge, *ratio*, and *razo*. When he commenced this romance, the narrator had faith in the reality of his existence as a historical individual; he thought he was a certain someone who was loved by a certain lady: "when I began this romance I thought I had a loyal love who loved me with a true heart." Here, however, he has no idea who he is, and his identity is strikingly multiplicitous and "unrealistic." In the beginning, he was the singular and "historical" subject of a realistic *razo*-like discourse; now, he is the radically undifferentiated lyric singer, a "no one" who knows nothing.

Yet what I have said so far about *Joufroi de Poitiers* is all just a prelude to our reading of that moment that draws our attention, the moment that theorizes the relation between lyric and narrative discourses. Immediately after the extensive outburst of lyric ignorance that we have just witnessed, the singing narrator announces his unwilling return to the story and his intention to quit the narrative path at the earliest opportunity:

> Or retornerai a l'estoire,
> Si vos en redirai avant;
> Ja nel lairai por mautalant,
> Que cest romanz voil a chief traire,
> Si ne voil ja mais autre faire,
> Que trop i ai travail et paine.
> Mais por savoir que *en demeine*
> Ai ma *lengue*, si faz ceste ovre,
> O ge en bien trover m'esprove. (ll. 4394–4402)

(Now I will return to the story, as I was telling it to you before; despite my annoyance I won't leave it, because I want to bring this romance to an end—and then I never want to make another one, because there's too much work and pain involved. But I have made this work, in which I prove myself a good composer, in order to know that I have my *langue under control*.)

The singing narrator speaks of a certain pain inherent in making romances, as if his endeavor were a sort of forced labor. We suspect that this pain is the product of the storyteller's harsh treatment of his own tongue. Storytelling is here said to be motivated not by any duty to tell the truth about the world but rather solely in order to assert its own domination over the singer's *langue*: "I have made this work in order to know that I have my *langue* under control." And domination is precisely the issue: the narrator wants to prove that his tongue is *en demaine*, which is to say under his "domain." The word *demaine* or *domaine* signifies "power," and it signifies the seigneurial estate, the property of the feudal *dominus* or lord. The phrase *en demaine* signifies "belonging to" or "property of"—the state of being under the power or dominion of the *dominus*. The aim of the narratorial voice is to prove that the tongue belongs to its owner. The composition of narrative romance is an assertion of one's lordship over his *langue*. The narrator figures himself as a feudal lord who would keep his tongue in a state of laborious serfdom, who would confine *langue* within the boundaries of the proper. Narrative discourse is here said to prove that the speaking subject dominates language. This narrator began this romance for one and only one reason: to prove that he controls his tongue and that his tongue does not control him. And this is exactly what we have come to see in these stories about singers: story is told and song is restricted precisely to defend against the fear that language dominates the speaking subject. The story is not recounted because of the intrinsic interest of its events. Rather, story is a discursive strategy meant to display the subject's authority, autonomy, integrity, power, propriety, and self-control. Yet if we have come thus to understand narrative's stake in lyrico-narrativity, we have also come to see the ease with which lyric in the end dominates the lyrico-narrative text. The discursive *demeine* ends up belonging to *langue*, and this domain simply ignores all boundaries of propriety.

Of course, there is great irony in the narrator's claim that he has proven himself a good composer ("I prove myself a good composer") by controlling his tongue in the composition of *Joufroi de Poitiers*. For just before this claim is made we have witnessed an exemplary lack of control in that violent eruption of courtly *langue* ("*Ne sai . . . , etc.*") in which the tongue clearly does not know what it is talking about. The voice that makes a claim for its own narrative composure seems to ignore all those lyric fits or attacks that mar the story's smooth unfolding. If the narrator has proven anything, it is precisely that he is a *bad* composer, that he cannot keep his composure, that he *cannot* control his tongue, that he cannot keep his lyric *langue* from disrupting the narrative text. The narrative voice, that is, appears blind to those moments of song that seem now more than ever to be symptoms of the text's linguistic unconscious. The voice of the narrator fears to speak of its own duplicity, refuses to acknowledge its captivity to courtly *langue*, and thus this voice maintains in all seriousness that it has composed a work of singular integrity, a work that is "under control." The narrator would conceal, ignore or repress the fact that his tongue is in fact "out of control." Yet this repressive narrative voice has just been betrayed by that explosive resurrection of Ignauré, by that return of the repressed lyric voice that sings "I don't know." That explosion of song that leaves the narrator weary and disillusioned with the entire storytelling project is a sort of "narrative breakdown," for by the end the narrator has simply had his fill of trying to "leash" or control that lyric voice that is always trying to force its way to the surface of his text.

Finally, in the end we witness the consequences of this narrative breakdown, as the story breaks off and is left "unfinished." Yet we would place *Joufroi de Poitiers* among the ranks of those great medieval works whose inachievement is motivated by a powerful textual logic.[6] Because the story itself (the events of the "plot") is secondary to the story's self-avowed primary task, which is to assert its dominance over the courtly *langue*, the story may end at any time. That is, the tale's dimension or length does not depend upon the unalterable dimension or length of a prior history that the story subsequently imitates. The narrator, satisfied that he has achieved the primary task, may simply bring his text to an end at will: *cest romanz voil a chief traire* ("I want to bring this romance to an end"). Yet the irrelevance of the actual "plot" to the achievement of the text turns against the assertion of story's dominance over language, since storytelling is thereby revealed to be a linguistic strategy rather than an after-the-fact imitation of history. The narrator announces that, as a continuation of his display of masterful control over his tongue, he will soon bring the romance to an end. Yet ultimately he never quite gets to the end, but rather he gives up storytelling and simply quits. In the end, as in those moments of lyric disruption, the text shows that the narrator's *langue* is not under his control. This narrative breakdown gives the final word to the tongue of the singing subject that can no longer stand to narrate. The story may simply end whenever the narrator pleases because there was really no story (no prior "history") to begin with. The singing narrator, after his recent and tremendous display of lyric ignorance, can no longer claim authoritatively to know anything: if he is the one who says *Ne sai* ("I don't know"), if he is marked above all by a generalized ignorance, then how can he claim to know "what happened," how can he claim to know the "history" that his story supposedly recounts? *Joufroi de Poitiers* must end, since the duplicitous voice that speaks the text can no longer pretend to know what it is talking about.

12. Chaucer's Evening Sickness

According to a commonplace of modern literary history, Chaucer's poetic career follows a definite trajectory. In his youth, he is "imitative," overly dependent on the courtly poetry of his French predecessors, Machaut and Froissart; he only truly becomes Chaucer in his maturity (i.e., in the *Canterbury Tales*), when he becomes "original," writes a more "realistic" or "historical" poetry, forges his own individual voice by grounding his writing in the personal and direct observation of life as it really is. Chaucer's writing appears to be transformed from a dependent, conventional, lyric discourse into an independent, novel, narrative discourse: he appears to reject song in favor of story. Chaucer's narrative poetry seems to herald the arrival of the Renaissance on English soil, to signal the end of an excessively "rhetorical" or conventional writing in which the poet merely imitates what has already been said.

The *Book of the Duchess* has come to be seen as the place where Chaucer renounces the courtly lyric tradition, where he moves beyond a conventional song sung by a collective *langue* to a biographical *historia* spoken by an individual. We shall see, on the contrary, that the *Book*'s chief significance is precisely its failure to escape the courtly tradition. I devote this lengthy final chapter to the *Book of the Duchess* because this text demonstrates, perhaps better than any other late medieval text, that the apparent triumph of story over song is an illusion, that a repressed lyricism returns to assert its primacy over narrative.

I

> due e nessun l'imagine perversa parea.
>
> (the perverse image appeared to be two and no one.)
>
> Dante, *Inferno* XXV

Chaucer's evening sickness is both a certain disease represented at a certain moment in the *Book of the Duchess* and a general pathological condition that afflicts the narrator of this remarkably odd poem. This general condition may be approximated arithmetically: the narrator is stricken by a chronic evenness that forever prevents contact with the singularity of the odd.[1]

The sickness is, for one thing, the poet/narrator's insomnia at the outset of the *Book*.[2] This lyric lamentation of sleeplessness is a certain malady occasioned by evening, by the evening out of difference, the leveling of the singular, the generalization of the subject. That is, the text's opening lyric verses tell the story of a radical sameness whereby one entity is indistinguishable and indivisible from another:

> I have gret wonder, be this *lyghte*,
> How that I lyve, for day ne *nyghte*
> I may nat slepe wel nygh noght.
> I have so many an ydel thoght
> Purely for defaute of slepe
> That, by my trouthe, I take no kepe
> Of nothing, how hyt cometh or gooth,
> Ne me nys nothyng leve nor looth.
> *Al is ylyche* good to me,
> Joy or sorowe, wherso hyt be,
> For I have felynge in nothynge,
> But as yt were a mased thynge. (ll. 1–12)

> (I greatly wonder, by this *light*, how I may be alive, for day nor *night* I cannot sleep at all. I have so many an idle thought purely for lack of sleep that, I swear, I don't care about anything, how it comes or goes, nor is anything pleasant or unpleasant to me. *All is alike* good to me, joy or sorrow, whatsoever it be, for I have no feeling at all but am, as it were, a dazed thing.)

To this lyric singer, evening and morning are subject to the evening effect of undifferentiation. The narrator's inability to sleep, which is a failure to respect the proper division between night and day, is a symptom of his failure to make other such proper divisions in other such binary constructs: he cannot divide coming from going, the lovely from the loathsome, joy from sorrow. The narrator is shackled by an evenness that prohibits him from definitely discerning a certain resting place, that keeps him from enjoying a state of semiotic repose. To one who would, as we learn in the second and third lines, be just as content to sleep during the day as during the night, night and day have become indistinguishable, have lost their positive, autonomous, or singular values. Night and day now amount to a bifold night-day just as I and I amount to II. Yet unlike the situation in the arithmetic realm, in the realm of lyric language the sum of the two singles cannot be divided, cannot yield, for separate consideration, its two singular components: night-day cannot be divided, by this lyric singer, into "night plus day" in the easy fashion that two can be divided into "one plus one." Thus the poem's first two verses (in an initial instance of the disease of oxymoronic undifferentiation from which the poem will not recover) couple by rhyme (*lyghte/nyghte*) two signifiers that are normally considered incompatible, that are naturally not seen together but rather remain apart. The text has already begun to say what it will say again and again until it ends: in the system of song the one cannot stand alone, independent from the other. This indivisibility of the mass thing or *mased thynge* (line 12) is inseparable from a critique of individuality: for what is individual or indivisible turns out in the *Book* to be the even twosome, and thus the individual turns out to be not singular but rather the duplicitous product of a multiplication. Arithmetical fact is flouted and reversed as the even number displays its oddness, its resistance to a divisive reduction to integral oneness.

The *Book*'s first eight lines, everything that immediately precedes the narrator's distressed recognition that *Al is ylyche* ("All is alike"), are much like the first nine lines of Froissart's *Paradys d'Amour*.[3] Yet contrary to the commonplace claim of the modern commentators, the interest of this resemblance lies not in the glimpse we are granted into Chaucer's "workshop," not in the spectacle of a young English poet struggling to forge a new language out of French sources, not in the notion that the juvenile poet sharpens his metrical skills through exercises in translation.[4] Rather, the interest of the resemblance between the opening of the *Book* and the opening of Froissart's poem lies in the very fact of the resemblance itself. As Chaucer evens the odd by translating Froissart's nine lines into eight of his own, the narrator of the *Book* is the passive object of another evening act: the difference between his voice and the voice of another is leveled, as the appearance of outstanding singularity is smoothed over. The narrator is robbed of individual subjectivity, transformed into one of "them," into a singer of conventional song. Thus the narrator initially finds himself in the place of all courtly singers—desiring but unable to express, in language, his special worth and the unique value of his desire. He is unable because there is no language that he can properly call his own. This revelation that one's language belongs to another is the compulsively repeated lesson of Chaucer's *Book*. The complaint that immediately follows the first eight lines, the recognition that *Al is ylyche* ("all is alike"), now appears as a lament specifically triggered by the undifferentiated generality of lyric language: what is so much alike is the language of Chaucer and Froissart that commences the poem. The *Book*'s opening verses are not at all singular, not the private expression of a self-standing or self-determining subject, and thus the poem's very premise is an insistence that language does not reveal the pre- or extra-linguistic experience of the individual heart. At the outset of the text is this eight-line evening (the first instance of the *Book*'s octo-mania), which the narrator cannot be said to speak. The poem opens with this duplicitous discourse, a narrator's voice which is not a narrator's voice, with an I which is not I. The *Book*'s initial voice, neither Froissart's nor Chaucer's, is in fact no one's: we are hearing not the youthful voice of the Father of English Poetry but rather the conventional voice of a voice that knows it is conventional. The ninth line—*Al ys alyche* . . . —is a commentary on the evenness, the sameness, of the previous eight, a commentary offered by a lyric voice which knows that the lyric voice is never odd but rather is constitutionally even, which knows that in the realm of song I is always II.

II

Chaucer's sickness is fed by the knowledge that he harbors a secondary and external voice within his heart, a secondary voice which is the source of the primary and cannot be distinguished from it, an external voice which prevents his own from being discerned. The famous eight-year sickness about which Chaucer complains is indeed a courtly love-sickness, but more specifically it is an impossible longing for singularity, the longing of a troubadour trapped in the multiplicitous world of the *losengiers*:

> I hold hit be a sicknesse
> That I have suffred this eight yeere—
> And yet my boote is never the nere,
> For there is phisicien but oon
> That may me hele. (ll. 36–40)

> (I consider it a sickness that I have suffered this past eight years—and yet my boat is never nearer, for there is but one physician that may heal me.)

These lines have been the site of a spate of scholarly sparring matches—the goal being to name the historical identity of the "physician" in question and the usual strategy being to claim that Chaucer had known, at the time of writing the *Book*, such-and-such a person for a period of eight years.[5] Yet this temporal span is more fruitfully read not as biographically referential but as working in relation to a specific series of crucial poetic effects in the literary system of the *Book*. In fact, the insistent point of the *Book* is, as we shall see, to deny that the historical affairs of the individual poet's life are either the privileged source or the guarantor of literary signification. Instead, the effect of Chaucer's insistence upon the eightness of the duration of his condition is both to recall a previous eightness—the eight opening lines lifted from Froissart that signified their own evenness, their sameness in relation to all lyric language—and to anticipate the future eightness implied in the name of the mysterious *Octo*vyen who rules the realm of Chaucer's dream—a figure whom we shall meet again as our reading unfolds. The second half of this eight-letter name, *Octo-vyen*, is a not so difficult anagram of perhaps the *Book*'s most frequently appearing word—*evene* or *yven* ("even"). The insistence on eight has nothing to do with a mystical numerological signification specific or intrinsic to eight and eight alone. Rather eight is the sign of the general principle of evenness. Chaucer's octomanic sickness is a symptom of a fetish or fixation on the even, a fixation we will have occasion to comment on again and again. Octovyen's world, the world of dreams, is a world of uncontrollable resemblance, a realm where everything is potentially like everything else, where *al ys alyche*, all is *yven*.

Now, I am aware that there are those who will never believe that Chaucer inscribed secrets into his *Book*. Yet such skeptics must entertain their doubt at the risk of dismissing Chaucer's expressed claim that his work is teeming with mathematical wonders. Indeed, in the passage where our act of reading the *Book* is most clearly foreseen by Chaucer, this act is represented as having everything to do arithmetic:

> That thogh Argus, the noble countour,
> Sete to rekene in hys countour,
> And rekene with his *figures ten*—
> For by tho figures mowe al ken,
> Yf they be crafty, rekene and noumbre,
> And tel of everything the noumbre—
> Yet shoulde he fayle to rekene *evene*
> The wondres me *mette* in my swevene. (ll. 434–442)

> (In short, it was so full of beasts that although Argus, the noble arithmetician, sat down to reckon in his calculator and reckoned with his decimal figures—for by those figures all who are crafty may know and reckon and number and tell the number of everything—yet he would fail to reckon evenly the wonders that I dreamt in my dream.)

The word *mette* signifies not only "dreamt" but also "measured," and we shall see later the manner in which Chaucer's dream is measured, in which the *Book* imbricates an *ars metryk* ("arithmetic") with the metric art of poetry.[6] It is enough at the moment to say that Chaucer here equates understanding the text with an act of reckoning or counting. Yet contrary to his claim that we cannot *rekene evene* his text, in fact we cannot fail to do so, since Chaucer has *mette* or measured his *swevene* in such a way that everywhere we turn we must take into account such even numbers as those *figures ten* by which the story of everything may be told. And the words of a certain man who will appear later in the *Book*—words that refer to the famous mathematician Pythagoras—similarly suggest that what is at stake is a question concerning the odd and the even:

> "But God wolde I had *oones or twyes*
> Ykoud and knowe the *jeupardyes*
> That kowde the Greke Pictagores!" (ll. 665–667)

> ("Would God that I had *once or twice* known the *jeopardies* that the Greek Pythagoras knew!")

This *oones or twyes* suggests that the numbers that count in this text's arithmetical world are the *oone*s and the *two*s, the Is and the IIs: all may be reckoned by this binary system of odd and even figures. These lines already tell us of the dominance of the even in such a world, of the even's possession of the upper hand, because a "jeopardy" (from the Old French *jeu parti*) is a game in which the odds are even, one in two. In a *jeu parti*, each player's chance is even with the other's, and thus the one is not marked by singular distinction but rather is indistinguishable from the other: the odd man out is made a member of an even twosome. The *jeu parti* is a perfect game for the *je parti*, for the partitioned or divided *je*, for the one who is two.

Traditional philological machinery will never settle beyond doubt the issue of the historical identity of the *physicien but oon* whose absence Chaucer mourns in lines 36–40. For in fact what the singer longs for is not a certain identifiable individual but rather identity itself. That is, the physician in question is nothing other *but oon*: what Chaucer desires is to be near the *oon* upon which his cure depends, and thus *oon*-ness is itself the object of desire. Oneness is the alternative to the eightness or evenness of Octovyen's and the courtly poet's world. Oneness is the principle of a stable and autonomous singularity that would transcend or escape the world of semiotic substitution. Only when the I is truly I—when the singing subject is truly singular—will the lyric narrator's ship have come in. Yet *I* cannot be self-identical, since as a grapheme it exemplifies duplicity—standing for both the sound that signifies first-person subjectivity ("I") and for the sound that signifies the first positive whole number (*oon*, "one"). Chaucer's eight-year evening sickness is a lyric longing for singularity, a longing to erase the difference between singing *I* ("I") and being *I* ("one"), a longing to be the one who rightfully says *I*. Though it seems odd to us, the roman numeral *I* is the numeral not of medieval lyric but rather of the medieval *roman*: narrative is the proper place of the singular ego in the late Middle Ages. Thus Chaucer's longing for *oon* or *I* is indistinguishable from a desire for story. In his lament for the physician *but oon* the singer wishes for a narrative cure for his lyric evening sickness.

III

> Thise loveres wolden speke in general.
> Chaucer, *Troilus and Criseyde*

Throughout his work Chaucer consistently represents the voice of the courtly lover as impersonal or plural: in the line from the *Troilus* under the rubric of which this section is written he uses a plural grammatical subject to refer to the speaker of courtly language, and he also uses the exact word by which we have repeatedly characterized the singing subject, "general." My point here is that our sense of medieval song's generality is not a modern distortion or a critical fable inspired by a post-Freudian or structuralist fetishization of impersonality. Instead, this sense accurately signifies the medieval poet's notion of lyric subjectivity.

Chaucer's keen recognition of the troubadour's plight is amply demonstrated elsewhere in his corpus—in, for instance, *The Franklin's Tale*.[7] In that tale a young squire, Aurelius, languishes in his secret desire for the wife of a knight. The woman in question has no cause to suspect the squire's love, since its only expression has been by means of the non-expressive, impersonal utterance that is song:

> He was despeyred; nothyng dorste he *seye*,
> Save in his songes somwhat wolde he *wreye*
> His wo, as in a *general* compleynyng. (ll. 943–945)

> (He was in despair; he dared *say* nothing, except in his songs he would somewhat hide [*wreye*] his woe, as if he were making a *general* complaint.)

Whereas our editor translates this *wreye* as "reveal," the verb in question is perhaps more properly regarded as *wryen*, "to hide." At any rate, there is no difference between the song of the true lover, Aurelius, and the song of the "they" who, like the *losengiers*, generally complain. This lack of difference between the truly motivated and the merely imitative songs of rival poets prevents Aurelius's public performance from communicating to his chosen lady his unique desire, from revealing the hidden contents of his heart's interior, from closing the distance between his heart and hers. Yet the incapacity of lyric language to *seye* his love is precisely the reason Aurelius sings, for in fact he dares not say his love in a manner that would be understood. These lines suggest that to sing is not truly to *seye*: saying one's love in song, in the manner of a *general compleynyng*, does not count as a real act of saying. To sing is to hide, to *wryen* one's woe. And indeed there is no communication between Aurelius and the woman whom he desires, despite her presence at those court gatherings at which the poet Aurelius performs his songs of sorrow. It is, of course, the fact that the subject and the object of this courtly love are immersed and thereby dissipated in a crowd or multitude that accounts for the nothingness of Aurelius' song. In the mass or collective situation, the singer dares *seye . . . nothyng*, and *nothyng wiste she of his entente* ("she knew nothing of his intent"; l. 959) The possibility of heart-to-heart communication is blocked by the fact that the place of song is a convention, a public coming together ruled by others.

If the lyric situation precludes saying it simultaneously precludes narrative, the temporal unfolding of story. *The Franklin's Tale* would surely be arrested at line 959 if nothing continued to happen, if the stasis of song were not swept away by a stream of story. What happens immediately after line 959 is the narration of happening itself and the telling of time, as Aurelius apparently acquires the ability truly to *seye* something:

> Nathelees *it happed*, er they thennes wente,
> By cause that he was hire neighebour,
> And was a man of worship and honour,
> And had yknowen hym of tyme yoore,
> They fille in speche; and forthe moore and moore
> Unto his purpos drough Aurelius,
> And whan he saugh his *tyme*, he *seyde* thus: (ll. 960–966)

(Nonetheless it happened, before they left there—because he was her neighbor, and was a worthy and honorable man, and she had known him for some time—that they engaged in conversation. And more and more Aurelius approached his purpose, and when he saw his time he said thus:)

This re-emergence of *historia* into the story is marked by the temporal signs of both the past (*it happed*, *er*, *tyme yoore*) and the future (*forthe moore and moore*). And indeed what Aurelius seeks is *his tyme*—an object that, once found, allows the singer to *seye*, to appear as a sort of narrator. Yet what Aurelius subsequently says to the woman—and herein lies the real interest for us of this excursion into *The Franklin's Tale*—turns out to be nothing other than the language of song:

> "For wel I woot my servyce is in vayn;
> My gerdon is but brestyng of myn herte.
> Madame, reweth upon my peynes smerte,
> For with a word ye mat me sleen or save.
> Heere at youre feet God wolde that I were grave!
> I ne have as now no leyser moore to *seye*;
> Have mercy, sweete, or ye wol do me deye!" (ll. 972–978)

("For I well know that my service is in vain; my reward is nothing but the breaking of my heart. Lady, have pity on my sharp pains, for with a word you may slay or save me. Would God that I were buried at your feet! I now have no more time to say; have mercy, sweet, or you will make me die!")

Despite, and because of, his discovery of *tyme*, Aurelius has not been transformed from singer to storyteller but rather from singer to singer of a lyric language redeemed by its historicity. For Dorigen, the woman whom he loves, now hears in Aurelius's song the signs of a true act of saying:

> She gan to looke upon Aurelius:
> "Is this youre wyl," quod she, "and *sey* ye thus?
> Nevere erst," quod she, "ne wiste I what ye mente.
> But now, Aurelie, I knowe youre entente." (ll. 979–982)
>
> (She began to look upon Aurelius: "Is this your will," she said, "and are you saying thus? Never before," she said, "did I know what you meant. But now, Aurelius, I know your intent.")

The rhetorical question Dorigen answers ("*sey* ye thus?") suggests the difference I have been suggesting between singing and saying, song and story. Her question does not ask whether Aurelius has actually said what he said but rather whether what he said was actually an act of saying. She does not wonder what he has spoken but rather whether his words actually have originated in his heart and whether they reflect an historically specific love entirely separable from and previous to the act of singing. And in fact she does not really wonder anything at all, since she immediately answers her own question, indeed taking Aurelius's song as an act of saying that properly communicates his prior *entente*. To *seye* song, then, is to sing in a manner that tells a story, that reveals the pre-linguistic interior life of the individual singer.

What this episode from *The Franklin's Tale* stages, then, is the drama or the fantasy of song's amelioration, its transformation into an apparently more expressive medium, its acquisition of a redeeming narrativity. The lyric impasse that marks Aurelius's public singing is overcome by a private singing that is marked by historicity and that is really nothing more than a stylized mode of narration. When Aurelius *seyes* his love in song, his previously generalized voice is made singular. Aurelius's transformation from lyric to narrative subjectivity is another version of that movement from song to story best exemplified by the Old Provençal *razos*. Both the *razos* and *The Franklin's Tale* claim that the lyric singer may be an *auctor* rather than merely an *actor*—may be, that is, the solitary and undivided origin of a discourse rather than merely one secondary relay point in a linguistic network of many. Indeed recent readers of medieval lyrico-narrativity have in their various ways accepted that the phenomenon is fundamentally the locus wherein the triumph of story over song is celebrated, wherein song is represented as having an identifiable and stable source in the lived experience of the specific poet, as if song were by virtue of its insertion into story "authorized" or seen to originate in the heart of the autonomous ego or individual subject.[8] Thus the model propagated by the orthodox *razos*—in which song is represented as more readable, more satisfying, and ultimately more valuable, in direct proportion to the extent to which it more nearly resembles story—still controls modernity's judgment of medieval texts. Yet what is not recognized is that many of these lyrico-narrative texts do not in fact celebrate the triumph of *historia*, of narrativity and its concomitant gesture toward pre-linguistic historicity, but rather they suggest that story is always secretly ruled by song and its anti-mimetic semiosis. Chaucer's *Book* is, as we shall see, precisely such a resistance to the purported ascendancy of narrative.

IV

Let us return to the *Book* to see the many ways that it formulates this resistance. As we have seen, at the opening of the *Book* the narrator is in fact a lyric singer lamenting his resemblance to all lyric singers. This singing storyteller speaks, until line 44, entirely in the present tense of song. Line 44 marks the point of a transition from song to story, as Chaucer begins to speak of the past, to narrate a former happening. We must, by the way, be suspicious of a turn to narrative oddness that takes place precisely at a point that pronounces so loudly its own evenness: 44, whose digits both double two and double themselves to equal the eightness of the Octovian realm, is the epitome of a doubling evenness. Yet this place of the proliferation of twos is the very place where the *Book* commences its first turn to story, the place where narrative singularity is supposed to emerge. What is first narrated is nothing other than this very turn to narrative, as Chaucer attempts to drive away his evening sickness by reading a story:

> So when I saw I might not slepe
> Til now late this other night,
> Upon my bedde I sat upright
> And bad oon reche me a booke,
> A romaunce, and he it me toke,
> To rede and drive the night away. (ll. 44–50)

(So when I saw I might not sleep until now late this other night, I sat upright in my bed and bade one to bring me a book, a romance, and he brought it to me, to read and drive the night away.)

Everything that precedes line 44 is, as I have said, the self-reflective and present tense language of a lyric singer lamenting the fact that he is nothing but a lyric singer. Line 44 is meant to be a turning point, the moment of the initiation of a cure, the moment that inaugurates the quest for *oon*-ness, the moment that begins to banish song from the *Book*, as the past tense emerges in Chaucer's narration of his decision to read a *romaunce*, a collection of narrative *fables* (52). Yet this turning point in the text turns out to be a return to rather than an escape from song:

So when *I saw I* might not sleep . . . (l. 44)

(So when I saw I might not sleep . . .)

The very line meant to adumbrate the triumph of story's singular ego is exemplary of a lyric duplicity that will continue to cast its shadow over story: there are not one but two "I"s, and the narrator is represented as one who uses his two eyes to look at himself. The first matter narrated in Chaucer's *Book*—the narrator's act of looking at himself (*I saw I*)—is a version of the story of Narcissus (a story recounted again and again throughout the *Book* as Chaucer continues constantly to see himself in others and others in himself). And insofar as the *Book* is above all an account of Chaucer's *avysyoun* (285) or "vision," the phrase *I saw I* tells us that the object of this vision is no different from its subject, tells that what the lyric "I" encounters in its dreams are various versions of itself. This story of an undifferentiated relation between the subject and the object of vision is the very paradigm of an unachieved or frustrated narrativity, of a drive toward story foiled by song's rule: Narcissus, as both *Sujet* and *Objet*, is trapped in a story that has nowhere to go, that can only signify unfulfilled desire.[9] Indeed the medieval response to Ovid's story was to transpose it into a lyric key—a fact witnessed by the many appearances of narcissistic reflection in the songs of courtly love.[10] The Middle Ages treated Narcissus as the lyric singer par excellence because he is the perfect figure for a subjectivity that is both doubled and divided. Narcissus is the courtly lover who is always both more and less than himself, never adequate to himself. Narcissus is a twosome that cannot rightly be divided into distinctive units; alternately, Narcissus is a unit that is always divided within itself. Chaucer's longing for the physician who is not a woman but rather is *oon*-ness or self-integrity clearly reflects a narcissistic longing to eliminate specularity, to become a *Sujet* pure and simple. Chaucer's longing is a desire to sever the ties that implicate the subject in the object and the object in the subject.

The *I saw I* of line 44 is thus difficult to think in an uncomplicated manner. In one sense the phrase signifies the fantasy of a clearcut distance between the one "I" and the other "I," a distance maintained yet traversed by the subject's field of vision. In other words, the phrase promises that one—a coherent ego—can adequately observe a coherent and objective external reality and can report the findings of that observation. Thus the phrase seems to fulfill the conditions of a cure, as Chaucer has in sight the *oon* or *I* for which he longs. Yet insofar as the phrase betrays its Ovidian and courtly subtext of specularity, what is seen is more of the same: the "I" is seeing nothing other than itself, the eye is not turned outward toward an objective externality, and thus nothing is really being seen. The *saw*, which normally signifies a discernible distance between subject and object, becomes senseless as the field of vision is turned into a non-distance. The *saw* is cut from the phrase, which thus becomes *I . . . I* or simply *II*. This exposure of the subject's duplicity, this transformation of the I into II, takes place in the locus of doubling proliferation signified by line 44's double digits—digits that, mirroring each other, each result from II's doubling and that add up to equal the even eight of the Octo-yven. The mysterious lord of Chaucer's dream, this Octovyen, has already extended his tentacular grasp beyond the recognized boundaries of his realm.

V

Let us return to the moment of Chaucer's turn to story in the *Book*. As we have seen, the narrator decides to take arms against his sea of songlike sickness by asking one to reach for a *romaunce*, for a *booke*:

Upon my bedde I sat upright
And bad oon reche me a booke. (ll. 46–47)

(I sat upright in my bed and bade one to bring me a book.)

Specifically, this therapeutic *romaunce* is a collection of brief narratives written in the vernacular. From among these tales, Chaucer chooses one to cure his evening sickness and to "drive the night away." The *Book* then recounts a version of Ovid's story of Ceyx and Alcyone—a version influenced by Machaut's telling of the same tale in *La Fonteinne amoureuse*. This choice of reading material has a specular relation to the *Book*'s lyric opening:

Chaucer, in an attempt to break the narcissistic circle of lyric resemblance, inadvertently (or perhaps inevitably) chooses this Ovidian tale, which tells nothing if not the story of a failed movement from song to story. He chooses, that is, to read narcissistically, to read another version of the same story, another version of his own story of lyric sameness.

I shall summarize the events of Ovid's tale a bit later. For the moment, I would like to dwell on the fact that Chaucer begins his version by foregrounding the name of its protagonist:

> This was the tale: There was a king
> That hight Seyes, and had a wife,
> The beste that mighte bere lyfe,
> And this quene hight *Alcyone*. (ll. 62–65)

(This was the tale: there was a king named Seyes who had a wife, the best alive, and this queen was named *Alcyone*.)

Alcyone's name provokes us to see her as the alter-ego of the generalized singing Chaucer who commenced the *Book*. The possibility that Alcyone's name, which is alternately spelled *Alcione* in the lines I am about to cite, conjures up "all" and "one" is confirmed by the rhyme with which her name is coupled in these lines:

> And doo hit goon to *Alcione*
> The quene, ther she lyeth *allone*. (ll. 145–146)

(And make it go to Alcione the Queen, there where she lies all alone.)

Insofar as *allone* signifies "alone," it is a sign of the discrete singularity denied the singing subject of lyric language. In other words, *allone* seems at first glance to signify the unitary wholeness, the type of "all-oneness" for which the lyric singer longs and that story seems tantalizingly to offer. Yet this rupture at the heart of *allone*—the rupture that separates the "all" from the "one"—reveals the duplicity masked by the word's apparent singularity. The very word meant to signify the individual singularity of that which is "alone" simultaneously signifies the communal plurality, the sameness, of the "all one." And, as we shall see, it is just when Alcyone is alone, precisely at the moment of her grief, when she most resembles Chaucer in his resemblance to Froissart in his resemblance to all lyric singers. The time of her suffering is the time of her most objective expression. It is just when she is apparently alone, apparently the singular "one," that she turns out to be the plural *on*, the generalized "they" of the Old French tradition. Alcyone's name is the perfect emblem of lyrico-narrativity, since at its center is an "I"—the *y* or the *i* (in Middle English both *Y* and *I* signify "I")—whose place is somewhere between the *Al* and the *one*, between the "all" and the "one": *AL-cY-ONE*. Her name, which conjoins the multitude and the individual, says that all is one and one is all. Her name signifies a subjectivity poised in the space between the plural and the singular, between *langue* and *parole*, between the even and the odd.

Insofar as *one*, *oon*, and *oo* are in Middle English interchangeable signifiers of "one" (a fact intimated by the presence of all three paradigmatic possibilities in the sytagmatic space of a single line: "and d*oo* hit g*oon* to Alci*one*"), Alcyone's name could well be written *Alcyoo*. It is this incarnation of her name that is present anagrammatically in the ninth line in the phrase "AL is ylYChe gOOd." Thus, Alcyone's name is first present at that early point in the *Book* where the narrator most explicitly laments the generality of his voice and thereby sounds most indistinguishable from all lyric singers. Alcyone's name names that lyric undifferentiation, that sameness of the would-be singular subject, that constitutional multiplication of the *oon* into the *al*, which inaugurated the *Book* and which is its continual concern. In short, Alcyone is, among other things, a figure for the generalized singer of courtly love lyric.

Yet what is most remarkable is that Alcyone's name condenses the entire actantial *dramatis personae* of troubadour and trouvère song: *AL-cY-ONE* signifies at once the *AL*, the "all," the "they," the *losengiers*; the *Y*, the "I," the courtly poet; and the *ONE*, the "one," the lady, the purportedly unique object of desire.

Let us very briefly recall the *récit* of Ovid's tale. King Ceyx, against the protest of his wife Alcyone, sets forth on a sea voyage. Ceyx drowns in a shipwreck. Meanwhile Alcyone prays to Juno for her husband's safe return. Juno bids Iris, her messenger, to command Sleep to send word of Ceyx's death by means of a dream to Alcyone. Sleep chooses for this task his son Morpheus, who is a masterful mimic of human beings. Morpheus appears to the sleeping Alcyone in the form and manner of Ceyx, and he informs her of her husband's death. The next morning, revisiting the place on the seacoast where Ceyx set sail, Alcyone watches a body as it washes ashore and finds to her great despair that it is her husband's. Leaping to her death, she is metamorphosed in mid-air into a bird. Ceyx is similarly metamorphosed, and the two birds live together in tranquility.

Now what Chaucer does to Ovid's tale of Ceyx and Alcyone is, through the mediation of Machaut's telling of the tale in his lyrico-narrative *La Fonteinne amoureuse*, to lyricize the story by insisting on the language of courtly love song. The mode of this transformation is twofold. First, Alcyone is represented as a lyric singer—not just because her name suggests that she is a figure for the plural *on*, for the "one" that is "all," but more importantly because she actually performs lyric, actually voices a song, in the course of her story. Thus the *romaunce* read by the *Book*'s narrator, meant to be a narrative antidote to song, turns out to be not a pure *fable* or *tale* but rather a text imbued with implicated lyric language. Secondly, in Chaucer's version of Ovid's story every "character" turns out to resemble another, to lose his or her integrity, as subjectivity is shown to be fluid, slippery, always prone to become what it is not. That is, in Chaucer's version the narrative positions of *Sujet* and *Objet* are not occupied with stability by singular and distinctive individuals but rather are, as in troubadour and trouvère song, the *loci* of continual substitution, the sites of the sort of exchange by which lover becomes beloved and vice versa, the places where desire is unceasingly displaced. The romance that he reads to drive away song turns out not only to contain song but to be entirely songlike.

Let us look closely at Alcyone's lyric, which previous criticism has failed to recognize as such, thus failing to see that it is the fact of Alcyone's courtly language that, more than anything else, accounts for the pertinence to the rest of the *Book* of Chaucer's account of the Ovidian *romaunce*. For the slippery language of Alcyone's song is exemplary of that lyric language that rules Chaucer's style from beginning to end.

Here is the lament that Alcyone speaks in the absence of Seyes:

> "A, mercy, swete lady dere,"
> Quod she to Juno, hir goddesse,
> "Helpe me out of thys distresse,
> And yeve me grace my lord to se
> Soone, or wete wher so he be,
> Or how he fareth, or in what wise,
> And I shal make yow sacrifise,
> And hooly youres become I shal
> With good wille, body, herte, and al.
> And but thow wilt this, lady swete,
> Send me grace to slepe, and mete
> In my slepe som certeyn sweven

Wherthorgh that I may know even
Wherther my lord be quyck or ded." (ll. 108–121)

("Ah, mercy, sweet lady dear," she said to Juno, her goddess, "Help me out of this distress, and give me grace to see my lord soon, or to know where he is, or how he is, and I shall make a sacrifice for you, and I shall become entirely yours with good will, body, heart, and all. And do but this, sweet lady: send me the grace to sleep, and to dream in my sleep some certain dream by which I may know exactly whether my lord is alive or dead.")

What we may or may not notice first about this song—and what marks its status as a song—is that there are precisely fourteen verses from the beginning to the end of Alcyone's lament. Alcyone, that is, speaks here a sort of sonnet. Yet this turns out to be an odd sonnet, since line 109 is a narrative exception that does not count. An odd state of affairs is revealed, as Alcyone speaks a thirteen-line sonnet. And we shall, by the way, witness a very similar odd evenness surrounding the *Book*'s most famous song when we come to read the *Book*'s most famous episode.

Alcyone's lyric language challenges in various ways the actantial fixity or the illusion of unified psychological realism proffered by historical narrative. Let us begin reading her song with another look at its beginning:

But doun on knees she sat anoon
And wepte that pittee was to here.
"*A, mercy, swete lady dere,*"
Quod she to Juno, hir goddesse,
"Help me out of thys distresse." (ll. 106–110)

In her grief the kneeling Alcyone speaks from the position of the troubadour, as if, flouting biological fact, her tongue here gives voice to male desire. Her words, addressed to and begging mercy and aid from a woman of elevated status, would properly belong in any courtly *canso* or *chanson*, and indeed her initial verse—*A, mercy, swete lady dere*—could well be called a perfect distillation of all troubadour and trouvère song. By attributing to Alcyone the words *A, mercy, swete lady dere*, Chaucer momentarily transforms her into a male courtly lover and singer of conventional song. Indeed, *mercy, sweete* is a phrase in Aurelius' lyric address to Dorigen in the episode of *The Franklin's Tale* we encountered earlier in this chapter, and the phrase *lady swete* is sung—later in the *Book* in what is surely its central episode—by a man whom Chaucer takes to be a troubadour. In the Chaucerian poetic universe, *mercy, swete lady dere* clearly signifies the plea of a courtly poet to his beloved.

Yet immediately following this most lyric of lines an odd state of affairs is exposed, as line 109's narrativity interrupts Alcyone's song to spell out the name of the *swete lady dear*: *Quod she to Juno, hir goddesse*. Besides complicating or rendering incoherent the lyric drama in ways we shall analyze below, this specification of the song's context signals the supplementation of the courtly register of Alcyone's song by a religious register. The song, that is, begins to resemble not just a courtly love lyric but also a prayer addressed to the Virgin—a resemblance that continues for several lines:

> "A, mercy, swete lady dere,"
> Quod she to Juno, hir *goddesse*,
> "Helpe me out of thys distresse,
> And yeve me *grace* my *lord* to se
> Soone, or wete wher so he be,
> Or how he fareth, or in what wise,
> And I shal make yow *sacrifise*,
> And *hooly* youres become I shal
> With good wille, body, herte, and al." (ll. 108–116)

The presence of certain words from the Christian lexicon—*grace, lord, sacrifise, hooly*—confirms our notion that Chaucer has, following a traditional continental practice, imbricated the rhetoric of courtly love with the rhetoric of prayer. In Alcyone's song neither the register of courtly desire nor the register of prayer is dominant. The phrase *hooly youres become I shal* could equally signify a "holy" and mariolatrous dedication to the Virgin or a courtly lover's promise to serve "wholly" and exclusively his lady. We cannot say whether the singer's *lord*, referred to in line 110, is the *Dominus* who rules the universe or the *dominus* who rules the aristocratic society of the feudal court, whether the *lord* is the Lord or the lord. On one hand, the *lord*'s metonymic association with the religiously charged word *grace* in the same line suggests that we are here in the presence of the discursive world ruled by the *Verbum* that is *Dominus*. Yet, on the other hand, we cannot forget that the phrase *my lord* of line 110 translates into Middle English the Old Provençal *midons*—a word, from the Latin *dominus*, meaning "my lord" and used by the troubadour to refer to the one who occupies the ruling political position in the hierarchy of courtly society.

Now, the possibility that the *my lord* of Alcyone's song signifies, despite the rhetoric of prayer by which it is surrounded, *midons* or *dominus* rather than *Dominus* produces some very curious effects. For in troubadour lyric *midons* quite often signifies not the feudal lord served by the courtly poet but rather the beloved lady, the object of the poet's desire. That is, for reasons that give rise to all sorts of speculations, the troubadour commonly addresses his lady as *midons* ("my lord") rather than as the grammatically proper *ma domna* ("my lady"). The possibility of this conventional inversion of the grammatically proper gender—saying "milord" when one means "milady," saying "Don" when one means "Donna"—means that the opening verses of Alcyone's song once again appear closely to imitate courtly love lyric. That is, the voice of the the male courtly lover, which we posited as the source of the troubadour-like line 108 (*A, mercy, swete lady dere*), is not entirely supplanted by the voice of the *she* who, dedicated to the Virgin, prays to see or to hear news of the *Dominus*. Instead, both voices remain and the song is thereby the site of a permanent, irrecuperable rupture. Bearing in mind the potential substitution of *midons* for *my lord* (we shall see below evidence that Chaucer translates Old Provençal poetic terminology into Middle English), we may re-read the opening lines of Alcyone's lament as if they belong more or less consistently to the courtly register, as if they consistently represent the desire of a male singing subject for a female beloved object:

"A, mercy, swete lady dere" . . .
"Helpe me out of thys distresse
And yeve me grace *midons* to se." (ll. 108–111)

("A, mercy, sweet dear lady" . . . "help me out of my distress, and give me grace to see *midons* [i.e., to see my lord/lady].")

Thus what Chaucer has done is to give Alcyone—who is, in the story, a biological female—the singing voice of a biological male. Alcyone is a Donna who, raising her voice in song, assumes the role of a Don who sings his desire for a Donna who is named "Don": she is a woman who sings as a man singing for a woman whom he addresses as a man. This vertiginous oscillation of gender—by which the Madonna is always ready to become the Lord—is another version of the registerial oscillation that blurs the distinction between courtly and religious language in Alcyone's song. For the confusion of both gender and rhetorical register prevents any definitive answer to the question "Who is speaking?"—an answer that would fix and locate the source and identity of subjectivity. We cannot say for certain whether Alcyone's song is sung by a man or a woman, by the *dominus* or the *midons*, nor can we even say which rhetorical tradition—courtly or religious—is singing the subject. Alcyone's song, as we shall continue to see, does not originate in and proceed from a coherent subject whose identity is established prior to the time of singing. Rather, the song produces various subject-positions that are variously filled in a continual and contradictory process of substitution.

Nor can we say for certain whether the song is addressed to a man or to a woman. It is not entirely clear who is the unique object of Alcyone's desire: either Juno or Seyes may alternately be regarded as Alcyone's *midons*. In other words, Alcyone's song is strange because initially Juno appears to occupy the position of the desired *midons* or *swete lady*, and then Seyes appears, in his role as *my lord* or *midons*, to reclaim his rightful position as the object of Alcyone's desire. Yet the man's rightful reclamation of the position of *midons* is a wrongful usurpation of that position of *midons* that, in a song which begins *A, mercy swete lady*, rightfully belongs to the woman. And this doubling of the desired object is inseparable from the doubling of discursive registers that disperses Alcyone's duplicitous lament.

The multiplication or pluralization of the desired object—the fact that the singer alternately desires both Juno and Seyes within the course of a single song—challenges the rationale of narrative fiction that would posit a singular subject desiring a singular object. The *oon*-ness of the beloved lady is violated, as she turns out to be two and to be both "she" and "he." What is more, and what is most remarkable, is that the very figure whose name pronounces the unity of her ego, *J'-uno*, is the one who is immediately subjected to the divisive multiplication of lyric language: in the first few lines of the song she is displaced from the position of desired *Objet* (*swete lady, midons* or *donna*) to the position of supplicated *Adjuvant* ["Helper"] (the feminine side of the Godhead, *Madonna*). She whose name most protests her integrity is revealed to have none.

Yet perhaps this multiplication or doubling of the object of Alcyone's desire is merely an illusion. Perhaps, that is, there is not such a clearcut difference between Juno and Seyes as we have just posited. After all, both Juno and Seyes may be seen as the *midons*, both Juno and Seyes are the object of Alcyone's desire. It is possible, in other words, to read the song as if Juno and Seyes are in fact *oon* and the same. Juno, who is a *goddesse*, is a feminized version of a *dominus*, just as Seyes, who is *my lord*, is a masculinized version of *midons*, a word that signifies a feminized *dominus*. Juno and Seyes both dominate Alcyone's lament. Our initial surprise at hearing the grieving Alcyone sing a love song to Juno rather than to Seyes, her absent beloved, subsides when we posit that Juno in fact is that selfsame beloved, that Juno and Seyes are interchangeable. To say that Alcyone longs for Juno is to say that she longs for the unified *je*, for the *J'uno* who is able sincerely to *seye*. The *J'uno*—the *je* who is *oon*, the one who *seyes*—is nothing other than the individualized narrative ego, and Alcyone's song is nothing other than a singing subject's desire for story.

So far we have read the first eight lines of Alcyone's song, which closes with these five lines:

> "And but thow wilt this, *lady swete*,
> Send me grace to slepe, and mete
> In my slepe som certeyn sweven
> Wherthorgh that I may know *even*
> Whether *my lord* be *quyck* or *ded*." (ll. 117–121)

> ("And do but this, sweet lady: send me the grace to sleep, and to dream in my sleep some certain dream by which I may know exactly whether my lord is alive or dead.")

Once again, bearing in mind that the *my lord* translates the troubadour's *midons*, which signifies the desired lady, we see that these lines could almost be taken as the words of the courtly lover to his lady. We say "almost," because there is a certain jarring oddity that signals the strangeness of Alcyone's song. For when a courtly lover sings to his lady it is typically *he*, not she, who is poised between the states of being *quyck* or *ded*. Indeed Chaucer, in the lyric that commences the *Book*, represents himself as a singing subject whose life or death hangs in the balance:

> And I ne may, ne nyght ne morwe,
> Slepe; and thus melancolye
> And drede I have for to *dye*.
> Defaute of slepe and hevynesse
> Hath sleyn my spirit of *quyknesse*. (ll. 22–26)

> (And I may not, morning nor night, sleep. And thus I am melancholic and fear that I will die. Lack of sleep and heaviness have slain the liveliness of my spirit.)

Yet in Alcyone's lament it is not the *Sujet* or "I" who hovers oxymoronically between life and death, but rather the *Objet*, the *dominus* or *midons*. To put it another way, Seyes—the object of Alcyone's desire—has in Alcyone's song usurped that position belonging to the one who balances precariously between life and death, a position rightfully reserved for the singing subject. In short, in Alcyone's song the objective appears in the guise of the subjective. Alcyone, the *swete lady* or *Objet* of the desire of Seyes, appears as the singing *Sujet*.

Let us sum up our account of Alcyone's song. Subjectivity, in Alcyone's lyric language, is anything but singular or psychologically unified. Rather, the singing subject is radically undifferentiated, ready at any moment to be that which it is not. In such a fluid semiotic system, "he" is in any verse on the verge of becoming "she," the *Sujet* is always ready to stand in the place of the *Objet*, and so forth. Chaucer condenses or intensifies in Alcyone's lament song's potential to represent a realm of uncontrollable resemblance or *all-oon*-ness. And—we recall—this exemplary model of song's sliding subjectivity is the prominent moment in that very story that the narrator had selected precisely as a cure for this very sort of rampant undifferentiation.

VI

What is represented after Alcyone's lyric lament, as Chaucer continues to recount the Ovidian tale he chose in his longing for story, is nothing other than the non-achievement, or rather the illusory achievement, of the singing subject's longing for narrativity. By means of an elaborate ruse orchestrated by Juno, Alcyone is duped into believing that she hears Seyes *seye*, that she hears the unitary *je*. Specifically, Alcyone is made to think that her prayer is answered by *J'uno*, by the unitary *je*. She thinks she hears a voice that properly belongs to Seyes and to Seyes alone, an interior voice that originates in the particular heart of a particular body:

> For as she prayede, ryght so was done
> In dede, for Juno ryght anone
> Called thus hir *messagere*
> To doo hir errande, and he come nere.
> Whan he was come, she bad hym thus:
>   "Go bet," quod Juno, "to Morpheus—

> Thou knowest hym wel, the god of slepe;
> Now understond wel and take kepe—
> Sey thus on my halfe, that he
> Go faste into the Grete Se,
> And byd hym that on alle thyng
> He take up Seyes body, the kyng
> That lyeth ful pale and nothyng rody.
> Bid hym crepe into the body
> And doo hit goon to Alcione
> The quene, ther she lyeth allone,
> And shewe hir shortly, hit ys no nay,
> How hit was dreynt thys other day;
> And do the body speke ryght soo,
> Ryght as hyt was woned to doo
> The whiles that hit was alyve." (ll. 131–151)

(For as she prayed, just so was it done in deed, for Juno right away called her messenger to do her errand, and he came near. When he had come, she bade him thus: "Go quickly," said Juno, "to Morpheus—you know him well, the god of Sleep. Now understand well and take note. Say thus on my behalf: that he go fast into the Great Sea, and bid him by all means to take up the body of Seyes the King, which lies all pale and not at all ruddy. Bid him to creep into the body and make it go to Alcyone the Queen, there where she lies all alone. And show her shortly—it cannot be denied—how it was drowned the other day. And make the body speak right so, just as it was wont to do while it was alive.)

Eventually Morpheus performs the deed requested by Juno through the messenger, placing the dead body of Seyes before the sleeping Alcyone (this manipulation of the corpse is a significant departure from Ovid, in whose tale Morpheus performs without this prop) and fostering the illusion that the lifeless corpse is inspired and able to speak:

> Anoon this god of slepe abrayede
> Out of hys slepe, and gan to goon,
> And dyd as he had bede hym doon:
> Tooke up the dreynte body sone
> And bar hyt forth to Alcione,

> Hys wif the quene, ther as she lay
> Ryght even a quarter before day,
> And stood ryght at hyr beddes fete,
> And called hir ryght as she hete
> By name, and sayede, "My swete wyfe,
> Awake, let be your sorwful lyfe,
> For in your sorwe there lyth no rede,
> For certes, swete, I am but dede—
> Ye shul me never on lyve yse." (ll. 192–205)

(Then this god of Sleep started up out of his sleep and began to go, and did as he had bade him to do: he soon took up the drowned body and carried it to Alcyone, his wife the Queen, there where she lay exactly a quarter [i.e., three hours] before dawn, and he stood right at the foot of her bed, and he called her by her name and said, "My sweet wife, wake up, leave off your sorrowful life, for there is nothing good in your sorrow, for certainly, sweet, I am but dead—you shall never see me alive.")

Significantly, it is not just Alcyone who is duped, by a phonocentric fallacy, to embrace the presence of this phony Seyes. For modern readers of Chaucer have systematically and symptomatically misread this episode, accepting at face value, time and again, that it is really the dead Seyes who speaks here to Alcyone.[11] A certain motivated carelessness or blindness has prevented Chaucer criticism from observing Morpheus's masquerade, from seeing that it is Morpheus, *not* Seyes, who *sayede, 'My swete wyfe'* ("said, 'My sweet wife'"). To disarm the scandal of a speaking corpse whose voice is not its own, modern readers attribute to the spirit of Seyes the words that are in fact so obviously voiced, in a jongleurian or theatrical manner, by the dissembling Morpheus. That is, critics routinely see Seyes as the *auctor* or originator of his language, as one who truly *seyes* in this episode—yet in fact Seyes is the mask behind which stands Morpheus, the *actor* of this speech. Thus it appears that the tradition of Chaucer criticism commonly cannot cope with a counterfeit Seyes or with a saying that is not one—cannot, in short, cope with the lyricism of the *Book*. What frightens such criticism is the lifeless corpse of Seyes, the body that is merely a body or merely a letter lacking spirit—a manipulated letter whose only inspiration is a ventriloquistic trick played by a minstrel. Or, perhaps even more unsettling is not the possibility that Seyes does not *seye*, but rather the recognition that what Seyes does *seye* is not said by Seyes. The scandal of the speaking corpse lies in the fact that the voice is not inside or within, not centered, phonocentrically, in the heart of the body, not an emanation from the *herte* of the one who says. Instead, in this scene the voice—not Seyes's but Morpheus's—is the voice of another located beside or behind the body, the voice of another who dons the body as if it were a mask.

Indeed the medieval audience would have heard and seen the name of Morpheus as a metamorphosis of the name of the greatest Ovidian lyric performer—namely, Orpheus. Thus the scene in the *Book* in which M-*Orpheus* appropriates another's words, in which Morpheus addresses Alcyone as *My swete* (or as *midons*), represents the conditions of lyric performance in the Middle Ages: the *jongleur* is given momentary license to sing "I," to sing of his love for the wife of another (*my swete wyfe*), while not actually referring to himself. But Alcyone's wishful thinking leads her to mistake the language of Morpheus for that of Seyes, to mistake song for story, to mistake the *jongleur* for the true lover.

Yet it would be a repetition of Alcyone's and modern criticism's error to think that the *Book* presents any such thing as "the language of Morpheus." For the words spoken to Alcyone by Morpheus are no more properly Morpheus's than they are the words of Seyes. In fact Morpheus's words do not originate within himself but rather are taught him by the *messagere*, by the messenger (who is left significantly anonymous in Chaucer's account) sent by Juno. It is this second-hand status of his speech that makes Morpheus a medievalized transformation of the singular and unique Orpheus, that makes Morpheus closer to an anonymous *jongleur* than to a legendary classical poet of great renown. Of course, the *messagere*'s very existence as *messagere* means that his language is nothing other than a transmission that originates elsewhere. And the *messagere* means something else as well, since he is an incarnation of the Old Provençal *messatger*, the messenger who is nothing other than the song itself. This *messatger* is the name by which the singing "I" addresses his song as he tells it to go elsewhere to continue the chain of jongleurian transmissions that is the courtly love song. At any given point in this chain the particular singer—the one temporarily in command of the song—will always be singing the *messatger*'s message rather than his own. The song speaks itself through the *jongleur*, producing merely the effect of rather than true singular subjectivity. The messenger is one who occupies only momentarily his place in a structure of relations.

Thus what we have in this episode of Juno's ruse is Chaucer's accurate account of the absence of historical individuality in lyric language. Not only is the language of Seyes not the language of Seyes, but also it is the language of no one in particular, a language that circulates from one messenger to another. The *J'uno* or unitary *je* who apparently originates the news told to Alcyone disappears from sight, as the singularity of her discourse is filtered out by its transmission through two lyric screens, the *messagere* and Morpheus. Insofar as the body of Seyes has a voice in the *Book*, this body is merely a vessel inhabited by the voice of others, by a voice that may alternately be appropriated by the *messagere*, by Morpheus, or indeed by any lyric singer. The voice heard by Alcyone does not belong to or emanate from any specific body but rather speaks through any body or anybody whatsoever. The speaking corpse of Seyes is thus a perfect figure for the generalized "I" of courtly song—an "I" that always incarnates a spirit not its own, an "I" that never coincides with or names the physical, individual body of the actual lover.

In the *Book*, then, the story of Alcyone and Seyes tells the story of a story that never arrives, of a longed-for saying that never comes to pass. What does arrive is, once again, an illusory singularity: the speaking corpse that says "I" is clearly not the self-present and unitary *je*, not the desired *J'uno*. Instead, what Alcyone hears is more of the same, which is to say more of herself. Wanting to hear a novel discourse from the heart of the *auctor*, instead she hears the generalized lyric language of the *jongleur*. She hears the "all-one," the plural *on*, the one that is many, the I that is II. And indeed this equivalence between Alcyone and Seyes has already been suggested in a passage that we have encountered before:

> And byd hym that *on alle* thyng
> He take up Seyes body the kyng,
> That *lyeth* ful pale and nothyng rody.
> Bid hym crepe into the body
> And doo hit goon to Alcione
> The quene, ther she *lyeth allone*. (ll. 141–146)

> (And bid him to take up that *one-all* thing—the body of Seyes the King—that *lies* quite pale and not at all ruddy. Bid him to creep into the body and make it go to Alcione, the Queen, there where she *lies all-one*.)

It now appears that the *on alle* thing that *lyeth* in line 143 (Seyes) and that Morpheus takes up and occupies is the same thing as the multiplicitous *on* or the "one-all" that is Alcyone. That is, the text here represents the King and the Queen as precise specular doubles of each other: he is the *one-all* that *lies*, whereas she *lies all-one*. Thus the tale of Alcyone and Ceyx, which the narrator reads to drive away his chronic evenness, ultimately insists on precisely that sort of evenness, that undifferentiated resemblance between the one and the other which the narrator longs to escape.

VI

After reading the Ovidian tale, the narrator's response is entirely narcissistic: he shows absolutely no interest in the love affair nor in the death and metamorphosis of Alcyone; instead he perversely glosses the tale as if Alcyone were initially suffering not from the absence of her husband but rather, just like himself, from sleeplessness—as if the tale's *raison d'être* were the narration of the possibility of sleeping, the possibility of distinguishing night from day, the possibility of establishing a difference between the one and the other, as if the story directly addresses his own obsession:

> Whan I had redde thys tale wel
> And overloked hyt everydel,
> Me thoght wonder yf hit were so.
> For I had never herde speke or tho
> Of *noo goddes* that koude make
> Men *to slepe* ne for *to wake*. (ll. 231–236)

> (When I had read this tale well and looked it over completely, I thought it a wonder if it were so. For I had never heard spoken of before then any gods that could make men sleep or wake.)

If we recall that at the opening of the *Book* the narrator's sleeplessness is the sign of the evening sickness that prevents the division of various binary or oxymoronic pairs into their odd or singular components—a sickness that prevents, for instance, the division of *nyghte* from *lyghte*, the division of the *quyck* from the *ded*, the division of the true lover from the false, of the I from the II, the odd from the even—then we see that what strikes the narrator as valuable about the Ovidian tale he has just read is its representation of *goddes* who are able to command and to effect precisely that sort of division into singularity, who are able to produce sleep and wakefulness, night and day, gods who are the instrument of differentiation.

Yet if upon finishing his reading the narrator recognizes difference or oddness as a distinct and desireable possibility, when he resumes telling his story his language is still decidedly songlike, still a language of both oxymoron and undifferentiated resemblance. Thus his first speech after he entertains the possibility of these gods of difference is a perfect model of undifferentiated contradiction:

> And *in my game* I sayede anoon—
> And yet *me lyst ryght evel to pley.* (ll. 238–239)
>
> (And than as a game I said—and yet I really hate to play.)

He who says he does not play here says that he is engaged in a game, as these verses proclaim the narrator's simultaneous dedication to both *ernest* ("seriousness") and *game*. In his evening sickness, the narrator cannot divide game from play any more than he can divide night from day.

And what he says in his ernest game is a prayer that seriously parodies Alcyone's song to Juno:

> "Rather then that y shulde dey
> Thorgh defaute of slepynge thus,
> I wolde yive thilke Morpheus,
> Or hys goddesse, dame Juno,
> *Or some wight elles, I ne roghte who,*
> To make me slepe and have som reste—
> I wil yive hym the alderbeste
> Yifte that ever he abode hys lyve." (ll. 239–247)
>
> ("Rather than die from lack of sleep I would give this Morpheus, or his goddess, Lady Juno, or someone else—I don't care whom—in order to make me sleep and get some rest I would give him the the best gift that he could ever hope for in his life.")

This expression of a desire to know sleep's difference is indeed a repetition of Alcyone's petition, but whereas Alcyone's prayer had at least pretended to be addressed to someone special, to *J'uno*, Chaucer's is sent to anyone, to whomsoever it may concern: *Or some wight elles, I ne roghte who* ("Or someone else—I don't care whom"). The language of the narrator's prayer is songlike insofar as it is addressed to no one in particular, insofar as it is set free to circulate and to find any destination that it happens to find. To the narrator—still in the wake of his chronic evening sickness that renders *al alyche*—Morpheus, Juno, and *some wight elles* ("someone else") are equally valuable addressees and are all one and the same.

VII

Immediately after addressing this prayer to Morpheus or Juno or *some wight* else, immediately after—in true troubadour manner—addressing his plea to no one in particular, Chaucer's prayer is answered:

> I hadde unneth that word ysayede,
> Ryght thus as I have tolde hyt yow,
> That sodeynly, I nyste how,
> Such a lust anoon me tooke
> To slepe that ryght upon my booke
> Y fil aslepe; and therwith *evene*
> Me *mette* so inly swete a swevene. (ll. 270–276)

> (I had hardly said that word, just as I have told it to you, when suddenly, I know not how, such a desire to sleep overcame me that I fell asleep right upon my book. And thereupon evenly I dreamt such an internally sweet dream.)

And so begins the dream that is supposed to be the pre-literary event that it is the purpose of the *Book* subsequently to report. Indeed everything we have glossed so far may be seen as a prologue to the *Book*. Yet this does not mean, as some arbiters of taste would claim, that the *Book* does not really get started until now and that everything that precedes the dream is more or less expendable, a waste of time that delays the one truly significant and singular episode of the *Book*—Chaucer's meeting with the Man in Black.[12] Rather all that we have read so far is truly a pro-logue, a *logos* that precedes or comes before, a word that speaks the event. Chaucer's dream is the product of a compulsion to repeat and what takes place therein has already taken place in one way or another before the dream. Yet there is also a compositional circularity that defies straightforward narrative logic: the prologue is written after the dream that is dreamt under the influence of the prologue. No event in the *Book* stands alone, no word or signifier stands alone, for the return or recurrence of the letter is Chaucer's poetic principle throughout.[13] The main event of the *Book*, the dream, is merely a grand or macroscopic version of what has come before.

The narrator's long-desired sleep does finally arrive, yet contrary to his expectations this sleep does not inaugurate or make visible a world of difference. The main event of the dream, Chaucer's encounter with the Man in Black, is another version of the narrator's encounter with another version of himself, another version of Alcyone's encounter with her own lyric language. That is, Chaucer's dream is not a revelation that imparts to its dreamer a knowledge of what is objectively there in the external world. Instead his relation to his dream exemplifies a hermeneutic circularity, as the object of his dreaming vision is inextricably bound up with his subjectivity.[14]

Chaucer's dream takes place in and around Octovyen's estate—in, that is, the proper realm of Octo-yven, Lord of Evening—and thus, if anything, the dream is more ruled by evenness than ever before. Just as Alcyone's prayer to Juno was answered by the appearance to her in her sleep of a false *oon*, the phony Seyes, so is Chaucer's prayer answered by the appearance to the dreamer of a false *oon*, a counterfeit speaker who is nothing other than a version of the dreamer himself.

The *Book*'s dream opens in the most lyrical of lyrico-narrative fashions, with the narrator's telling of finding himself in a place surrounded by song:

> Me thoghte thus, that hyt was May,
> And in the dawenynge I lay—
> Me mette thus—in my bed al naked
> And loked forth, for I was waked
> With smale foules a gret hepe
> That had affrayed me out of my slepe,
> Thorgh noyse and swetnesse of her songe.
> And as me mette, they sate amonge
> Upon my chambre roof wythoute,
> Upon the tyles overal aboute,
> And songen everych in hys wyse
> The most solempne servise
> By noote that ever man, y trowe,
> Had herd; for some of hem song lowe,
> Some high, and *al of oon a*cor*de*. (ll. 291–305)

(I thought thus, that it was May, and at dawn I lay—I dreamt thus—in my bed all naked, and I looked forth, for I was awakened by a great heap of small birds that had startled me out of my sleep by the noise and sweetness of their song. And as I dreamt, they sat here and there outside upon my chamber roof, up on the tiles that covered over all, and they each in his way sang the most solemn service in birdsong that ever anyone, I believe, had ever heard. For some of them sang low, some high, and all of one accord.)

This surrounding of the subject by birdsong is the narrativized version of the typical springtime opening of the typical troubadour song. And the *cor* or heart that gives voice to this accordant lyric language is a collective one, as the songbirds are marked by a discursive *al-oon*-ness. Thus the dream, supposedly the site of the *Book*'s story, begins just as the *Book* began, with the representation of the generalized voice of song.

Following this aviary concert the narrator is motivated to leave his chamber by the sound of a horn—a hunting horn that announces the pursuit of the *herte*. This *herte* is, as has been often noted, not only the stag or "hart" but the "heart" and the "hurt."[15] Chaucer learns that the commotion means that the emperor Octovyen is in pursuit of the *herte*—and Chaucer watches as this dramatization of his own pursuit of interiority is played out and passes by before his eyes: he sees a mass of desiring subjects—Octovyen and his entourage—chasing the object; he sees the even eight named Octo-vyen chasing the *oon herte*. Yet the *herte* is elusive:

This herte rused and staal away. (l. 381)

(This heart made a ruse and stole away.)

Then a small puppy, unequal to the task of pursuit, is left straggling behind. Chaucer follows this straggler into a *floury grene* (398), into a sort of *locus amoenus* that, still part of the Octo-yven realm, is ruled by numerical evenness, by its lack of *oon*s:

For both Flora and Zephirus,
They *two* that make floures growe,
Had mad her dwellynge ther, I trowe. (ll. 402–405)

(For both Flora and Zephirus—those two who make flowers grow—had made their dwelling there, I believe.)

This doubly inhabited dwelling is perceived by the narrator as a place wherein flourish a magnitude or multiplicity that he describes in terms of numerical evenness:

> Hyt ys no nede eke for to axe
> Wher there were many grene greves,
> Or thikke of trees so ful of leves;
> And every tree stood *by hymselve*
> Fro other wel *ten* foot or *twelve*—
> So grete trees, so huge of strengthe,
> Of *fourty* or *fifty* fadme lengthe. (ll. 416–422)

(There is no need to ask whether there were many green bushes or thick trees so full of leaves. And every tree stood by himself from the other a good ten or twelve feet—such great trees, so huge of strength, forty or fifty fathoms long.)

Now, what sort of solitude is this or in what sense is a tree *by hymselve* when it stands in a *selva* or forest *thikke of trees* that are so evenly spaced as to be each like every other? Clearly the "self" of this *selva* is a collective one, and this wood is a perfect figure for the mass solitude, for the conventional sorrow, of the courtly lover. And this representation of the *al-oon*—which is expressed with the aid of the even numbers ten, twelve, forty, and fifty—is followed by an inventory suggesting the great zoological multiplicity of this realm, a realm that includes *many an hert* (427), many stags but also many hearts and sorrows—the mass sentiments of a plurality rather than the singular sentiment of an individual.

Here is where, as we have seen before, Chaucer poses to the reader—whom he figures as a counter, an acountant or arithmetician—a grandiose hermeneutic challenge:

> Shortly, hyt was so ful of bestes,
> That thogh Argus, the noble *countour*
> Sete to rekene in hys *countour*,
> And rekene with his figures *ten*—
> For by tho figures mowe al ken,
> Yf they be crafty, rekene and *noumbre*,
> And tel of everything the *noumbre*—
> Yet shoulde he fayle to rekene *evene*
> The wondres me *mette* in my swevene. (ll. 434–442)

(In short, it was so full of beasts that although Argus, the noble arithmetician, sat down to reckon in his calculator and reckoned with his decimal figures—for by those figures all who are crafty may know and reckon and number and tell the number of everything—yet he would fail to reckon evenly the wonders that I dreamt in my dream.)

On one hand Chaucer's claim that we cannot *rekene evene* his dream means that there will always be an interpretive surplus for which we cannot account, that there is in the text an overdetermined plenitude of odd wonders that will elude our reckoning. Yet more significantly, his claim that we cannot *rekene evene* his dream is a resistance, a denial: in fact, we cannot help but reckon it *evene*, since the *noumbres* inscribed by this singing storyteller or ra-*countour* are, with the sole exception of the *oon*, of the one *herte*, which recurs as the elusive object of desire, so persistently *evene*. This passage itself is a prime instance of the insistence of the *evene* in the narrator's discourse: *countour* and *noumbre* are both doubled, rhymed with themselves, oddly enough, to make even pairs. And even this Argus is oddly determined by the narrator's evening sickness. Argus is, according to our editor's account, really Algus, "the 9th-century Arabian mathematician through the translation of whose writings arabic numerals and the decimal system (called alegorism or augrim) were introduced into Europe after 1200."[16] Yet if the narrator confuses this arithmetician's name, this confusion is no accident but is motivated by his chronic condition: multiplying the *ten* associated with Algus by itself, the narrator comes up with 100, and this figure dictates Algus's appearance in the guise of the hundred-eyed Argus. Argus is thus not one who reckons externally and prior to the *Book*, since he is the product of the discourse of *hys countour*—the product of his counter or *raconteur*, of the narrator of the *conte*, of Chaucer's evening sickness.

Insofar as *mette* means "measured" as well as "dreamt," we see that Chaucer himself is responsible for the doubled *noumbres* of his dream. The narrator reports his measurements in a language whose only signifying elements are even numbers. Regardless how tall the trees really were or how much distance really separated them, the only figures we are given by which to measure these distances are the even numbers ten, twelve, forty, and fifty. The narrator forces us to *reckene evene* because he *metes* or measures the objects in his *swevene* or dream so evenly. That which he dreams may well really be odd, but once it passes through his *countour*, his songlike storytelling faculty, it comes out even, doubled, matched with its *mete* or mate.

This propensity to see evenly, to read lyrically, rules the encounter with the Man in Black:

> But forth I romed ryght wonder faste
> Doun the woode; so at the laste
> I was war of a man in blak
> That sete and had yturned his bak
> To an ooke, an huge tree.

> "Lord," thoght I, "who may that be?
> What ayleth hym to sitten here?"
> Anoon-ryght I wente nere;
> Than found I sitte *even* upryght
> A wonder wel farynge knyght—
> By the maner me thoghte so—
> Of good mochel, and ryght yong therto,
> Of the age of *foure and twenty* yere,
> Upon hys berde but lytel here,
> And he was clothed al in blake.
> I stalked *even* unto hys bake,
> And there I stood as stille as ought
> That, soth to saye, he saw me nought,
> For-why he heng hys hed adoune,
> And with a dedely sorwful soune
> He made a ryme of *ten* vers or *twelfe*
> Of a compleynt to hymselfe. (ll. 443–464)

(But I roamed forth wondrously fast down through the woods, so in the end I was aware of a man in black who sat and had his back turned next to an oak, a huge tree. "Lord," I thought, "who might that be? What ails him that he is sitting here?" Right then I went near. Then I found sitting evenly upright a wondrously attractive appearing knight—I thought by his manner that he was such—of good size, and also quite young, twenty-four years of age, few whiskers on his face, and he was clothed all in black. I stalked evenly up to his back, and there I stood so still that, truly, he did not see me, because he hung his head down, and with a deadly sorrowful sound he made a rhyme of ten verses or twelve, a complaint to himself.)

This man in black is sitting in solitude, by himself, at one of those trees that has just been described, unconvincingly, as solitary, as standing *by hymselve*. Yet, whether or not this man is truly himself *oon*, Chaucer cannot help but regard him as not *oon*: *found I sitte even* ("I found sitting evenly").

Now, this man is, according to scholarly consensus and in accordance with certain anagrammatical hints Chaucer drops near the end of the *Book*, John of Gaunt.[17] And indeed, more than any other work by Chaucer, the *Book* tempts the reader to posit the primacy of the biographical "occasion" in the task of interpretation. But this is not simply because we can be more certain about the biographical facts and circumstances surrounding the *Book* than we can about the similar context of other works in Chaucer's *corpus*. Rather, the notion of "occasional" poetry, of literary production as biographical history, lies at the very heart of the *Book* itself and is the very issue at stake in the dreamer's encounter with the Man in Black. In other words, one quite reasonable reading of the *Book* sees it as a claim that literary discourse is biographical and does originate in and flow forth from the heart of the individual. If readers are tempted by the lure of the "occasion" it is because certain elements of the *Book* tell us that poetry is occasioned by the facts of biography. Yet what readers have failed to realize is that these elements are there precisely to be discounted as irrelevant.

Let us return to that Man in Black whom we left sitting underneath an *ooke*. Biographically inclined readers are disturbed to find that this man is said to be *foure and twenty* years old, whereas John of Gaunt was at the time of composition "nine and twenty." This contradiction has been resolved by the invocation of the medievalist's favorite *deus ex machina*—scribal error.[18] Yet is it not much more likely that, as a side effect of his insertion into the Octo-vyen world of Chaucer's dream, Gaunt's age is naturally subject to a linguistic revaluation? Whatever the true age of the Man in Black, in the thought and language of the dreamer/narrator of the *Book* his age is determined by the factor of an even eightness. That is, the man's age is not an objective entity that exists before the writing of the *Book* but rather is a production of the dreamer's evening discourse. Chaucer here represents himself as simply unable to see or to think the odd. The one who is sitting near an *ooke* is, according to Chaucer, sitting *even (found I sitte even upryght)*. The dreamer is an evening stalker (*I stalked even unto hys bake*) who considers all that he comes upon to be even.

This incapacity to recognize the singular *oon*, this failure to see the distinctive, this persistent pattern of evening the odd rules the dreamer's recollection of that troubadour-like song sung by the Man in Black. In what is perhaps the most remarkable outbreak of his evening sickness, the most stark symptom of his blindness to outstanding singularity, Chaucer fails to accurately count and recount the number of verses in the Man's lyric lament. Chaucer tells us that, after stalking evenly behind the one sitting under the *ooke*, he overheard him singing a song of ten or twelve verses (*He made of ryme ten vers or twelfe*). The imprecision of Chaucer's account of the Man's verses is contradicted by the manifest precision with which Chaucer transcribes those very verses:

> And was thys, for ful wel I kan
> Reherse hyt ryght. Thus hyt began:
> "I have of sorwe so grete wone
> That joye gete I never none
> Now that I see my lady bryght,
> Which I have loved with al my myght,
> Is fro me ded, and ys ag*oon*.
> *All*as, dethe, what ayleth the
> That thou noldest have taken me,
> Whan thou toke my lady swete,
> That was so faire, so freshe, so fre,
> So goode, that men may wel se
> Of all goodnesse she had no *mete*?" (ll. 473–486)

(And it was this, for I can fully well repeat it exactly. Thus it began: "I have such a great plenty of sorrow that I can never have any joy now that I see that my bright lady, whom I have loved with all my might, is from me dead and gone. "Alas, Death, what ails you that you would not have taken me when you took my sweet lady, who was so fair, so fresh, so generous, so good, that men can clearly see that she had no equal in goodness?")

It does not take an accountant as crafty as Argus to see that the very song that Chaucer inexactly quantifies as *ten vers or twelfe* has, according to the narrator's boastfully exact transcription of the song in his *Book*, exactly *eleven* verses. Chaucer simply fails to acknowledge that digit, that *1* (or, to use the numeral of the *roman*, that *I*), which would make a difference and would prompt a decision. He cannot count that prime number produced by the proliferation of the *oon*. He will not admit into his measured dream the possibility of an irreducible difference, of a number that will not take part in an algebra of equivalence and substitution. To the dreaming Chaucer, *x* or *y* is all the same: there is no difference between *ten vers or twelfe*. Banished from his thought is any positivistic unit that would escape the economy of relational value or semiotic exchange. The *Book*, which Chaucer elsewhere (in the *Prologue* to the *Legend of Good Women*) calls the book of *Blaunche the Duchess*, is indeed a book of Blanks and Deuces, a book that can acknowledge the 10 and the 12 but not the 11, the 0 or the 2 but not the 1. The discourse of the *Book* is not adequate to represent singularity.

Now, Chaucer has quite cleverly inscribed into this eleven-line song the opposition between two ways of thinking about the foundation of value—an opposition which comes to rule the rest of the *Book* and which is another way of saying the conflict between song and story. The song's first stanza is odd, the second even. The first stanza's final word ends up declaring the *oon*, the singular, the unmatched, the autonomous; the second stanza begins with an instant transition from the *oon* to the *all* and ultimately insists on the *mete* ("mate" or "equal"), the matched, the metonymic couple witnessed everywhere in the *sw-evene* that Chaucer has *mette* ("dreamt," "measured," or, we suspect, "matched"). The first stanza speaks for that side of the *Book* that champions an odd notion of value as stable, unitary, and self-determined; the second for that side that supports an even notion of value as a relational function of pairs or matched couples. It is thus no accident that stanza number one of this song, the oddly numbered five-line stanza, is the place of narration: the Man in Black, telling us that his lady is *fro me ded*, recounts that historical event that apparently inspired—*razo*-like—his singing. (This is, by the way, the same story told at the end of the narrator's telling of the Ovidian tale, a tale about how Alcyone *deyde*.) Stanza number two of this song, the evenly numbered, six-line stanza, returns to a purely lyric language, an interrogative apostrophe, a desire to hear an answer from one who cannot speak. And the rest of the *Book* asks whether the *oon* can ever break free from its *mete*, whether one can stand unequaled.

To say that we suspect that the dream that Chaucer has *mette* is "matched" is merely to acknowledge that the dream's value depends upon its relation to something else, that the dream must be paired and compared with the prologue, a prologue that is by no means gratuitous and whose value depends upon its relation to the dream. Indeed virtually everything in the *Book* meets its match. But this coupling is promiscuous, as every *oon* encounters more than one *mete*, more than one mate. The evenness or equivalence of elements means that any *oon* may be swapped for another. The *lady swete* whose death is briefly narrated in the first stanza of the Man in Black's song couples with Alcyone, whose death is briefly narrated in Chaucer's version of the Ovidian tale; yet Alcyone, who sings to an absent *lady swete* (who turns out to be her *dons* or her "lord"), couples with the Man in Black who sings to an absent *lady swete*; the Man in Black, a troubadour, couples with the troubadour Chaucer who narrates the *Book*; the troubadour Chaucer who narrates the *Book* couples, in the first eight lines, with Froissart; both Froissart and Chaucer couple—or triple—with Alcyone, the lyric singer. But then who is not invited to this congregation of courtly lovers? Chaucer, Froissart, Alcyone, Seyes, Morpheus, the Man in Black, Gaunt, Octovyen and his familiars—even the messenger is asked to stay. And what brings them all together is their common desire for the *lady swete*, *J'uno*, *midons*, my lord, the physician, the one who has *no mete*, the *oon* who is not there. This swapping, powered by equivalence, among those who stand for the singing subject is just the most obvious, and perhaps the least interesting, of the *Book*'s rampant semiotic substitutions by which any *oon* element will always meet or *mette* ("dream") its mate. For such displacement of the signifier is Chaucer's style throughout and on every level of the *Book*. That is, throughout the *Book* phonemes and graphemes, words, phrases, verses, songs, stories, and entire discourses or genres are engaged in a metonymic free-for-all, in an unending search for one's *mete* conducted over a slippery territory. We come to see that the language of Chaucer's *mette* ("dream") is the language of the *mete* ("equal"). And such is the language of song.

IX

What has always and rightly appeared to readers as the interpretive crux of the *Book* is Chaucer's apparent failure to take the Man in Black's song seriously as the realistic expression of lived experience. Yet with a few notable exceptions the question of Chaucer's misprision of the man's lyric language has foundered on psychologistic speculations concerning the dreamer's "personality," motivation, and degree of stupidity. Yet it is clearly Chaucer's evening sickness that accounts for his misrecognition of the song's apparent singularity. The dreamer cannot admit the song's oddness, cannot conceive that the song tells a story, cannot imagine that song refers to the history of the individual singer.[19] That is, Chaucer comes upon one whom he takes to be a troubadour or, more precisely, a *jongleur*—one who sings the words of another.[20] The dreamer hears the song not as the heartfelt expression of an *auctor* but rather as the virtuoso performance of an *actor*. For after the song is sung Chaucer exchanges pleasantries with the very one who, in keeping with the dramatic role of lovesick courtly lover, had *made al/Hys hewe chaunge and wexe grene* ("made all the color of his body change and turn green" [496–497]). And it is in the exchange of these pleasantries, after the Man's hue has been restored, that the dreamer confirms his suspicion that the language of the lyric is not bound to the body of the Man in Black:

> Loo, how godoely spak thys knyghte,
> As hit had be *another wyghte*:
> He *made* hyt nouther *towgh ne queynte*. (ll. 529–531)

(Lo, how pleasantly this knight spoke, as if he were another person: he made it neither tough nor quaint.)

Our editor translates this *towgh ne queynte* as "arrogant nor affected" and claims that "in this line we observe Chaucer's 'good ear' for voice as a clue to character."[21] Yet this notion that *towgh ne queynte* lends an air of verisimilitude or realism to Chaucer's depiction of the man's voice misses the boat in every way. The whole point of this little exchange is that voice has no necessary connection with and carries no information about the body from which it emanates. Chaucer criticism, operating under the influence of its twin chief assumptions—that Chaucer fathers or originates his own poetic language and that this language conveys his observation of natural phenomena—cannot hear or see in the phrase *towgh ne queynte* Chaucer's translation of technical terminology from the field of continental poetics. Chaucer opposes to the Man's song the pleasantries that do not appear to have been *made* or "composed." The verb *to make* is one way for Chaucer to say the Old Provençal *trobar* ("to compose"). Thus the Man's song, which in comparison with the pleasantries is a *made* or "composed" speech, is seen by the dreamer as the product of a troubadour tongue. Now, the *towgh ne queynte* is there to subtly spell out the pertinence of continental lyric practice to this encounter between Chaucer and the Man in Black. For *towgh* is Chaucer's translation of the *trobar clus*, the "closed" or "difficult" style of troubadour lyric, while *queynte* is his translation of the *trobar ric*, the "rich" or "intricate" style. When Chaucer says that, in speaking pleasantries to him, the Man in Black *made hyt nouther towgh ne queynte* he is saying that the Man "composed it neither *clus* nor *ric*." Thus Chaucer proclaims that the Man in Black with whom he is engaged in pleasant conversation appears not to be the composer who made the song, that the troubadour is *another wyghte*, another person, some one else not there with him. The language of the song, the language that may be *clus* or *ric*, is the language of *another wyghte*: the voice of song comes from elsewhere, from without rather than from within the heart of the Man. Chaucer sees the man as a *jongleur*, as one who temporarily appropriated the words of another. In the eyes of the dreamer, the Man as singer briefly occupied the position occupied by Morpheus in his representation of a counterfeit Seyes, of a saying that was not one—the position of he who feigns singing from the heart. In short, when the song passes through Chaucer's evening faculty it can only appear as a circulating message—no different from all such messages—that momentarily passed through the body of the Man in Black.

X

The rest of the *Book* is the Man's failed attempt to convince Chaucer otherwise, the Man's attempt to gain the proper recognition for the singularity of his song, to convince Chaucer that the song really refers to his individual historical life. This attempt is indistinct from a parade of discursive possibilities, as the Man in Black searches by trial and error for that novel language which will disclose the heart of the individual. As one critic persuasively demonstrates, the Man in Black, in his attempt to reveal the historical event that lies at the source of his sorrow—namely, the death of his *lady swete*—uses three discursive or generic strategies before apparently getting it right, before finding the capacity to narrate and thereby to move beyond song.[22] That is, the Man recounts the same story—the love affair ended by death—in three different ways before the dreamer appears to accept that the Man's language reports the biography of the individual, thereby appearing to receive the odd narrative cure for which he has been longing. The first attempt to tell the story comes in the song—specifically, in the fifth verse of the eleven-line song—that we have just come across. The second attempt comes, as we shall see, when the Man in Black renounces song for an allegorical narration. The third attempt comes, as we shall see, when the Man finally turns to a realistic, novelistic, biographical narration that in the end appears to lay the heart bare and to tell—*razo*-like—the true history of the Man's lived experience.[23]

It is not difficult to see in this quite reasonable account of the discursive or generic trajectory of the Man in Black's language another version of recent criticism's dominant stance on medieval lyrico-narrativity. The view that sees the *Book* as the place in which mimesis ultimately breaks free from semiosis, in which historical or realist narrative finally emerges from the shackles of song, in which lyrico-narrativity is a necessary but in the end expendable catalyst in the production of pure story—this view quite easily becomes an allegory of medieval literary history in general and of Chaucer's career in particular. Such a view is meant to make us congratulate Chaucer for his progressive foresight. We are supposed to think that Chaucer, frustrated with the tired conventionality of love song, points toward historical narration as the agent of literature's future salvation.[24] The *Book* would thus tell the story of Chaucer's renunciation of his youthful dalliance with the lyrico-narrative compositional strategies of Machaut and Froissart. And the *Book* would intimate Chaucer's turn from France toward Italy and his encounter there with the discourse of novel historicity that is the *novella* (and, perhaps, with the novel lyrico-narrativity of Dante's *Vita Nuova*, which may be seen to say, as its title implies, something *newe* concerning "life"). The *Book* would proclaim a poetics of novelty or *newe tidynges*, thereby clearing a path for one of the all-time crowning achievements of narrative, those *Tales* for which Chaucer is so universally admired.[25]

XI

This notion that the *Book* traces a positive progressive journey from song to story is quite compelling insofar as the notion itself makes an excellent story, yet it is rendered entirely suspect when we return to reading the *Book*. The apparent triumph of story, the evidence that the literary work is grounded in a historical "occasion," is indeed there for our consideration. Yet there is even more evidence that this apparent triumph is a deception that the *Book* means at every level and at every moment to expose as such. The *Book* reveals the fraudulence of its own claim to herald or adumbrate the interior language of the individual heart.

The transition in the Man in Black's discourse from song to allegory is initiated by the Man's own interpretation of his own significance. The Man interprets himself for the dreamer:

> For whoso seeth me first on morwe
> May seyn he hath mette with sorwe,
> For y am sorwe and sorwe ys y. (ll. 595–597)

(He who sees me first in the morning may say that he has met with Sorrow, for I am Sorrow and Sorrow is I.)

Here the man clearly states that his identity is not self-standing: he does not say *y am y* ("I am I") but rather *y am sorwe and sorwe ys y*. He is defined, he says, by his mutual relation with something else. More precisely, he is both himself and not himself. When the Man in Black says "I" he means more than he says and, indeed, he says one thing and means another. He now speaks not so much the language of song as the language of allegory.

Yet as the *Book* continues it seems to suggest that song and allegory cannot be kept apart, that there is a fundamental resemblance between the two discourses. Thus, following the institution of allegorical language that takes place when the Man reads himself as an allegorical sign, lyric and allegory appear to be discursive companions. The commencement of the Man's allegorical tale, which is meant to signify the death of his *lady swete*, is represented as the culmination of an outburst (of which I here cite but the latter verses) of conventional courtly oxymora:

> "To derke ys turned al my lyghte,
> My wytte ys foly, my day ys nyghte,
> My love ys hate, my slepe wakynge,
> My merthe and meles ys fastynge,
> My countenaunce ys nycete,
> And al abawed whereso I be
> My pees, in pledynge and in werre.
> Allas, how myghte I fare werre?
> My boldenesse ys turned to shame
> For *fals Fortune hath pleyde a game*
> *Atte chesse with me*." (ll. 609–619)

("All my light is turned to darkness, my sense is folly, my day is night, my love is hate, my slepe waking, my mirth and feasting is fasting, my seriousness is foolishness, and I'm all abashed whether I'm at peace, in litigation, or at war. Alas, how could I fare worse? My boldness is turned to shame, for false Fortune has played a game of chess with me.")

This allegorical personification of Fortune at the end of this lyric passage is the beginning of the Man's allegorical narrative. Thus this personification has, as it were, one foot in song and the other in allegory or, let us say, it has a massive tangle of lyric roots. From this position the Man goes on to tell a tale of how he played chess against Fortune and lost his queen. Still, the dreamer does not grasp the historical event—the death of the Man's lady— that this tale is meant to signify. Chaucer cannot see what is hidden by the allegorical figure. Whereas the dreamer previously would not consider that the Man's song was literally about events in the Man's life, this time the dreamer's reading of the Man's language is too literal, too ready to assume that the man actually did play chess with Fortune. He thus tries to comfort the Man by saying that the loss of a queen in a game of chess is no great loss:

> "But ther is no man alyve here
> Wolde for a fers make this woo." (ll. 740–741)

> ("But there is no man alive here who would be so upset over a chess-queen.")

The man responds by telling the dreamer that the tale of the chess game means more than it seems to mean:

> "Thou woste ful lytel what thou menest.
> I have lost more than thow wenest." (ll. 743–744)

> ("Little do you know the meaning of what you're saying. I have lost more than you know.")

Here the man is saying that he himself, in saying that he lost his queen in a chess game with Fortune, has meant more than he said. He has, he says, said one thing and meant another. Neither his tale nor the Man himself (*y am sorwe and sorwe ys y*) are what they seem to be on the literal or "historical" level of their appearance. His tale, like himself, is a sign of something else— a sign ruled by the fundamental principle of semiosis, dependent for its value on its relation to something outside or beside itself. Neither the Man nor his language is *oon*, but rather each is inextricably bound up with a *mete*, with another.

Much of the Man's allegorical tale is spent in a vilifying portrait of Fortune. What is striking about this personification is that Fortune appears in the Man's portrait to be not so much the traditional goddess *Fortuna* as she is a figure for Allegory itself. Thus in vilifying Fortune as an allegorical figure the man appears to be vilifying the very language that makes such vilification possible. Fortune is, to the Man, primarily a linguistic goddess: she is the principle of representation or signification upon which allegory is founded.[26] Fortune is the goddess of a deceptive surface whose value turns out to be otherwise than it seems:

> "An ydole of fals portrayture
> Ys she, for she wol sone wrien.

> She is the mowstres hed ywrien,
> As fylthe *over-ystrawed with floures*.
> Hir moste worshippe and hir flour ys
> To lyen, for that ys hyr nature,
> Withoute feyth, lawe, or mesure.
> She ys fals and ever *lawghynge*
> With one eye, and that other *wepynge*." (ll. 626–634)

("She is an idol of false representation, for she will soon turn away. She is the hidden monster's head, like filth overstrewn with flowers. Her greatest renown and the flower of her achievement is to lie, for that is her nature, without faith, law, or restraint. She is false and always laughing with one eye and weeping with the other.")

What Fortune hides is always *over-ystrawed with floures*, overstrewn with flowers of rhetoricity. And she is the personification of lyric oxymoron, one who both laughs and cries.

Fortune is thus not unlike the Man in Black, who tells us, in his lengthy outburst of lyric oxymora, that his *lawghtre* easily becomes *wepynge* (600). Indeed the dreamer is convinced that the Man in Black is a *jongleur* rather than a true lover precisely because, when the dreamer first meets him in the forest, the man is at one moment overcome with grief and at the next moment pleasantly cheerful, as if the man were *another wyghte*, another person. The *jongleur* is he who, like Fortune, laughs with one eye and cries with the other. In accusing Fortune the Man is accusing himself: it is he who propagates *fals portrayture* by telling this tale of a chess game that does not truly say what it means, and it is he who speaks the lyric language of oxymoronic undifferentiation.

The Man's view of Fortune is summed up in the following verses:

> "She ys pley of en*chaunte*ment
> That *semeth oon* and ys not soo." (ll. 648–649)

Clearly it is not only Fortune that *semeth oon and ys not soo*. The Man's allegorical tale seems to be one about a game of chess and is not so. The Man himself seems to be one and is not so: he is more than one man, since he sings with the voice of *another wyghte*, and he is in fact not a man but rather a personification of Sorrow ("I am Sorrow and Sorrow is I"). The Man is not so much a man as he is a figure for the various discourses—song, allegory and, a bit later, historical or biographical narrative—that he speaks. Fortune, whom the Man violently rails against, is a figure for the Man's own language—a figure for both allegory and song. She figures allegory insofar as she *semeth oon and ys not so*, insofar as the apparent unity of each *seme* or seed that she sows reveals a duplicity. She figures song insofar as she is the *pley of en-chaunte-ment*, the "play of en-song-ment." This *chaunte* signifies—as in the name of the singing rooster *Chauntecleer* of the *Nun's Priest's Tale*—the Old French *chant*, which is to say the trouvère *chanson* or the troubadour *canso*. Fortune, who is the *pley of en-chaunte-ment, / That semeth oon and ys not soo*, is the songlike play of the signifier always ready to signify something else. Fortune is both allegory and song, and Fortune is the Man himself, who has served thus far in the *Book* as the personification of both song and allegory. The Man, like all singing subjects, rails against his own language, the language of Fortune, the language that has been dealt him and with which he has no choice but to deal.

XII

> Thus among numbers all are measured against one, and are considered to be larger or smaller as they are farther from, or nearer to, one; and among colors, all are measured against white, for they are considered more or less visible to the degree that they approach or depart from white.
>
> Dante, *De Vulgari Eloquentia* I, 16

So far we have witnessed the failure of both song and allegory to communicate to the dreamer the story of the Man in Black's real-life individual love affair. There follows a turn to a third discourse—to a straightforward storytelling or realist narrative. It seems that story finally arrives in the *Book*, as the Man recounts the history of his love for a certain lady. He tells of selecting one from among the ladies at court:

> "Among these ladyes thus echon,
> Soth to seyen *y sawgh oon*
> That was lyk noon of the route." (ll. 817–819)

("To tell the truth, among all these ladies I saw one who was like none of the others in the crowd.")

The Man goes on to tell the story of his love for this *oon* whom he discerns as unlike any other, and thus the commencement of narration is simultaneous with the singularization of his desire.[16] The phrase *y sawgh oon* ("I saw one") repeats, with a difference, the narrator's *I saw I* of the crucial line 44. The earlier phrase signified, as we saw, the narrator's narcissistic, specular relation with the object of desire—signified, that is, the mutual interdependence of subject and object. The significant difference in the Man in Black's repetition of the earlier phrase is that *oon* has replaced *I* as the object of vision. The Man in Black believes that he sees one who is truly *oon*, that the object of his desire is purely objective, that there is a definite difference between him and his lady. In this narrative discourse he now seems able to speak of the *oon* who does not *semeth* but who truly is *oon*:

> "*Trewely* she was to myn eye
> The *soleyn fenix* of Arabye;
> For ther levyth never but *oon*,
> Ne swich as she ne knowe I noon." (ll. 981–984)

("Truly she was to my eye the solitary phoenix of Araby, for there never lives but one. And I know none such as she.")

But this lady who is the object of the Man's narrative turns out, despite his insistence on her absolute singularity and her freedom from the world of resemblance and semiotic substitution, to be other and more than she seems, to be not merely a certain unique lady of the court whom the man happened to love. For she comes to be in the Man's tale an allegorical figure for the *oon*, the real, the true, the non-lacking, the singular, the self-defining, and for the corresponding heartfelt language of the individual—for, in short, everything that all the singing subjects have sought since the beginning of the *Book*. She is the purely objective, that which depends on no *mete* and therefore transcends semiosis.

Her face is a place that forbids the signifier:

> And yet moreover, thogh alle thoo
> That ever levede were not alyve,
> Ne sholde have *found to diskryve*
> Yn al hir face a *wikked sygne*,
> For hit was sad, symple, and benygne. (ll. 914–918)

("And yet moreover, all those who ever lived could not have been able to describe in all her face a wicked sign, for it was sober, simple, and benign.")

Though *diskryve* may seem to mean "descry" or "discern," there is good reason to say that it means "describe." For a few lines earlier the Man uses the same word to describe the indescribability of the lady's face:

> "But which a visage had she thertoo!
> Allas, myn herte ys wonder woo
> That I ne kan *discryven* hyt;
> Me lakketh both Englyssh and wit." (ll. 895–898)

("But what a face she had as well! Alas, my heart is wondrously sad because I cannot describe it; I lack both English and wit.")

In any case, her face is a place without signification. Her face is no place for the *scryveyn*—the scribe or writer—to exercise his craft. No wicked signs may be found inscribed on her face, and thus she is the opposite of Fortune, idol of false representation. Insofar as the face is traditionally analogous to the sign (and the heart to the thing), to say that her face is without a sign is to say that her face is without a face. Her face is without figure, and she is faceless. In short, this lady is blank—a point to which we shall return momentarily.

What the Man claims to see in looking at her is the absence of the rhetorical or semiotic—the absence of his own mode of being. This is not to say that she is entirely without language. Rather, her language does not come from the outside, from elsewhere as if *another wyghte* had inscribed signs upon her face, but from within, from its foundation in the heart. Thus her speech is said to be a sort of edifice solidly built on a stable place of interior depth:

> "And which a goodely, softe speche
> Had that swete, my lyves leche!
> So frendly, and so wel *ygrounded*,
> Up al *resoun* so wel *yfounded*." (ll. 919–920)

("And what a good, soft speech that sweet lady had, my life's physician! So friendly, and so well grounded, upon all reason so well founded.")

The lady is figured as a constructed space in whose depths, inner chamber, or heart resides the very principle of Truth:

> "And I dar seyn and swere hyt wele—
> That *Trouthe* hymselfe over al and alle
> Had chose hys maner principalle
> In hir, that was his restyng place." (ll. 1002–1005)
>
> ("And I dare say and swear it well—that Truth himself over each and everybody had chosen his principal residence in her, who was his resting place.")

She is the *maner*, the manor or house of Truth, whose *restyng place* or bedroom is the inner chamber of her heart. Her language, says the Man, originates from and is contained within this manorial fortress of truth, and thus she is protected from contamination by the false language of others.

Let us remark in passing on the troubling power that this personification of Truth wields against those who would see the Man's third telling of his story as the renunciation of allegory and the inauguration of realist, historical narration. And this Truth is not the only allegorical personification that signals the continued persistence of false representation or semiosis in the Man's biographical tale: elsewhere in this supposedly anti- or post-allegorical tale the Man speaks, in the manner of personification allegory, of both Fortune (811) and Youth (797). And the *lady swete* herself is no lady but rather is meant to be the personification of a proper self-integrity or unity that precedes the duplicity of writing. When the Man tells us the lady's name, which is itself, as we shall see, an allegorical sign, it is clear that in speaking of her he says one thing and means another. To argue that the Man eventually tells his story in a straightforward or realist manner is to remain blind to the very highly allegorical quality of this telling. Just as lyric language was carried over to or was not purged from the Man's allegory about the game of chess against Fortune, so allegorical language is carried over to or is not purged from his biographical narration. And with this language of Fortune is brought the pestilent language of song, which plagues the Man's story and rules our reading in the end.

The lady's name is White. This name, says the Man, is proper: it properly corresponds, in good cratylistic fashion, to her essence:

> "And goode faire *White* she hete,
> That was my lady name ryghte,
> She was both faire and bryghte:
> She hadde not hir name wronge." (ll. 948–951)

(And she was named good fair White, that was my lady's proper name. She was both fair and bright: she was not wrongly named.)

We shall leave aside for the moment the fact that the lady's name is not in fact a proper name (it is, rather, a sort of *senhal* or sign that does not fully disclose historical identity and that may thus be the place of semiotic substitution). The Man here claims that her name properly discloses her being. In the Man's view, the sign that names her is appropriate, properly belongs to her—unlike the signs appropriated by the *jongleur*, which always belong to someone else. Indeed, the Man contends that White is defined by her own name, by the language that is properly hers. She comes to stand for a self-contained semiotic system in which meaning is self-determined and value self-defined:

"She loved so wel hir oune name." (l. 1018)

("She loved so well her own name.")

She—who will have nothing to do with the *wikked sygne*, with the language of others—desires and is granted her own language, an autonomous language comprised of a single sign that properly reveals her essence. She is that which rightly refers only to herself, that which depends on no *mete* for her value and which knows no lack:

"I knewe on hir noon other lack."

("I knew about her that she lacked nothing other.")

The Man sees her as the language of the *oon*, a language in which there is but a single Word, which is White.

Yet her name, as scholars tell us, does refer to something beside or outside herself. For she is quite reasonably supposed to represent Blanche, the Duchess of Lancaster, recently deceased wife of Chaucer's patron John of Gaunt. That "white" is a translation of the Old French *blanc* is indisputable, nor would anyone doubt that we are supposed to think that the *Book*'s White represents Blanche. Still, there may be those who would dispute that Blanche represents the White of the *Book*, the Blank parchment prior to the inscription upon its face of wicked signs.[28]

The Man says that he himself was, prior to his initiation into the order of particularized desire, ready and able to fall in love—and this readiness made the Man resemble that blank book or prepared parchment upon which nothing is written:

> "Paraunter I was therto most able,
> As a *white walle* or a *table*,
> For hit ys redy to cachche and take
> Al that men wil theryn make,
> Whethir so men wil *portreye* or peynt." (ll. 779–783)

> ("As it happened I was for that [desire] quite prepared, as is a white wall or a tablet, for it is ready to catch and take all that men will thereupon make, whether they will portray or paint.")

Ironically—let us mention in passing—it is upon seeing White that the story of the Man's love affair is written. White is the ink that fills the Man in Black's book. Now, if the man was a sort of *white walle* or *tabula rasa* prior to the inscription upon him of a certain desire for a certain lady, White is instead a *tabula* that remains permanently *rasa*, remains uninscribed, remains a *white walle* or blank slate untainted by *fals portrayture*. If there is any doubt that this passage concerning the Man's adolescent blankness suggests the blankness of Blanche as well, this doubt is dispelled near the *Book*'s very end, in the line that, scholars agree, cryptically spells out the identity of the Man's lady:

> With that me thoghte that this kynge
> Gan homwarde for to ryde
> Unto a place was there besyde,
> Which was from us but a lyte,
> A *longe castel* with *walles white*,
> Be Seynt Johan, on a riche hille. (ll. 1314–1319)

> (With that I thought that this king began to ride home, to a neighboring place that was but a little distance away, a long castel with white walls, by Saint John, on a rich hill.)

The phrase *longe castel* refers anagrammatically to "Lancaster," and thus the line that ends in *walles white* refers to Blanche, Duchess of Lancaster. In the next verse, by the way, is hidden the name of John of Gaunt, who was Earl of Richmond prior to his marriage to Blanche: one substitutes the Old French *mont*, which translates *hille*, and one finds *riche mont* or "Richmond."²⁹ If Chaucer is here, according to philological consensus, playing cryptic, anagrammatical, and bilingual games, why could he not compose in this manner elsewhere and indeed throughout the *Book*? Upon what is founded the authority to exile significant linguistic effects from the domain of philological fact?

But—after this excursion meant to prove that Blanche is the *white walle*—let us return to our reading of the previous passage. The fact that Blanche is a blank slate or *tabula rasa* may be taken in two ways. First, she may have no need of the *wykked sygne* that is absent from her face. She who loves so well her own name may have nothing to do with inscription, *fals portrayture*, false representation, the language of Fortune, allegory, song, and others. White may remain blank because her value does not depend upon her being written on, does not depend upon her subjection to a language that comes from elsewhere. Her continued blankness would represent—and this fact in itself is ironic—her freedom from or immunity to signification, and her whiteness would be a sign of her extra-linguistic and, may we say, pre-scriptive identity. Her value would be a function of her self-definition: since she is the total absence of the sign, she cannot be inserted into a system of semiotic exchange. The Man's story of winning White's love would thus recount his attainment of the truly Other, the Real, the *Oon* that has no *mete*. This would be the story of the Man's own conquest of *oon*-ness, his acquisition of the language of the heart, the successful cure of his evening sickness as he gains the capacity properly to tell the story that is uniquely his—a story whose value does not depend upon and which could not be exchanged for other stories in the semiotic system of literary discourse, a story that would appear as

The soleyn fenix of Arabye;
For ther levyth never *but oon*. (ll. 982–983)

(The solitary phoenix of Araby, for there never lives but one.)

and a story whose Truth would be prior to inscription.

Or, the blankness of Blanche may be taken to mean something entirely different, for it raises the specter of a danger that will come to haunt the Man's story and to put in question the objective reality or the extra-discursive existence of that which the story supposedly represents. For it is possible that Blanche is truly blank, not *oon* but rather *noon*, none, nothing, a cipher. White may be, like that *white walle* of which the man speaks,

>   . . . redy to cachche and take
>   Al that men wil theryn *make*. (ll. 781–782)
>
>   (. . .ready to catch and take all that men will thereupon make.)

White, whose face is without figure, may in fact have no language of her own. She may be like that blank parchment prepared to receive that which others *make* ("compose"). Blanche—or should I say Blank?—can readily be written on, appropriated, used by any and everybody. Thus her value depends upon others, upon her submission to the power of the common tongue. She comes to resemble nothing more than the *jongleur*, who is merely a convenient blank place wherein may be recorded the language of *another wyght*, of someone else. The mere fact that both the Man in Black and Blanche are appropriately signified by the phrase *white walle* means that there is no clearcut difference between them, that she resembles him, that she is not truly the autonomous *oon*, that she is not purely objective. And our suspicion of a hidden similitude between the Man and his lady is confirmed when we realize that, just as he is both black and white (he is white insofar as he resembles a white wall), so is she both White and Blanche. Her resemblance to the man means that she, like the Man, is always ready to *cachche and take* the *portrayture* of others. And she does, in the end, catch the Man's evening sickness.

If White loves her own name, unfortunately for her this name is promiscuously unfaithful. For in the very verses that speak of White's devotion to her own name, this name names any and every *other wyght*:

>   "Therwith she lovede so wel ryght,
>   She wrong do wolde to *no wyght*.
>   *No wyght* myght doo hir noo shame,
>   She loved so wel hir oune name.
>   Hyr lust to holde *no wyght* in honde,
>   Ne, be thou siker, she wolde not fonde
>   To holde *no wyght* in balaunce." (ll. 1015–1021)
>
>   ("Also she loved so rightly that she would do wrong to no one. No one could do her any shame, she loved so well her own name. She did not desire to deceive anyone, nor, you may be sure, would she contrive to hold anyone in the balance.")

The difference between *White* as that which names the singular, phoenix-like *Oon* and *wyght* as that which names, generally, any person whosoever is the difference between the two notions of subjectivity that have ruled our readings. And this is the same difference as that between the two alternative meanings of her blankness, which signifies either her autonomous objectification or her subjection to the language of others. She cannot keep her name in her private possession, since it is properly the name of any *wyght*. The name *White* is significantly absent from the central verse of the passage I have just cited: it has been dissolved to precipitate elsewhere, in the outlying verses, as *no wyght*. White has been transformed into no one, into a sign potentially appropriated by any and everyone.

And this dissolution or disappearance of White is precisely what happens near the end of the *Book* and at the end of the Man's story: she loses her objective, autonomous identity as her blankness is defaced by, we imagine, the figures traced by the Man in Black's ink. After telling of his courtship—which begins with his composition of a love song whose reference to the real she fails to recognize and ends with his act of "saying," of telling her the true story of his desire (and thus this courtship mimics the passage from song to story attempted everywhere in the *Book*)—the Man tells of his final possession of the *oon* whom he had sought:

> "She took me in hir governaunce.
> Therwyth she was alway so trewe,
> Our joye was ever *ylyche* newe.
> Oure hertes wern so *evene a payre*
> That never nas that *oon* contrayre
> To that other for noo woo.
> Forsothe, *ylyche* they suffred thoo
> *Oo* blysse, and eke *oo* sorwe bothe,
> *Ylyche* they were bothe glad and wrothe.
> *Al* was us *oon*, without were.
> And thus *we* lyved ful many a yere." (ll. 1286–1296)

("She took me in her governance. Thereupon she was always so true, our joy was ever like new. Our hearts were such an even pair that one was never contrary to the other for any woe. Truly, alike they both suffered—one bliss and also one sorrow. Alike they both were glad and angry. All was one with us, without doubt. And thus we lived for many years.")

Clearly what predominates, here in the end of the *Book* as it has throughout, is the insistence of an even *oon*-ness, of a "one" that is in fact "two," "we," or "all." Indeed it is not difficult to discern near the end of this passage another cryptic and anagrammatical inscription of *Alcyoon*—she who gets around from the beginning to the end of the *Book*. The relation between the Man in Black and White is in the end one of *ylyche*-ness—of likeness or resemblance. She who, according to the Man, is like no other is here defined only insofar as she is inextricably bound up with her relation to her *mete*, her "equal." She, who is supposed to be the self-standing, phoenix-like *oon*, is consumed by her insertion into a relational duo. She has indeed, like that blank tablet she is, been ready to *cachche and take* all that the Man would *make*. And what she has caught and taken, what has become the wicked signification inscribed on her heretofore figureless face, is nothing but the Man's own language, a lyric language driven by a chronic propensity toward the evening out of difference. For if she here remains anything like an *oon*, she is that *oon* that is simultaneously an "all" or a "we." Her *mete*-less or matchless *oon*-ness has given way to the *oon*-ness of the pair, of the indivisible twosome—an *oon* that always speaks the voice of another. She is now clearly that *white walle* that catches and reflects his own evenness. To say that she reflects his evenness is to say that she is now a "we," the Old French *on*, "they"—the plural pronominal unit that is the singing subject, who when it sings "I" is always singing with the voice of *another wyght*. The Man's search for *oon*-ness, his quest for a progressive discourse that would represent a difference, has come up short, and what he gets turns out to be more of the same: he gets his *mete*, his equal. She is equal to him because she is no longer Blank or Blanche but rather the *portrayture* of his semiotic singing self that he has made upon her face. The man's *y sawgh oon* ("I saw one")—the remark, we recall, that signified the autonomy of the object of his vision (and, by implication, the objective reality of the prior historical "occasion" or event later represented, *razo*-like and after the fact, by the act of narration)—is discredited, since what he sees in Blank is more of himself: the even, the all-one, the plural subject, the I which is II. Instead the man should have more truthfully said *I saw I*—the remark, we recall, that signified Chaucer's inability to see an external place of autonomous, prediscursive objectivity.

If the Man and his lady form, as he says they do, *so evene a payre*, then the pair they form—a pair we may signify by the couplet White/Black—is the very exemplar of the oxymoronic. The coupling of White and the Man in Black recapitulates the *Book*'s opening couplet, which—as we remarked near the outset—coupled the normally incompatible *lyghte* and *nyghte*. And at the culmination of his supposedly singular story the Man speaks in the generalized lyric language of oxymora: *Oo blysse, and eke oo sorwe bothe*. Thus the very story of the Man in Black, which—according to the view that sees the *Book* as championing a progressive renunciation of lyric resemblance and conventionality in favor of novel distinction and realist narrative—is meant to spell story's triumph over song, instead turns out ultimately to celebrate the return of the most conventional of lyric conventions. The heart laid bare by the Man in Black's story is not singularly different but is the heart of all lyric singers.

As the dream and the *Book* come to an end, it becomes clear that neither has left behind the Octovyen realm of resemblance. After the Man's portrait of his evening relationship with White, her death is—like the death of Alcyone in Chaucer's retelling of the Ovidian tale—summarily stated in a single line:

"She ys ded."—"Nay!"—"Yis, be my trouthe" (l. 1309)

("She is dead."—"No!"—"Yes, truly")

The entire argument that the *Book* progresses toward the inauguration of a biographical, realistic narrative discourse must—since nothing that precedes or follows can be considered "realistic"—rest on the weight of this single moment.[30] Yet this narration is so minimal as to represent not the triumph but rather the absence of narration. What is not told in the *Book* is this story of the death of Gaunt's wife. Like the story of Alcyone's death, this story is, as it were, squeezed out or displaced by the mass of surrounding lyric language. The *Book* exiles true narration from its domain. For just after this supposed breakthrough of novel or realist discourse we are reminded under whose rule we continue to be:

With that me thoghte that *this kynge*
Gan homwarde for to ryde. (ll. 1314–1315)

(With that I thought that this king began to ride homeward.)

This *kynge* is that Octovyen whose empire of evening is the locus of Chaucer's dream. And as the *Book* comes to a close we see the continued insistence of Octovyen's arithmetical discourse:

. . . But thus hyt fille,
Ryght thus me mette, as I yow telle,

> That in the castell ther was a belle,
> As hyt hadde smyten oures *twelve*.
> Therewith I awook myselve
> And fonde me lyinge in my bedde,
> And the book that I hadde redde
> Of Alcione and Seyes the kyng,
> And of the goddes of slepynge,
> I fond hyt in myn honde ful *evene*.
> Thoghte I, "Thys ys so queynt a sw*evene*
> That I wol, be processe of tyme,
> Fond to put this sw*evene* in ryme
> As I kan best, and that a*noon*."
> This was my swevene; now hit ys *doon*. (ll. 1320–1334)

(. . . but thus it happened, I dreamed exactly this, as I tell you, that there was a bell in the castle, and it struck the hour of twelve. Then I woke up and found myself lying in bed, and I found right in my hand the book that I had read about Alcione and King Seyes and about the gods of sleep. I thought, "this is such a strange dream that I will, in time, try to put this dream in rhyme, and right away." This was my dream; now it is done.)

If the book tells of Chaucer's aquisition of the language of the individual *oon*, such a story is nowhere to be seen at the end of the *Book*. The even still prevails as Chaucer awakes without having found the cure for his evening sickness. For—far from tracing a progressive, linear trajectory toward a positive gain—the *Book*'s compositional temporality is songlike in its circularity. That is, Chaucer announces at the end that he will begin writing the *Book*. And what he begins writing is, as we saw in the beginning, the lyric language of *another wyght*, Froissart. Clearly Chaucer has not learned the writing lesson concerning the triumph of realist or historical discourse supposedly formulated in his dream. After the dream he is still that singing subject who lacks the physician *but oon*. And, fittingly, the *Book*'s closing couplet rings with the sound of evening: the *noon* and *doon* signify the "none" and the "duo," the zero and the two, which surround and falsify every *oon* in Chaucer's Book of Blanks and Deuces.[31]

Notes

Introduction

1. Georg Simmel, "Das Individuum und die Freiheit," in *Brücke und Tür: Essays des Philosophen zur Geschichte, Religion, Kunst und Gesellschaft* (Stuttgart: Köhler, 1957), p. 260. Simmel died in 1918, and this essay was only published posthumously. The English translation is from Georg Simmel, *On Individuality and Social Forms: Selected Writings*, ed. Donald N. Levine (Chicago and London: University of Chicago Press, 1971), pp. 217–218.

2. Jakob Burckhardt, *The Civilization of the Renaissance in Italy*, trans. S. G. C. Middlemore (London: Phaidon Press, 1955), p. 81.

3. For an account of modern criticism's false construction of a uniform or monolithic medieval Other against which it defines the diversity and complexity of the Renaissance—an account that puts into question the novelty of Renaissance individualism, see Lee Patterson, "On the Margin: Postmodernism, Ironic History, and Medieval Studies," *Speculum* 65 (1990): 87–108.

4. See Georg Simmel's trenchant analysis of the paradoxes of the "fashion system"—chief among which is that the desire to be different is the sign of conformity—in his "Die Mode," in *Philosophische Kultur* (3rd ed., Potsdam: Kiepenheuer, 1923), pp. 31–64 (English translation in Simmel, *On Individuality and Social Forms*, pp. 294–323).

5. Dante Alighieri, *De Vulgari Eloquentia*, I, 16; trans. Robert S. Haller in *Literary Criticism of Dante Alighieri* (Lincoln and London: University of Nebraska Press, 1973), p. 28.

6. Ibid., I, 9 (Haller, p. 15): "They invented it [i.e., grammar], then, out of a fear that, because of the change in language which issues from the will of individuals, we would be able to understand either not at all or at least imperfectly the authoritative ideas and histories of the ancients or of peoples whom the difference of place makes different from us."

7. Dante remarks (I, 19; Haller, p. 30) that "our illustrious vernacular wanders like a stranger": the voice of courtly lyric is an alien voice, the voice of an unknown stranger.

8. Jonathan D. Culler, *On Deconstruction: Theory and Criticism After Structuralism* (Ithaca, NY: Cornell University Press, 1982), p. 120.

9. On the medieval notion of the pronoun as signifying pure or undetermined Being (i.e., God), see Giorgio Agamben, *Il linguaggio e la morte: un seminario sul lungo della negatività* (Turin: Giulio Einaudi, 1982). For Priscian's text, which is cited by Agamben, see C. Thurot, "Extraits de divers manuscrits latins pour servir à l'histoire des doctrines grammaticales au moyen âge," in *Notices et Extraits des Manuscrits de la Bibliothèque Nationale*, vol. 22 (Paris, 1974).

10. As Agamben remarks (*Il linguaggio e la morte*, p. 63; English translation mine), "the name *qui est* ["he who is"], formed from a pronoun and the verb 'to be,' is thought [in the Middle Ages] to be the most adequate and 'absolute' name of God." Agamben continues (p. 64) by citing Thomas Aquinas:

> it is necessary to say that other names [i.e., nouns rather than pronouns] signify being according to a certain further determination; thus the name "scholar" expresses a certain being: but this name *qui est* signifies absolute being and is not determined by any other specification that is added to it; this is why Damascenes says that it does not signify what God is (the "what" of God), but, in a sense, the infinite and nearly undetermined sea of substance.

The purely pronominal name does not specify; its significance remains indeterminate and potentially infinite, and its qualities, remaining unnamed, are limitless.

11. A. J. Minnis, *Medieval Theory of Authorship* (2nd ed.; Philadelphia: University of Pennsylvania Press, 1988), p. 132.

12. Dante, *De Vulg. Eloq.*, II, 1 (Haller, pp. 31–32).

13. It is customary in recent criticism to reject the term "courtly" (as in "courtly love") on the grounds that it is an invention of nineteenth-century philology. If I retain it, this is because Dante himself uses the term. For Dante, "courtly" means "general" or "universal": "And my reason for calling it courtly is this, that if we Italians had a royal court, this vernacular would be spoken in the palace. For if a court is the common house for the whole kingdom and the august ruler of each part of the kingdom, it is right that *everything common to the whole and not peculiar to any part* should frequent it and reside in it. There is no other dwelling worthy of so great a resident, so great, that is, as the vernacular to which I refer would certainly seem to be" (*De Vulg.*, I, 18; Haller, p. 30; emphasis added). The courtly language is the *public* language, that which properly belongs to each member of the *gens* yet is not the private property of any individual. The only "quality" signified by such a language is that one common to all and particular to no one—namely, pure, undetermined, undifferentiated Being. The least illustrious of the lesser vernaculars (i.e., non-grammatical or non-courtly language) is "that which belongs to one household alone" (*De Vulg.*, I, 19; Haller, p. 31). That is, the private language of the individual (the language spoken in but one single household) is, in relation to the public or courtly language, at the opposite end of the spectrum of grammaticality. (For Dante, "grammaticality" means language's capacity to resist historical change.)

14. Cf. Agamben, *Il linguaggio e la morte*, pp. 124–125 (English translation mine; slightly modified for clarity):

> Later [i.e., after the troubadours] . . . love became a feeling, one among others that the poet could, eventually, put into verse. The modern idea of a lived experience as a material that the poet must express in his poem is born precisely from this misunderstanding concerning the experience of the art of composition of the troubadours. . . . (The error consisting in seeing a biographical experience in the composition is so old that it is already at the origin of the first

attempt to explain Provençal lyric: the *razos* and the *vidas* composed between the thirteenth and fourteenth centuries, in the Provençal language but in an Italian *milieu*. In these brief narratives, which also represent the earliest example of Romance biography, there takes place a veritable reversal of the relation between poetry and life which characterized the poetic experience of the troubadours.... But, on second thought, the authors of the *razos* were only radicalizing the process which the troubadours themselves had inaugurated: they construct a biographical anecdote to explain a poem, but the lived experience is here invented, "found," beginning with the poeticized and not the reverse, as would be the case when the troubadours project had been forgotten.

This "forgetting of the project of the troubadours"—that is, the birth of a way of thinking that locates the origin, source, or foundation of song in the lived experience of a specific, named individual, is precisely what I am calling the "death of the troubadour." The troubadour, who is no one in particular, who always appears as a stranger or an unknown entity, dies when inserted into *historia*, when he becomes someone special.

15. Jean Renart, *Le Roman de la Rose ou de Guillaume de Dole*, ed. Félix Lecoy (Paris: Honoré Champion, 1979), ll. 8–23. Throughout this book, all translations are mine unless otherwise indicated.

Chapter 1: Song as Langue

1. On the politics of the troubadours, see Martin Aurell, *La vielle et l'épée: troubadours et politique au XIII siècle* (Paris: Éditions Aubier Montaigne, 1989).

2. Here follows a very brief, by no means all-inclusive, bibliographical history of the notion that we are calling courtly lyric's "grammatical ego"—the notion of the anonymity or impersonality of the lyric *je*: Robert Guiette, "D'une poésie formelle en France au moyen âge," *Revue des Sciences Humaines* (April–June 1949): 61–68; Roger Dragonetti, *La technique poétique des trouvères dans la chanson courtoise: contribution à l'étude de la rhétorique médiévale* (Bruges: Rijksuniversiteit te Gent, 1960); Paul Zumthor, *Essai de poétique médiévale* (Paris: Éditions du Seuil, 1972) and *Langue, texte, énigme* (Paris: Éditions du Seuil, 1975); Eugene Vance, "The Châtelain de Coucy: Enunciation and Story in *Trouvère* Lyric," in Vance, *Mervelous Signals: Poetics and Sign Theory in the Middle Ages* (Lincoln: University of Nebraska Press, 1986), pp. 86–110; Jean-Charles Huchet, *L'amour discourtois* (Toulouse: Éditions Privat, 1987).

3. If courtly love lyric is marked by its lack of historical, individual subjectivity, this lack does not mean that it differs fundamentally from other medieval literary modes. On the contrary, courtly love lyric magnifies the tendency of all medieval literature to present a generalized, grammatical, rather than historical speaking subject, and thus we may begin to see why the *chanson* was considered, as Dragonetti suggests (*La technique poétique*, p. 545), "comme le plus noble des genres, celui donc qui incarne au plus haut point l'idée du poème dans la conscience du

public et du poète." In other words, the Old Provençal *canso* and the Old French *chanson* were the most obviously rhetorical literary types in an age that was keenly aware of and that highly esteemed the rhetoricity of poetry. The fact that the fictional "I" who sings the song is no one in particular reflects the historical conditions of poetic performance: any number of actual singers, indeed anyone whosoever, may have performed a particular song. Thus the "I" of courtly lyric is a general figure for the speaker of the medieval text in any genre, who similarly is most frequently no one in particular but rather a formal function of the text:

> Normalement transmise (par chanteur, récitant ou lecteur public) de bouche à oreille, l'oeuvre poétique médiévale possède un énonciateur concret, visuellement perceptible (alors qu'elle-même ne l'est pas), mais qui change, en principe, à chaque nouvelle audition. Si l'auteur (peut-être identique à l'un des récitants successifs) a fait d'un *je* le sujet de l'énoncé, ce *je* fonctionne comme une forme virtuelle, dont l'actualisation varie selon les circonstances: il est peu vraisemblable que l'auditeur médiéval ait pu l'interpréter dans un sens autobiographique. (Zumthor, *Langue, texte, énigme*, p. 168)

4. Dragonetti:

> *Exprimer* signifie dorénavant pour l'écrivain, sentir ou voir en dehors des formes de sensibilité et des visions imposées aux hommes pendant des siècles par la rhétorique, s'écarter par conséquent des sentiments communs, et poursuivre en soi une image assez unique pour que l'expression qui en résulte ne puisse être comparable à nulle autre. L'originalité et l'effet de sincérité, tel est dorénavant le double but que se propose d'atteindre l'écrivain romantique. Ecrire, c'est donc avant tout, remonter la pente de la rhétorique, et en tout cas, sinon pratiquement, du moins en théorie, faire profession de rupture avec le lieu commun. Or, les *lieux* avaient constitué pendant des siècles le moyen, la substance et le fondement de la littérature. Ils avaient servi à l'éclosion des plus belles oeuvres lyriques. . . . Le lecteur a pu se rendre compte qu'ils assument un rôle essentiel dans la poésie courtoise. Mais la conception romantique de lyrisme a si fortement imprégné la sensibilité esthétique contemporaine, que la poésie courtoise s'est vue elle-même assimilée aux oeuvres dont l'expression individuelle faisait tout le prix. Elle fut appréciée ou dépréciée en fonction d'un système étranger à ses conventions propres. (*La technique poétique*, p. 541)

5. "Le *je* du grand chant courtois . . . fournit un modèle à l'influence duquel aucun des discours «littéraires» des XII, XIII, XIV siècles n'échappa entièrement" (Zumthor, *Langue, texte, énigme*, p. 172).

6. See Elizabeth Wilson Poe, *From Poetry to Prose in Old Provençal: The Emergence of the "Vidas," the "Razos," and the "Razos de trobar"* (Birmingham, AL: Summa Publications, 1984), pp. 78–79.

7. J. H. Marshall, ed., *The "Razos de trobar" of Raimon Vidal and Associated Texts* (London: Oxford University Press, 1972), p. 2.

8. Poe, *From Poetry to Prose*, p. 78.

9. Marshall, *"Razos de trobar"*, p. 2.
10. See Joan Ferrante, "Was Vernacular Poetic Practice a Response to Latin Language Theory?" *Romance Philology* 35 (1982): 586–600.
11. Marshall, *"Razos de trobar"*, p. lxxxv.
12. Ibid., p. 22.
13. Ibid., p. 4.
14. Raimon's claim that "no one entirely encompasses" song is a striking anticipation of Saussure's claim (*Course in General Linguistics*, ed. Charles Bally and Albert Sechehaye in collaboration with Albert Reidlinger, trans. Wade Baskin [New York: Philosophical Library, 1959], p. 14) that the grammatical system of language "is not complete in any speaker" but rather "exists perfectly only within a collectivity."
15. Émile Benveniste:

> There is no concept "I" that incorporates all the *I*'s that are uttered at every moment in the mouths of all speakers, in the sense that there is a concept "tree" to which all individual uses of *tree* refer. . . . Then, what does *I* refer to? To something very peculiar which is exclusively linguistic: *I* refers to the act of individual discourse in which it is pronounced, and by this it designates the speaker. It is a term that cannot be identified except in what we have called elsewhere an instance of discourse and that has only a momentary reference. (*Problems in General Linguistics*, trans. Mary Elizabeth Meek [Coral Gables, FL: University of Miami Press, 1971], p. 226)

16. The possibility that Raimon uses "no one" to signify a grammatical subjectivity is perfectly consonant with a longstanding ludic medieval literary tradition. Mikhail Bakhtin:

> The most interesting example of this carnivalesque game of negation is the famous "History of Nemo," *Historia de Nemine*, one of the most unusual pages of Latin recreative literature. . . . Radulfus Glaber, a French monk, composed the *Historia de Nemine* in the form of a sermon. *Nemo* is a hero whose nature, position, and exceptional powers are equal to those of the second person of the Trinity, that is, the Son of God. Radulfus discovered the great *Nemo* in a number of Biblical, Evangelical, and liturgical texts, as well as in Cicero, Horace, and other writers of antiquity; the word *nemo* (nobody), which in Latin is used as a negation, was interpreted by Radulfus as a proper noun. For instance, in the Scriptures *nemo deum vidit* (nobody has seen God) in his interpretation became "Nemo saw God." Thus, everything impossible, inadmissible, inaccessible, is, on the contrary, permitted for *Nemo*. Thanks to this transposition, *Nemo* acquires the majestic aspect of being almost equal to God, endowed with unique, exceptional powers, knowledge (he knows that which no one else knows) and extraordinary freedom (he is allowed that which nobody is permitted). . . . Hence the exceptional attraction of this game for medieval man. All the endless gloomy sentences: "no one may," "no one can," "no one knows," "no one dares" are transformed into gay words: "Nemo

may," "Nemo can," "Nemo knows," "Nemo must," "Nemo dares." . . . No one can have two wives, but *Nemo* is allowed bigamy. According to the Benedictine rule, it was forbidden to talk after supper, but *Nemo* was an exception, he could talk (*post completorium Nemo loquatur*). (*Rabelais and His World*, trans. Helene Iswolsky [Bloomington: Indiana University Press, 1984], pp. 413–414)

17. Marshall, *"Razos de trobar"*, p. 2 (emphasis added).
18. Dante, *De. Vulg.* I, 16 (Haller, p. 28).

Chapter 2: "Everyone Loves Thus"

1. On the *envoi* and its absence from trouvère lyric, and for the suggestion that this absence signifies a strategic suppression of the proper noun, see Roger Dragonetti, *La technique poétique des trouvères dans la chanson courtoise: contribution à l'étude de la rhétorique médiévale* (Bruges: Rijksuniversiteit te Gent, 1960), pp. 304–306.

2. Peter Haidu proposes that

insofar as we can use the text as the basis on which to construct a notion of the self as it might have been lived or experienced in the twelfth century (even though it may not have been formulated in our terms, or formulated at all), it is a loose self, one whose subordinate parts are not bound to remain subsumed and enclosed under and within the overriding category of the self. It is a notion of selfhood allowing a simultaneous presence *in* and presence *out* of the normal bounds of the self, a dissociation of self and consciousness of self that is quite remarkable from our point of view. In terms of contemporary theory, it is a notion of selfhood that is not so much the product of having been decentered as one whose *decenteredness* is an assumption. There may be some similarity to the sense of dispersal of self in our modern experience, but that similarity is to be located at opposite ends of the historical process of development. The contemporary sense of dispersal occurs as a result of a historical process of deconstruction of the self and its surrounding ideological context. The medieval sense of dispersal is probably to be attributed to the opposite historical process of constructing the notion of the self out of members already disjected. It is as if we found ourselves, in the closing years of the twentieth century, at the same level on a developmental triangle as did the men of the twelfth, only we are moving in a descending direction at the vertical leg opposite the one they were ascending. We are perhaps living the liquidation of a process they began, and it may be their creation we are deconstructing. ("Text and History: The Semiosis of Twelfth-Century Lyric as Sociohistorical Phenomenon," *Semiotica* 33 [1981]: 26)

3. "Desconfortez, ploins de dolour et d'ire," ll. 1–8, in Emmanuèle Baumgartner and Françoise Ferrand, eds., *Poèmes d'amour des XII et XIII siècles* (Paris: Union Générale d'Éditions, 1983), p. 40.

4. For an inventory of songs lamenting the undifferentiation of the true and false languages of desire, see Dragonetti, *La technique poétique*, pp. 21–30.

5. On the *losengier*'s status as the literary rival of the courtly poet, see Emmanuèle Baumgartner, "Trouvères et *Losengiers*," *Cahiers de Civilisation Médiévale* 25 (1982): 175–176: "Ils [i.e., the *losengiers*] tiennent sur l'amour un discours faux—c'est du moins le trouvère qui le déclare tel—mais strictement identique en apparence au discours vrai. . . . [L]es *losengiers* deviennent ainsi les rivaux, mais en écriture, du trouvère authentique. Ils sont ceux qui, parce que le langage est un bien commun à tous les hommes . . . , récupèrent et s'appropient les mêmes schèmes formels, les mêmes thèmes . . . , mais sans les ressourcer à un sentiment vrai." On the *losengiers* as an undifferentiated mass to which everyone, from the perspective of someone else, may be seen to belong, see Erich Koehler, "Observations historiques et sociologiques sur la poésie des troubadours," *Cahiers de Civilisation Médiévale* 7 (1964): 43: "chacun est toujours le *lauzengier* de quelqu'un."

6. Heidegger argues that

> in utilizing public means of transport and in making use of information services such as the newspaper, every Other is like the next. This Being-with-one-another dissolves one's own Dasein completely into the kind of Being of "the others," in such a way, indeed, that the Others, as distinguishable and explicit, vanish more and more. In this inconspicuousness and unascertainability, the real dictatorship of the "they" is unfolded. We take pleasure and enjoy ourselves as *they* take pleasure; we read, see, and judge about literature and art as *they* see and judge; likewise we shrink back from the "great mass" as *they* shrink back. (*Being and Time*, trans. John Macquarrie and Edward Robinson [New York: Harper and Row, 1962], pp. 126–127)

The courtly singer's violent aversion to the *losengiers* is nothing other than this shrinking back from the all too familiar "great mass."

7. Conon de Béthune, "Belle doce dame chiere," in *Les Chansons de Conon de Béthune*, ed. Axel Wallensköld (Paris: Champion, 1921), p. 12.

8. Wallensköld (*Conon*, pp. xii–xiii) says that the love songs of Conon de Béthune are of two categories, "celles où le poète apparaît comme l'amant fidèle et humble . . . et celles où il accuse sa dame de trahison et de félonie." He continues with the following remark concerning the song in question: "le couplet I appartient à la première catégorie et le couplet II à le seconde, ce qui a fait supposer, non sans raison, qu'il y a là *deux* chansons incomplètes, dont l'une serait l'imitation extérieure de l'autre." And he later says (p. 27), concerning the same song, that the "second couplet du texte est peut-être le fragment d'une autre chanson parodiant le premier couplet."

9. For examples of this strategy, see Dragonetti, *La technique poétique*, pp. 55–59.

10. Marie-Claire Zai, ed., *Les chansons courtoises de Chrétien de Troyes* (Berne and Frankfurt: Lang and Lang, 1974); cited in Haidu, p. 13.

11. See Haidu, pp. 13–18, for his reading of this stanza.

12. Cf. Jacques Lacan: "Who, then, is this other to whom I am more attached

than to myself, since at the heart of my assent to my own identity it is still he who agitates me?" (*Écrits: A Selection*, trans. Alan Sheridan [New York: Norton, 1977], p. 172). For a brief but quite helpful overview and bibliography of Lacanian criticism of courtly lyric in particular and medieval literature in general, see Eugene Vance, *From Topic to Tale: Logic and Narrativity in the Middle Ages* (Minneapolis: University of Minnesota Press, 1987), pp. xxviii–xxix.

13. See Haidu, pp. 21–26, for his reading of this stanza.

14. Lacan glosses these lines at the beginning of one of his seminars. See Jacques Lacan, *The Four Fundamental Concepts of Psychoanalysis*, trans. Alan Sheridan (New York: Norton, 1977), p. 17. The translation of Aragon is Sheridan's.

15. Pierre Bec, ed., *Anthologie des troubadours* (Paris: Union Générale d'Éditions, 1979), pp. 110–112.

16. "Au titre de l'Autre, la Dame est avant tout un lieu vers lequel tend le désire et le chant qui le supporte. *Lai on es ma volontatz*, dit Bernard de Ventadorn. 'Là est mon désir,' peut-on traduire. . . . *Lai* se tient non seulement l'objet qui suscite le désir, mais le désir lui-même, aliéné au sens le plus littéral du terme car il est situé au lieu de l'Autre" (Jean-Charles Huchet, *L'amour discourtois: la "Fin'amours" chez les premiers troubadours* [Toulouse: Privat, 1987], p. 35).

17. In Old Provençal terminology, *tenso* signifies a song in which two singers carry on a debate concerning a given topic, *cobla* signifies what we would call a "stanza," and *coblas tensonadas* are stanzas that contain two debating voices.

18. Bec, pp. 254–256.

19. "Le descort est en effet un genre qui rompt délibérément la belle ordonnance strophique de la chanson, puisqu'il constitue par définition un ensemble désorganisé, tant du point de vue poétique que musical: ce désordre formel étant d'ailleurs fonctionnellement lié à un certain désarroi psychique et sentimental, réel ou poétiquement valorisé, du troubadour" (Bec, *Anthologie des troubadours*, p. 295).

20. Ibid., p. 258.

21. "De la Dame vient la parole que *je* lui adresse" (Huchet, p. 41).

Chapter 3: The Speculum *of Song*

1. Guillaume de Machaut, *Le Livre du Voir-Dit de Guillaume de Machaut*, ed. Paulin Paris (Paris: Société des Bibliophiles Français, 1875), letter XXVII, p. 201.

2. On the undifferentiation of Machaut and his lady in *Le Voir Dit*, see Jacqueline Cerquiglini, *"Un engin si soutil": Guillaume de Machaut et l'écriture au XIVe siècle* (Geneva and Paris: Éditions Slatkine, 1985), 139–155.

3. Maurice Delbouille, ed., *Le Lai d'Aristote* (Paris: Bibliothèque de la Faculté de Philosophie et Lettres de l'Université de Liège, 1951).

4. Machaut similarly represents the effect of song as an enchantment to which the subject is literally subjected:

> Plus douce que voix de seraine,
> De toute melodie plaine
> Et sa voix, car quant elle *chante*
> Mon cuer endort, mon corps *enchante*,

Ainsi com Fortune *enchantoit*
Ses subgés quant elle *chantoit*
Et les decevoit au fausset.
(*Le Voir dit*, BN fr. 22545, ll. 8303–8309)

(Sweeter than the Siren's voice, full of melody is her voice, for when she sings my heart [or, "self"] sleeps, she enchants my body as Fortune enchants her subjects when she sings and deceives them falsely.)

5. In the glossary to his edition of the *Lai d'Aristote*, Delbouille maintains that *mireors* is a figure of speech and thus must mean other than it says, that the proper meaning here is *chef-d'oeuvre* or *modèle*; so too, the editors and translators of a 1984 Old French/Modern English edition of the tale do not take *mireors* at face value but translate it as "wonder" (*The French Fabliau, BN Ms. 837*, ed. and trans. R. Eichmann and J. Duval [New York: Garland Publishing, 1984]). Why this modern reluctance to take the text at its word? The response lies in the double scandal of specularity, which exposes both the object's non-existence and the subject's objectivity. In fact Aristotle means literally what he says, that the woman whom he sees, not a "*chef-d'oeuvre*" or a "wonder," is a *mirror*, the *speculum* of his own alienated and objectively constituted ego. The modern editors gloss over this transparent truth, turning it into an opacity that can only be resolved by a paraphrase.

6. On the mirror as the object of the courtly lover's desire, and on the undifferentiation of interiority and exteriority in the poetry of the *dolce stil nuovo*, see part three of Giorgio Agamben's very fine *Stanze: la parola e il fantasma nella cultura occidentale* (Turin: Giulio Einaudi, 1977). Agamben argues that the great novelty of courtly love poetry was an epistemological specularity that revealed the unreality of the desired woman, her existence as a phantasm.

7. Jean Renart, *Le Roman de la Rose ou de Guillaume de Dole*, ed. Félix Lecoy (Paris: Honoré Champion, 1979), ll. 329–332.

8. Mikhail Bakhtin, *The Dialogic Imagination: Four Essays*, ed. Michael Holquist, trans. Caryl Emerson and Michael Holquist (Austin: University of Texas Press, 1981).

Chapter 4: The Burgher and the Bird

1. As the twelfth-century writer Walter Map says: "My only fault is that I am alive. I have no intention, however, of correcting this fault by my death." And Map continues: "I know what will happen after I am gone. When I shall be decaying, then, for the first time, it [i.e., his text] shall be salted; and every defect in it will be remedied by my decease, and in the remote future its antiquity will cause the authorship to be credited to me, because, then as now, old copper will be preferred to new gold. . . . In every century its own present has been unpopular, and each age from the beginning has preferred the past to itself" (cited in A. J. Minnis, *Medieval Theory of Authorship*, p. 12).

2. Dante, *De. Vulg.*, II, 8 (Haller, p. 50).

3. *Le vilain et l'oiselet* is printed in Étienne Barbazan, *Le Castoiement, ou*

Instruction, du père à son fils (Paris, 1760); *Le lai de l'oiselet* is printed in Albert Pauphilet, ed., *Poètes et romanciers du moyen âge* (Paris: Gallimard, 1939). I have distinguished the two poems by source in my *ensemble* below.

4. Dante, *De Vulg.*, II, 8 (Haller, pp. 48–49).

5. Saying "mine" and "yours" was regarded in the Middle Ages as a consequence of the desire for private property that resulted in the Fall from Eden: "It was original sin which introduced private property to this world. Men began to lust for the common goods as their own, and to utter those chilling words, 'mine' and 'thine'. When this happened, said John Chrysostom, quarrels and contention arose" (Odd Langholm, *Economics in the Medieval Schools* [Leiden and New York, E. J. Brill, 1992], p. 73). Indeed our *fabliau*, in which the burgher appropriates for himself that birdsong which was previously the "common good" of all who resided in the garden, resounds with obvious echoes of this medieval economic understanding of the Fall from Eden.

6. According to Gianni Vattimo,

> the preliminary understanding of the world which constitutes being-there [i.e., the human subject] is an unthinking and acritical participation in a certain socio-historic world, in its prejudices, its tendencies, its refusals and its "common" way of seeing and judging things. In other words, if we ask what it means to say that being-there always already has a certain understanding [i.e., *fore-knowledge*] of the world, the first answer is that, in fact, being-there always already encounters the world in the light of certain ideas that he has absorbed from the social atmosphere in which he lives. (*Introduzione a Heidegger* [Bari and Rome: Gius. Laterza & Figli, 1971], p. 48 [translation mine])

Vattimo continues:

> For being-there, being-in-the-world is equivalent to being, at the origin, familiar with a totality of meanings. The world is not first of all given to him as a collection of objects to which he later attributes functions and meanings. Things are always already given to him provided with a meaning, and they can only appear as things insofar as they are inserted in a totality of meanings which he already possesses. . . . We could say in other words that the world is only given to us if we always already have (originarily, before any particular experience) a certain "patrimony of ideas" or certain "prejudices" that guide us in the discovery of things. It is like reading a book: everyone has experienced the fact that a book only speaks to us when we are "searching" for something in it. Or, as Plato says, we only recognize the true when we encounter it because, in some way, we already know it. (Vattimo, p. 38)

*Chapter 5: Anti-*Vida, *Anti-*Razo

1. As Dragonetti demonstrates in *La vie de la lettre au moyen âge* (Paris: Éditions du Seuil, 1980), pp. 13–40, the name "Chrétien de Troyes" signifies a set of

binary oppositions generated by the differences between the Middle Ages (Christendom) and Antiquity (Troy). Historically, it was never possible to be a "Chrétien de Troyes," a "Christian from Troy." The name is a conjunction of contradictions. One might regard song's anonymity as a "Christian" humility while regarding story's concern with individual and heroic fame as a classical, epic or "Trojan" impulse. Thus "Chrétien de Troyes" is the name of lyrico-narrativity, the name of the twelfth century's concern with contrary representations of the self.

2. "Just as the writer of narrative must withdraw from human company into his *clausum cubiculum*, as Quintilian puts it, in order to thrash out the text that he will later perform before the public, so too the questing knight must withdraw from the court, enclose himself in his armor, and depart alone into the wilderness in order to invent, by his deeds, a story that he will later submit to the *iudicium* of his peers in the court. A hero's quest as a knight, like Chrétien's as a writer, is to produce the best possible story" (Eugene Vance, *From Topic to Tale: Logic and Narrativity in the Middle Ages* [Minneapolis: University of Minnesota Press, 1987], p. 8).

3. Georges Duby:

> The exemplary figure that literature placed at center stage was that of the knight on the march, alone in the wilderness, surrounded by dangers and face to face with the disquieting presence of the woman or the fairy. So far from the scrutiny of others, however, who was in a position to judge him, who could appreciate his value and award his prize? The action of romance therefore takes place in two different settings, one solitary, the other crowded with people: the forest and the court. The literature to which I refer is rightly named *courtly* literature. It has a predilection for sylvan settings, but these are depicted as the obverse of the real world, a countervalue. In reality, the instruction of which the romances were one instrument was carried out in the courts. The knight who wished to advance in the eyes of his master had to outdo his rivals. Knights lived in private communities as regimented as the monks of Cluny; for younger sons who had no hope of inheritance, distinction was everything, the basis of all social action. What the literature of escape evokes with its images of the forest is the series of selection procedures by which some knights distinguished themselves from others. Like the saintly hero to whom contemporary iconography was just beginning to give individualized features, the knightly hero separated himself from the mass of other knights and affirmed his valor through individual exploit. He exhibited his unique prowess in public victory and alone reaped the reward—it, too, unique. ("Solitude: Eleventh to Thirteenth Century," in *A History of Private Life*, vol. 2: *Revelations of the Medieval World*, ed. Georges Duby, trans. Arthur Goldhammer [Cambridge, MA: Belknap Press of Harvard University Press, 1988], pp. 517–518)

Yet Duby, like other modern readers of medieval romance, sees the knight's desire for difference as a purely positive goal unquestioned by the text. Similar in its insistence that individuality is invariably championed in romance narrative and that the pursuit of distinction is represented as an unambiguously noble quest is Robert W. Hanning's *The Individual in Twelfth-Century Romance* (New Haven, CT: Yale

University Press, 1977). As Vance points out (*From Topic to Tale*, p. 115n) Hanning's work is, from the point of view of contemporary theory, marred by its romantic notion of subjectivity (by, we might add, its pop psychological glorification of self-fulfillment that borders on a New Age divinization of the "inner being" of the individual). I cite as an example of this neo-romanticism the following passage:

> . . . the chivalric romance makes of its adventure plot the story, nay the celebration, of the necessity of men (and women) to face the fact of their private destiny, and to attempt to attain that vision which, born within the recesses of the self, makes of life a process of dynamic self-realization. The great adventure of chivalric romance is the adventure of becoming what (and who) you think you can be, of transforming the *awareness* of an inner self into an *actuality* which impresses upon the external world the fact of personal, self-chosen destiny, and therefore of an inner-determined identity. . . . Thus the chivalric romance urges the centrality of inner awareness on its audience as the key to happiness, and in the process effectively defines man as the product of inner vision shaping external experience. (Hanning, pp. 4–5)

4. See Vance, *From Topic to Tale*, pp. 8–13.

5. Sylvia Huot:

> Overall, it is possible to document a general shift of focus, in the later thirteenth and fourteenth centuries, from lyric performance to lyric composition, with the latter defined ever more insistently as an act of writing rather than one of song or declamation. Romance and *dits* with lyric insertions tend increasingly to recount the genesis of the lyrics in question, rather than to describe their performance. This concern with composition is associated with a more writerly concept of the song as specifically referential, documenting a particular experience; the fiction of many a fourteenth-century *dit amoureux* is that of the poet-lover who uses both lyric and narrative verse forms to record, in writing, the vicissitudes of his love. As the lyric voice is assimilated to that of the narrator or writer, a new poetics is defined. . . . The growth of this lyrico-writerly poetics, centered on the lyric poet as writer and author of books, reaches new heights in the fourteenth century. (*From Song to Book: The Poetics of Writing in Old French Lyric and Lyrical Narrative Poetry* [Ithaca, NY: Cornell University Press, 1987], pp. 4–5)

Unfortunately Huot simply equates—as in the phrase "lyrico-writerly," in which "writerly" substitutes for "narrative"—writing and narration, and throughout her study "writing" means the language of the individual, coherent, *auctor*-ial self. She thus argues that song, when written, must take a narrative, individualist turn. I would argue, on the contrary, that this turn is in the lyrico-narrative text the very object of the text's resistance and scorn. For the view that medieval lyrico-narrativity is meant to redeem song's historicity and to grant an "authority" to the individual writer which is valued as progressive, see also Thomas Stillinger, "Authorized Song" (Ph.D. dissertation, Cornell University, 1987); and, for the view that

Dante's *Vita Nuova* attempts to move "beyond lyric" toward narrative, see Robert Pogue Harrison, *The Body of Beatrice* (Baltimore: Johns Hopkins University Press, 1988).

6. This strategy had, as Zumthor points out, been anticipated by the late troubadours Raimon de Miraval and Uc de Saint-Circ, who had grouped songs together so that a certain ordered chronology of the love affair was suggested. See Paul Zumthor, *Langue, texte, énigme* (Paris, Éditions du Seuil, 1975), pp. 171–172.

7. On the sense of *razo* as "reason" (with implications of "reasonable"—i.e., referential, mimetic, true, serious) in troubadour usage, and on *razo*'s opposition to "foolish" or "facetious" interpretation, see Laura Kendrick, *The Game of Love: Troubadour Wordplay* (Berkeley: University of California Press, 1988), pp. 24–25 and ch. 4.

8. Laura Kendrick's otherwise excellent *The Game of Love* fails, except for a very brief mention of a single case, to recognize the ludic and self-subverting possibilities of the *razos* themselves. Instead she regards the *razos* as a monolithically "serious" genre, as a "didactic" reaction to an already existing tradition of playful and linguistically grounded hermeneutic practice (see Kendrick, ch. 4). Yet numerous *razos* may turn out to be anti-*razos*, may parody and belittle the very notion that a song could be founded upon a pre-discursive "reason."

9. Bernard de Ventadour, "Quan vei la lauseta mover," in Pierre Bec, ed., *Anthologie des troubadours*, pp. 132–134.

10. Jean Boutière and Alexander H. Schutz, *Biographies des troubadours* (Paris: A.-G. Nizet, 1964), p. 29.

11. Ibid., pp. 62–63.

12. Cf. Heidegger: "On the usual view, the work arises out of and by means of the activity of the artist. But by what and whence is the artist what he is? By the work; for to say that the work does credit to the master means that it is the work that first lets the artist emerge as master of his art. The artist is the origin of the work. The work is the origin of the the artist. Neither is without the other" ("The Origin of the Work of Art," in *Poetry, Language, Thought*, trans. Albert Hofstadter [New York: Harper & Row, 1971], p. 17).

13. "For *sens* can mean in Old French 'sign,' 'sense,' but also 'seed' or 'semen' (Latin *semino*)" (R. Howard Bloch, "The Medieval Text—'Guigemar'—as a Provocation to the Discipline of Medieval Studies," *Romanic Review* 79 [1988], p. 67).

14. Boutière and Schutz, pp. 351–352.

15. "Cette histoire se base apparemment sur la métaphore imperial dont Peire Vidal se sert souvent dans ses poésies" (Margarita Egan, ed., *Les vies des troubadours* [Paris: Union Générale d'Editions, 1985] p. 155).

Chapter 6: Lyric Secrecy

1. Guido Favati, ed., *Il Novellino* (Genoa: Fratelli Bozzi, 1970).

2. The most intelligent reading practice founded on this view of narration as a positive "breakthrough"—a view contradicted by the texts that draw our atten-

tion—is found in chapter 6 ("Beyond the Lyric") and chapter 7 ("The Narrative Breakthrough") of Robert Pogue Harrison's *The Body of Beatrice* (Baltimore: Johns Hopkins University Press, 1988).

    3. Favati, ed., *Il Novellino*, pp. 269–273. Page numbers of further citations will be given in parentheses in the main body of the text.

    4. On Old Provençal narrative, see Alberto Limentani, *L'eccezione narrativa* (Turin: Guilio Einaudi, 1977).

    5. Dragonetti:

> Un certain nombre d'envois attestent l'existence . . . d'une académie littéraire appelée le *Pui* où les trouvères étaient invités à présenter leurs chansons en vue d'un tournoi poétique. . . . Qu'était-ce au juste ce *pui*? probablement une confrérie religieuse en l'honneur de la Vierge. . . . Comment expliquer à présent les rapports entre la confrérie religieuse et l'académie poétique? . . . Il est à peu près certain . . . qu'une assemblée composée pour la majeure partie de poètes, autorisait sans doute, après les solennités pieuses, des récitations de poésies profanes d'où le *Pui* tire ses origines. . . . Ils l'appellent *Puy Notre-Dame*. (*La technique poétique des trouvères dans la chanson courtoise: contribution à l'étude de la rhétorique médiévale* [Bruges: Rijksuniversiteit te Gent, 1960], p. 371–373)

The *Pui*, which appears to have originated in Arras, was also a widespread institution throughout the region of the *langue d'oc*.

    6. Favati, ed., *Il Novellino*, p. 269. For a thorough treatment of various philological questions raised by this tale, see Favati's "La novella LXIV del *Novellino* e Uc de Saint Circ," *Lettere Italiane* XI (1959): 133–173.

    7. This representation of the individual's separation or distinction from the crowd is perhaps the most significant of the discursive transformations that mark the late Middle Ages: E. B. Vitz:

> Je soutiendrai que la période médiévale a presque exclusivement pratiqué le placement des personnages (spécialement, mais non exclusivement, des héros) sur l'axe vertical, tenant compte de ce qui les plaçait *au-dessus* ou *au-dessous*, mais non point *à part*, du commun des mortels. Au Moyen Age, les héros (les protagonistes) sont définis par la *quantité* de leurs qualités, et non par la *qualité* de leurs qualités, non par la forme particulière que ces qualités prennent. Les héros possèdent, soit dans l'absolu, soit, dans certains cas, à un très haut degré, certaines caractéristiques, et ils les possèdent sans autre précision ni différenciation. ("Type et individu dans l'autobiographie médiévale," *Poétique*, 1975, pp. 430–431)

Vitz's excellent article fails to see that it is just that differentiation of the hero from courtly society—which is to say the differentiation of the "author" from the *jongleur* (I am thinking once again of one of the first romances, Chrétien's *Yvain*, and of the prologue of Chrétien's *Erec et Enide*)—that is one of the announced aims, one of the novelties, of medieval narration.

    8. Georges Duby:

In the final third of the twelfth century the hermit played a leading role in stories devised for the amusement of knights, most of them composed in northwestern France. There were two main reasons for this: first, the forest was one of the two primary sites of action in medieval romance, and the hermit's natural place in this period and region was in the woods; second and most important, the chansons and romances were composed as compensations for the frustrations of private life in the feudal era, which so severely cramped individual aspirations. The works depicted in imaginary form that which the young men who formed the most receptive part of their audience had to do without. Literature exalted the individual and celebrated his flourishing in freedom from all constraint. Alone and unsupervised, the hermit represented a tolerant form of Christianity, a religion freed from the straitjacket of ritual. And freedom, too, from domestic promiscuity: the knight errant traveled alone, led solely by his desires. ("Solitude: Eleventh to Thirteenth Century," in *A History of Private Life*, vol. 2: *Revelations of the Medieval World*, ed. Georges Duby, trans. Arthur Goldhammer [Cambridge, MA: Belknap Press of Harvard University Press, 1988], p. 517)

9. The phrase *gentil cuore* is perhaps the most frequently repeated linguistic convention of the Italian tradition of courtly love lyric known, since Dante called it such, as the *dolce stil nuovo*.

10. The *auctor*, the origin or source of a discourse, is regarded by the official or orthodox Middle Ages with great respect; the *actor* or *mimus*, performer of another's language, is regarded with relative scorn. The distinction between *auctor* and *actor* also refers to "a distinction between mere writers (*actores*) and writers who are authorities (*auctores*)" (A. J. Minnis, *Medieval Theory of Authorship* [2nd ed.; Philadelphia: University of Pennsylvania Press, 1986], p. 26).

11. On the resistance to novelty/narrativity in *La Châtelaine de Vergi*, see Paul Zumthor, *Langue, texte, énigme* (Paris: Éditions du Seuil, 1975), pp. 219–36.

12. Natalino Sapegno, ed., *Poeti minori del trecento* (Milan: Riccardo Ricciardi, 1952), p. 824.

Chapter 7: Four Lovers

1. Marie de France, *Lais*, ed. Jean Rychner (Paris: Champion, 1968), pp. 142–150.

2. As Giorgio Agamben remarks (*Il linguaggio e la morte: un seminario sul longo della negatività* [Turin: Giulio Einaudi, 1982], p. 50), the Middle Ages regarded the pronoun as signifying *substantiam sine qualitate* ("substance without qualities")—i.e., pure existence *prior to* any specific determination of its "individualizing" qualities.

3. On the probability that Marie, generally throughout her *Lais*, uses the word *reisun* or *raison* to mean *conte* or "story," see Mariantonia Liborio's introduction to her edition of *Storie di dame e trovatori di Provenza* (Milan: Bompiani, 1982), pp. 12–14.

4. For an excellent treatment of some related issues in Marie de France, see R.

Howard Bloch's "New Philology and Old French," in *Speculum* 65 (1990): 38–58, as well as Bloch's "The Dead Nightingale: Orality in the Tomb of Old French Literature," *Culture and History* 3 (1988): 63–78.

Chapter 8: Nameless Lovers

1. Achille Jubinal, ed., *Jongleurs et trouvères* (Paris: Merklein, 1835), pp. 119–122.

Chapter 9: The Eaten Heart

1. Jean Boutière and Alexander H. Schutz, *Biographies des troubadours* (Paris: A.-G. Nizet, 1964), pp. 530–531.
2. On the literalization of the metaphorical heart, see Giuseppe Mazzotta, "The Heart of Love," in his *The World at Play in Boccaccio's 'Decameron'* (Princeton, NJ: Princeton University Press, 1986), esp. p. 149.
3. Giovanni Boccaccio, *Decameron*, ed. Cesare Segre (Milan: Mursia, 1966), p. 309.
4. Ibid., p. 307.
5. Mazzotta, "The Heart of Love," p. 152.
6. "the self-mirroring of the two knights, of which friendship is the symbol, hides a desire for a difference which violence seals" (ibid., p. 153).
7. *Decameron*, p. 309.
8. On questions concerning the "entombment of the voice" in medieval literature, see Alexandre Leupin, *Le Graal et la littérature: étude sur la vulgate arthurienne en prose* (Lausanne: L'Âge d'Homme, 1982).

Chapter 10: Lyric Ignorance

1. *Le Lai d'Ignauré ou Lai du prisonnier*, ed. Rita Lejeune (Brussels: Académie Royale de Langue et de Littérature Françaises de Belgique, 1938).
2. This *topos* stems from

> a long exegetical tradition centered upon the powerful parable in Matthew 13 where Christ compares the revelation of the Word of God to the sowing of seeds, a parable that gave rise in the Middle Ages to daring analogies between speaking and the ejaculation of semen. . . . Alain de Lille had gone especially far in underscoring the analogy between laws of copulation that must govern the proper regeneration of natural species and laws of grammar, dialectics, and rhetoric. . . . He is no less forceful in depicting the relationship between the misdirected seminal flows of phallus and pen, an analogy that would later be made more famous by Jean de Meung. (Eugene Vance, "The Differing Seed: Dante's Brunetto Latini," in *Mervelous Signals: Poetics and Sign Theory in the Middle Ages* [Lincoln: University of Nebraska Press, 1986], pp. 239–240)

3. Pierre Bec, ed., *Anthologie des troubadours* (Paris: Union Générale d'Éditions, 1979), p. 79.
4. Achille Jubinal, ed., *Jongleurs et trouvères* (Paris: Merklein, 1835), p. 182.
5. Jean Boutière and Alexander H. Schutz, *Biographies des troubadours* (Paris: A.-G. Nizet, 1964), p. 441.
6. See Rita Lejeune, "Le personnage d'Ignauré dans la poésie des troubadours," *Bulletin de l'Académie Royale de Langue et de Littérature Françaises de Belgique* 18 (1939), 140–172. See also Maurice Delbouille, "Les 'senhals' désignant Raimbaut d'Orange," *Cultura Neolatina* 17 (1957), 59–63.
7. Or, according to Delbouille ("Les senhals," p. 63), Raimbaut's *senhal* (*Linhaura*) may have been inspired by an earlier version of the *Lai d'Ignauré* (which itself post-dates Raimbaut). Yet we cannot definitively decide whether Raimbaut d'Aurenga was named after Ignauré or whether Ignauré was named after Raimbaut d'Aurenga.
8. On the relation between private confession and the rise of the notion of the individual self in courtly literature, see R. Howard Bloch, *Medieval French Literature and Law* (Berkeley: University of California Press, 1977), pp. 229–231.
9. Cited by Delbouille ("Les senhals," p. 63), who makes the following comment: "Raimbaut d'Orange raconte, en effet, qu'il a été châtré par un mari jaloux.... Enorme plaisanterie où le poète, sans pourtant invoquer aucun précédent, se vante d'avoir connu mésaventure pareille à celle qui rendait fameux le nom d'*Ignaure-Linhaura*." And, incidentally, near the end of this same song Raimbaut speaks of this castration as a loss of *podér* ("power," "potency," *puissanche*).
10. On the relation between the *trou* and the *trouvère*, see R. Howard Bloch, "Silence and Holes: The *Roman de Silence* and the Art of the Trouvère," *Yale French Studies* 70 (1986): 81–99.
11. The anagrammatical inscription of names in the text is extremely common in the thirteenth and fourteenth centuries—and especially so in the lyrico-narrative tradition. For numerous examples, see Sylvia Huot, *From Song to Book: The Poetics of Writing in Old French Lyric and Lyrical Narrative Poetry* (Ithaca, NY: Cornell University Press, 1987), passim.

Chapter 11: Narrative Breakdown

1. For an excellent reading of aspects of *Joufroi de Poitiers* that I shall leave unexamined, see Roger Dragonetti, "Joufroi, Count of Poitiers and Lord of Cocaigne," *Yale French Studies* (1984): 95–119.
2. See Michel Zink, *Roman rose et rose rouge: le Roman de la Rose ou de Guillaume de Dole, de Jean Renart* (Paris: A.-G. Nizet, 1979), p. 29: "Il n'a pas révélé un accord en réunissant un roman et des chansons préexistantes. Il a créé cet accord en jouant du seul élément dont il était maître, le roman, puisqu'il recueillait les chansons telles quelles. Autrement dit, il a composé son roman à partir des chansons."
3. Percival B. Fay and John L. Grigsby, eds., *Joufroi de Poitiers* (Geneva: Droz, 1972).

4. Cf. Fay and Grigsby, p. 20: "On pourrait conjecturer que cette *Vida* de Guillaume VII, sous une autre forme peut-être, était tombée sous les yeux de notre auteur, et que celui-ci s'était complu à l'idée de mettre en rime une nouvelle « vie » du célèbre troubadour."

5. But this "realism" is, as Dragonetti's essay on *Joufroi* amply demonstrates, a ruse—since the lives of the "characters" turn out to be dictated and determined by the play of the letter.

6. Chrétien's *Perceval* and Chaucer's *House of Fame* come readily to mind as works that are significantly incomplete.

Chapter 12: Chaucer's Evening Sickness

1. In medieval numerical theory, the distinction between odd and even numbers is, among other things, a distinction between the principles of self-identity and self-difference, between stability and mobility. R. Howard Bloch:

> If Adam exists fully and Eve only partially, it is because he participates in what is imagined to be an original unity of being, while she is the offshoot of division and difference. This association translates even into what might be thought of as a medieval metaphysics of number, according to which, under the Platonic and Pythagorean schema, all created things express either the principle of self-identity (*principium ejusdem*) ["oddness"] or of continuous self-alteration (*principium alterius*) ["evenness"]. The first is associated with unity, the monad; the second with multiplicity, dyadic structures.... "It must be said," we read in a fragment from Eudorus, "that the Pythagoreans postulated on the highest level the One as a first principle, and then on a secondary level two principles of existent things, the One and the nature opposed to this.... One of them is called by them ordered, limited, knowable, male, *odd*, right, and light; the one opposed to this is called disordered, unlimited, unknowable, female, left, *even*, and darkness." Of the two principles, "one expresses stability, the other endless variation," writes Boethius. "Here [i.e., in the even] is change and alteration, there [i.e., in the odd] the force of fixity. Here [i.e., in the odd], well determined solidity, there [i.e., in the even] the fragmentation of infinite multiplicity. (Bloch, *Medieval Misogyny and the Invention of Western Romantic Love* [Chicago: University of Chicago Press, 1991], pp. 25–26 [emphasis added])

As our reading unfolds, we shall see that the narrator of *The Book of the Duchess*, in representing himself as constitutionally *even*, is representing himself as ruled by the *principium alterius*, the principle of "continuous self-alteration" and "infinite multiplicity."

2. I am using the text of the *Book of the Duchess* edited by John H. Fisher in his *The Complete Poetry and Prose of Geoffrey Chaucer* (New York: Holt, Rinehart and Winston, 1977). All citations will be noted parenthetically by line numbers in the main body of the text.

3. On Chaucer's knowledge of the continental lyrico-narrative tradition and its manifestation in the *Book*, see James I. Wimsatt, *Chaucer and the French Love Poets: The Literary Background of "The Book of the Duchess"* (Chapel Hill: University of North Carolina Press, 1968).

4. "These lines, modeled upon ll. 1–9 of Froissart's *Paradys d'Amour*, reveal how these early pieces were exercises in adapting the French poetic idiom to English" (Fisher, in *Chaucer*, p. 544).

5. "Margaret Galway has proposed that it is a specific tribute to Joan of Kent.... In 1369, she had been married for eight years to the Black Prince, eldest son of Edward III" (Fisher, in Chaucer, p. 544). See also John N. Palmer, "The Historical Context of the Book of the Duchess: A Revision," *Chaucer Review* 8 (1974): 253; John M. Hill, "The *Book of the Duchess*, Melancholy, and That Eight-Year Sickness," *Chaucer Review* 9 (1975): 35–50; Edward I. Condren, "Of Deaths and Duchesses and Scholars Coughing in Ink," *Chaucer Review* 10 (1976), 87–95.

6. One may wish to consider in this regard Chaucer's use, in the *Summoner's Tale*, of the phrase *ars-metrik* to name that hermeneutics concerned with the discourse of the *arse*. The arithmetical question posed by the tail at the end of that tale concerns the problem of division with specific reference to the even number twelve and the odd number thirteen.

7. Citations of *The Franklin's Tale* are from Fisher's edition.

8. See Sylvia Huot, *From Song to Book: The Poetics of Writing in Old French Lyric and Lyrical Narrative Poetry* (Ithaca, NY: Cornell University Press, 1987); Thomas Stillinger, "Authorized Song," Ph.D. diss., Cornell University, 1987; Robert Pogue Harrison, *The Body of Beatrice* (Baltimore: Johns Hopkins University Press, 1988).

9. For a reading of courtly lyric in terms of A. J. Greimas' actantial scheme, see Eugene Vance, "The Châtelain de Coucy: Enunciation and Story in *Trouvère* Lyric," in his *Mervelous Signals: Poetics and Sign Theory in the Middle Ages* (Lincoln: University of Nebraska Press, 1986) pp. 86–110.

10. See Frederick Goldin, *The Mirror of Narcissus in the Courtly Love Lyric* (Ithaca, NY: Cornell University Press, 1967).

11. For an example of criticism's habit of attributing these words to Seyes, see Donald R. Howard, *Chaucer: His Life, His Works, His World* (New York: E. P. Dutton, 1987), p. 154: "The simple words of the deceased Seyx to the living Alcione." And even a reader so accutely aware of hermeneutic complexities as Judith Ferster speaks, in her *Chaucer on Interpretation* (Cambridge: Cambridge University Press, 1985), of Morpheus's words as if they were "the king's [i.e., Seyes's] command."

12. Fisher, in *Chaucer*, p. 543: "In spite of attempts to show how appropriate it is as an introduction, the story of Seyes and Alcyone remains a distraction. The poem does not really get started until the dream begins at l. 291."

13. On repetition in the *Book*, with special reference to Freud, see A. C. Spearing, *Medieval Dream Poetry* (Cambridge: Cambridge University Press, 1976), pp. 49–73.

14. For a very good account of Chaucer's dream-visions from the perpective of Gadamarian hermeneutics, see Ferster.

15. See, for instance, Sandra Pierson Prior, "*Routhe* and *Hert-Huntyng* in the *Book of the Duchess*," *Journal of English and Germanic Philology* (1986): 3–19.

16. Fisher, in *Chaucer*, p. 550.

17. Ibid., p. 562.

18. Ibid., p. 550: "John of Gaunt . . . was 29 in 1369, about the same age as Chaucer himself. Manly suggested that 24 may have resulted from scribal misreading of xxiv for xxix. . . . Perhaps, as sometimes today, it was a compliment to underestimate the age of a prince."

19. Donald R. Howard nicely formulates an account of the dreamer's failure to understand the Man's song, yet in the end this account falls back into a humanist privileging of the "core" or signified that is absolutely typical of modern critical approaches to the *Book*:

> On the surface of things it seems absurd that the narrator cannot understand what is so plainly stated in the complaint, and critics of a previous generation reckoned this a flaw because it seemed improbable. But what the narrator hears is an entirely conventional verse, the complaint of a forlorn lover; there is no reason for him to suppose it states a fact or explains, rather than expresses, the Knight's sorrowful mood. What the narrator cannot understand is that beneath the conventionality of the verse lies a stark reality. Why should he? If you came upon a cowboy in a field singing to himself a typical cowboy song about death, would you conclude that someone had really died? That is exactly the narrator's circumstance: he wants to know why the knight is sad, wants to help him, tells him it may ease his heart to tell his story, but doesn't see that the conventional song stated the facts. This central moment in the poem serves as an instruction to the reader about how to read the poem: we must seek beneath—or in—its conventionality its core of human feeling and human truth. (*Chaucer*, p. 156)

20. This point was perhaps first formulated in W. H. French's excellent article, "The Man in Black's Lyric," *Journal of English and Germanic Philology* 56 (1957): 231–241.

21. Fisher, in Chaucer, p. 551.

22. See Diane M. Ross, "The Play of Genres in the *Book of the Duchess*," *Chaucer Review* 19 (1984), 1–13, esp. p. 7:

> The *Book of the Duchess* . . . asserts that narrative must overpower lyric if a story is to be told and communication achieved. This is not to deny that lyric can accomplish anything on its own. Chaucer permits lyric to convey emotion, both in the *Book of the Duchess* and elsewhere. Yet in a number of poems Chaucer insists that lyric and song in themselves leave us unsatisfied. Despite the medieval belief that music and words together might foster spiritual harmony, Chaucer's poems move beyond lyric to narrative. During the heavenly journey in the *House of Fame* the narrator Geffrey moves through and beyond the spheres in which music is produced, to the House of Rumor, in search of non-musical "tidings." Similarly, at the end of the *Parliament of Fowls*

the charming lyric conclusion provided by the birds is followed by the narrator's resolution to "rede alway." Song is not enough.

23. See Piero Boitani, *English Medieval Narrative in the Thirteenth and Fourteenth Centuries* (Cambridge: Cambridge University Press, 1982), p. 141: " If it is true that Chaucer wrote many lyrics—including love lyrics—that have not survived, and if it is true that the *Book of the Duchess* is the earliest of his surviving narrative works, than we can see in it a transposition of lyric into narrative. The transformation takes place before our eyes."

24. This line of thought is championed by Jerome Mandel in his "Courtly Love in the *Canterbury Tales*," *Chaucer Review* 19 (1985), 277–289, an article that concludes (p. 288) that there is no courtly love in Chaucer's great narrative collection: "Though Chaucer ranks among the great poets of love in the English language, by the time he came to write the *Canterbury Tales* he no longer looked upon the language, tenets, or characteristics of courtly love as a viable way of expressing what occurs in the human heart."

25. It has become in recent years a commonplace of Chaucer criticism that the *newe tydyngs* announced, anticipated, yet not delivered at the end of the *House of Fame* signify a new mode of literary representation—the realistic mimesis of local history that is finally delivered in the *Canterbury Tales*.

26. On the relation between language and Fortune in Chaucer (and for some very good speculation concerning the singularization of plural signs), see Julian N. Wasserman, "Both Fixed and Free: Language and Destiny in Chaucer's *Knight's Tale* and *Troilus and Criseyde*, in *Sign, Sentence, Discourse: Language in Medieval Thought and Literature*, ed. Julian N. Wasserman and Lois Y. Roney (Syracuse, NY: Syracuse University Press, 1989), pp. 194–222.

27. Consider Fisher's gloss (Chaucer, p. 556) on the Man in Black's description of his lady—a gloss which gives the lie to the Man's claim that she is like no other, for in fact she is like all other such ladies: "The following moving description of the lady is in fact pieced together from lines translated from the *Romance of the Rose*, poems of Machaut and Deschamps that Chaucer had used throughout, and examples in Geoffrey of Vinsauf's handbook of rhetoric, *Poetria Nova*."

28. For a good treatment of blankness and inscription in the *Book*, see Ferster.

29. See Fisher, in Chaucer, p. 562.

30. See Phillip C. Boardman, "Courtly Language and the Strategy of Consolation in the *Book of the Duchess*," *English Literary History* 44 (1977):

> The narrator must finally give over all attempts at courtly poetry. . . . The language the knight must use to describe his lady and his grief has proved inadequate to the depth of his feelings; while the knight gains some consolation by remembering the bliss he formerly had, the dreamer-poet is not brought into understanding and sympathy until faced with the blunt, unpoetic, uncourtly truth, "She ys ded!" The fragile distance at which the courtly vision must be held can be seen in the way the narrator struggles to interpret the knight's experience at the level of his own eight-years suffering. In the end, the courtly vision which had shaped the narrator's understanding of love,

death, and poetry shrivels in the face of the real experience of love and death expressed in the knight. (p. 574)

31. Is it mere chance that the *Book* numbers exactly 1,334 verses—a number that disarms, by evening, the exemplary oddness of the more numerologically significant 1,333?

Bibliography

Agamben, Giorgio. *Il linguaggio e la morte: un seminario sul longo della negatività*. Turin: Giulio Einaudi, 1982.
———. *Stanze: la parola e il fantasma nella cultura occidentale*. Turin: Giulio Einaudi, 1977.
Aurell, Martin. *La vielle et l'épée: troubadours et politique au XIII siècle*. Paris: Aubier Montaigne, 1989.
Bakhtin, Mikhail. *The Dialogic Imagination: Four Essays*. Ed. Michael Holquist, trans. Caryl Emerson and Michael Holquist. Austin: University of Texas Press, 1981.
———. *Rabelais and His World*. Trans. Helene Iswolsky. Bloomington: Indiana University Press, 1984.
Barbazan, Étienne, ed. *Le Castoiement, ou Instruction, du père à son fils*. Paris: 1760.
Baumgartner, Emmanuèle. "Trouvères et *Losengiers*." *Cahiers de Civilisation Médiévale* 25 (1982): 171–178.
Baumgartner, Emmanuèle and Françoise Ferrand, eds. *Poèmes d'amour des XII et XIII siècles*. Paris: Union Générale d'Éditions, 1983.
Bec, Pierre, ed. *Anthologie des troubadours*. Paris: Union Générale d'Éditions, 1979.
Benveniste, Émile. *Problems in General Linguistics*. Trans. Mary Elizabeth Meek. Coral Gables, FL: University of Miami Press, 1971.
Bloch, R. Howard. "The Dead Nightingale: Orality in the Tomb of Old French Literature." *Culture and History* 3 (1988): 63–78.
———. *Medieval French Literature and Law*. Berkeley: University of California Press, 1977.
———. *Medieval Misogyny and the Invention of Western Romantic Love*. Chicago: University of Chicago Press, 1991.
———. "The Medieval Text—'*Guigemar*'—as a Provocation to the Discipline of Medieval Studies." *Romanic Review* 79 (1988): 63–73.
———. "New Philology and Old French." *Speculum* 65 (1990): 38–58.
———. "Silence and Holes: The *Roman de Silence* and the Art of the Trouvère." *Yale French Studies* 70 (1986): 81–99.
Boardman, Phillip C. "Courtly Language and the Strategy of Consolation in the *Book of the Duchess*." *English Literary History* 44 (1977): 567–579.
Boccaccio, Giovanni. *Decameron*. Ed. Cesare Segre. Milan: Mursia, 1966.
Boitani, Piero. *English Medieval Narrative in the Thirteenth and Fourteenth Centuries*. Cambridge: Cambridge University Press, 1982.
Boutière, Jean and Alexander H. Schutz. *Biographies des troubadours*. Paris: A.-G. Nizet, 1964.

Burckhardt, Jakob. *The Civilization of the Renaissance in Italy*. Trans. S. G. C. Middlemore. London: Phaidon Press, 1955.

Cerquiglini, Jacqueline. *"Un engin si soutil": Guillaume de Machaut et l'Écriture au XIV siècle*. Geneva and Paris: Éditions Slatkine, 1985.

Chaucer, Geoffrey. *The Complete Poetry and Prose of Geoffrey Chaucer*. Ed. John H. Fisher. New York: Holt, Rinehart and Winston, 1977.

Condren, Edward I. "Of Deaths and Duchesses and Scholars Coughing in Ink." *Chaucer Review* 10 (1976): 87–95.

Conon de Béthune. *Les chansons de Conon de Béthune*. Ed. Axel Wallensköld. Paris: Champion, 1921.

Culler, Jonathan D. *On Deconstruction: Theory and Criticism After Structuralism*. Ithaca, NY: Cornell University Press, 1982.

Dante. *De Vulgari Eloquentia*. In *Literary Criticism of Dante Alighieri*. Trans. Robert S. Haller. Lincoln: University of Nebraska Press, 1973.

Delbouille, Maurice. "Les 'senhals' désignant Raimbaut d'Orange." *Cultura Neolatina* 17 (1957): 59–63.

Delbouille, Maurice, ed. *Le Lai d'Aristote*. Paris: Bibliothèque de la Faculté de Philosophie et Lettres de l'Université de Liège, 1951.

Dragonetti, Roger. "Joufroi, Count of Poitiers and Lord of Cocaigne." *Yale French Studies* (1984): 95–119.

———. *La technique poétique des trouvères dans la chanson courtoise: Contribution à l'étude de la rhétorique médiévale*. Bruges: Rijksuniversiteit te Gent, 1960.

———. *La vie de la lettre au moyen âge: le conte du Graal*. Paris: Éditions du Seuil, 1980.

Duby, Georges. "Solitude: Eleventh to Thirteenth Century." In *A History of Private Life*, vol. 2: *Revelations of the Medieval World*. Ed. Georges Duby, trans. Arthur Goldhammer. Cambridge, MA: Belknap Press of Harvard University Press, 1988.

Egan, Margarita, ed. *Les Vies des troubadours*. Paris: Union Générale d'Editions, 1985.

Favati, Guido. "La novella LXIV del *Novellino* e Uc de Saint Circ." *Lettere Italiane* 11 (1959): 133–173.

Favati, Guido, ed. *Il Novellino*. Genoa: Fratelli Bozzi, 1970.

Fay, Percival B. and John L. Grigsby, eds. *Joufroi de Poitiers: Roman d'adventures du 13e siècle*. Geneva: Droz, 1972.

Ferrante, Joan. "Was Vernacular Poetic Practice a Response to Latin Language Theory?" *Romance Philology* 35 (1982): 586–600.

Ferster, Judith. *Chaucer on Interpretation*. Cambridge: Cambridge University Press, 1985.

French, W. H. "The Man in Black's Lyric." *Journal of English and Germanic Philology* 56 (1957): 231–41.

The French Fabliau, B.N. MS. 837. Ed. and trans. R. Eichmann and J. Duval. New York: Garland, 1984.

Goldin, Frederick. *The Mirror of Narcissus in the Courtly Love Lyric*. Ithaca, NY: Cornell University Press, 1967.

Guiette, Robert. "D'une poésie formelle en France au moyen âge." *Revue des Sciences Humaines* (April–June 1949): 61–68.

Haidu, Peter. "Text and History: The Semiosis of Twelfth-Century Lyric as Sociohistorical Phenomenon," *Semiotica* 33 (1981): 1–62.
Hanning, Robert W. *The Individual in Twelfth-Century Romance*. New Haven, CT: Yale University Press, 1977.
Harrison, Robert Pogue. *The Body of Beatrice*. Baltimore: Johns Hopkins University Press, 1988.
Heidegger, Martin. *Being and Time*. Trans. John Macquarrie and Edward Robinson. New York: Harper and Row, 1962.
———. "The Origin of the Work of Art." In *Poetry, Language, Thought*, trans. Albert Hofstadter. New York: Harper and Row, 1971.
Hill, John M. "The *Book of the Duchess*, Melancholy, and That Eight-Year Sickness." *Chaucer Review* 9 (1975): 35–50.
Howard, Donald R. *Chaucer: His Life, His Works, His World*. New York: E. P. Dutton, 1987.
Huchet, Jean-Charles. *L'amour discourtois: la "Fin'amours" chez les premiers troubadours*. Toulouse: Privat, 1987.
Huot, Sylvia. *From Song to Book: The Poetics of Writing in Old French Lyric and Lyrical Narrative Poetry*. Ithaca, NY: Cornell University Press, 1987.
Jubinal, Achille, ed. *Jongleurs et trouvères*. Paris: Merklein, 1835.
Kendrick, Laura. *The Game of Love: Troubadour Wordplay*. Berkeley: University of California Press, 1988.
Koehler, Erich. "Observations historiques et sociologiques sur la poésie des troubadours." *Cahiers de Civilisation Médiévale* 7 (1964): 27–47.
Le Lai d'Ignauré ou Lai du prisonnier. Ed. Rita Lejeune. Brussels: Académie Royale de Langue et de Littérature Françaises de Belgique, 1938.
Lacan, Jacques. *Écrits: A Selection*. Trans. Alan Sheridan. New York: Norton, 1977.
———. *The Four Fundamental Concepts of Psycho-Analysis*. Trans. Alan Sheridan. New York: Norton, 1977.
Langholm, Odd. *Economics in the Medieval Schools*. Leiden and New York: E. J. Brill, 1992.
Lejeune, Rita. "Le personnage d'Ignauré dans la poésie des troubadours." *Bulletin de l'Académie Royale de Langue et de Littérature Françaises de Belgique* 18 (1939): 140–72.
Leupin, Alexandre. *Le Graal et la littérature: étude sur la vulgate arthurienne en prose*. Lausanne: L'Âge d'Homme, 1982.
Liborio, Mariantonia, ed. *Storie di dame e trovatori di Provenza*. Milan: Bompiani, 1982.
Limentani, Alberto. *L'eccezione narrativa*. Turin: Giulio Einaudi, 1977.
Machaut, Guillaume de. *Le Livre du Voir-Dit de Guillaume de Machaut*. Ed. Paulin Paris. Paris: Société des Bibliophiles Français, 1875.
Mandel, Jerome. "Courtly Love in the *Canterbury Tales*." *Chaucer Review* 19 (1985): 277–89.
Marie de France. *Lais*. Ed. Jean Rychner. Paris: Champion, 1968.
Marshall, J. H., ed. *The 'Razos de trobar' of Raimon Vidal and Associated Texts*. London: Oxford University Press, 1972.
Mazzotta, Giuseppe. *The World at Play in Boccaccio's "Decameron"*. Princeton, NJ: Princeton University Press, 1986.

Minnis, A. J. *Medieval Theory of Authorship*. 2nd ed. Philadelphia: University of Pennsylvania Press, 1988.

Palmer, John N. "The Historical Context of the Book of the Duchess: A Revision." *Chaucer Review* 8 (1974): 253–261.

Patterson, Lee. "On the Margin: Postmodernism, Ironic History, and Medieval Studies." *Speculum* 65 (1990): 87–108.

Pauphilet, Albert, ed. *Poètes et romanciers du moyen âge*. Paris: Gallimard, 1939.

Poe, Elizabeth Wilson. *From Poetry to Prose in Old Provençal: The Emergence of the "Vidas," the "Razos," and the "Razos de trobar."* Birmingham, AL: Summa, 1984.

Prior, Sandra Pierson. "*Routhe* and *Hert-Huntyng* in the *Book of the Duchess*." *Journal of English and Germanic Philology* (1986): 3–19.

Renart, Jean. *Le Roman de la Rose ou de Guillaume de Dole*. Ed. Félix Lecoy. Paris: Honoré Champion, 1979.

Ross, Diane M. "The Play of Genres in the *Book of the Duchess*." *Chaucer Review* 19 (1984): 1–13.

Sapegno, Natalino. ed. *Poeti minori del trecento*. Milan: Riccardo Ricciardi, 1952.

de Saussure, Ferdinand. *Course in General Linguistics*. Ed. Charles Bally and Albert Sechehaye in collaboration with Albert Reidlinger, trans. Wade Baskin. New York: Philosophical Library, 1959.

Simmel, Georg. "Das Individuum und die Freiheit." In *Brücke und Tür: Essays des Philosophen zur Geschichte, Religion, Kunst und Gesellschaft*. Stuttgart: Köhler, 1957.

———. "Die Mode." In *Philosophische Kultur*, pp. 31–64. 3rd ed. Potsdam: Kiepenheuer, 1923.

———. *On Individuality and Social Forms: Selected Writings*. Ed. Donald N. Levine. Chicago and London: University of Chicago Press, 1971.

Spearing, A. C. *Medieval Dream Poetry*. Cambridge: Cambridge University Press, 1976.

Stillinger, Thomas. "Authorized Song." Ph.D. dissertation, Cornell University, 1987.

Thurot, C. "Extraits de divers manuscrits latins pour servir à l'histoire des doctrines grammaticales au moyen âge." In *Notices et extraits des manuscrits de la Bibliothèque Nationale*, vol. 22. Paris: 1974.

Vance, Eugene. "The Châtelain de Coucy: Enunciation and Story in *Trouvère* Lyric." In Vance, *Mervelous Signals: Poetics and Sign Theory in the Middle Ages*, 86–110. Lincoln: University of Nebraska Press, 1986.

———. *From Topic to Tale: Logic and Narrativity in the Middle Ages*. Minneapolis: University of Minnesota Press, 1987.

Vattimo, Gianni. *Introduzione a Heidegger*. Bari and Rome: Gius. Laterza & Figli, 1971.

Vitz, E. B. "Type et individu dans l'autobiographie médiévale." *Poétique* 21 (1975): 426–445.

Wasserman, Julian N. "Both Fixed and Free: Language and Destiny in Chaucer's *Knight's Tale* and *Troilus and Criseyde*." In *Sign, Sentence, Discourse: Language in Medieval Thought and Literature*, ed. Julian N. Wasserman and Lois Y. Roney. Syracuse, NY: Syracuse University Press, 1989.

Wimsatt, James I. *Chaucer and the French Love Poets: The Literary Background of "The Book of the Duchess."* Chapel Hill: University of North Carolina Press, 1968.

Zai, Marie-Claire, ed. *Les chansons courtoises de Chrétien de Troyes*. Berne and Frankfurt: Lang and Lang, 1974.

Zink, Michel. *Roman rose et rose rouge: le Roman de la Rose ou de Guillaume de Dole, de Jean Renart*. Paris: A.-G. Nizet, 1979.

Zumthor, Paul. *Essai de poétique médiévale*. Paris: Éditions du Seuil, 1972.

———. *Langue, texte, énigme*. Paris: Éditions du Seuil, 1975.

Index

Agamben, Giorgio, 199–201, 207, 213
Alain de Lille, 214
Algus, 175
allegory, 56, 184–87, 190
Andreas Cappellanus, 25
Aragon, Louis, 26
Arnaut Daniel, *razo* of, 62–65
auctor, 43–44; 50–51, 74, 152, 166, 168, 180, 213
Augustine, Saint, 18, 43, 71, 116
Aurell, Martin, 201

Bakhtin, Mikhail, 203–4
Baumgartner, Emmanuèle, 205
Bec, Pierre, 206
Bernart de Ventadorn, 61–62
birdsong, 44–46, 173
Blanche (Duchess of Lancaster), 192
Bloch, R. Howard, 211, 214–16
Boardman, Phillip C., 219
Boccaccio, Giovanni (*Decameron* IV, 9), 104–8
Boethius, 18, 43, 216
Boitani, Piero, 219
Bonaventure, Saint, 7–8
bourgeois subject, 51–55
Burckhardt, Jakob, 2–4, 199

castration, 66, 121, 123, 125–26, 129
Cerquiglini, Jacqueline, 206
Chaucer, Geoffrey, 143–98; *Book of the Duchess*, 143–49, 153–98; *Canterbury Tales*, 183, 219; "The Franklin's Tale," 149–52, 159; *House of Fame*, 216, 219; "Prologue to the *Legend of Good Women*," 178; "The Summoner's Tale," 217; *Troilus and Criseyde*, 149
chiasmus, 29, 40
Chrétien de Troyes, 23–25, 208–9; *Perceval*, 216; *Yvain*, 58–59
citationality, 35
Condren, Edward I., 217

Conon de Bethune, 21–23
Court of the Puy, 72
courtly lyric, 5–7, 12–14, 20–21, 25, 42, 45–46, 49
Culler, Jonathan, 199

Dante Alighieri, 10, 32, 213; *De Vulgari Eloquentia*, 4–5, 7–9, 14–15, 33, 43–44, 50–51, 187, 199–200; *Inferno*, 97, 143; *Vita Nuova*, 183, 211
Delbouille, Maurice, 207, 215
Des Deux Amans, 97–100
descort, 29–30
Dragonetti, Roger, 201–02, 204–05, 208, 212, 215–16
Duby, Georges, 209, 212–13

Egan, Margarita, 211
envoi, 20
Eudorus, 216
evenness, 144, 146–47, 149, 153, 173–75, 177, 179, 195–96, 216

Favati, Guido, 212
Ferrante, Joan, 203
Ferster, Judith, 217
Fisher, John H., 217, 219
fore-knowledge, 54–55
French, W. H., 218
Freud, Sigmund, 20
Froissart, Jean, 143, 183; *Paradys d'Amour*, 145, 179–80, 198, 217

Gace Brulé, 21
Goldin, Frederick, 217
grammar, 5, 13, 15–17
grammatical ego, 8, 12, 14
Greimas, A. J., 217
Guiette, Robert, 201
Guillaume de Machaut, 143, 183; *Le Voir Dit*, 33, 206–7; *La Fonteinne amoureuse*, 155, 158

Index

Guillaume de Poitiers, 136
Guillem de Cabestaing, *vida* of, 101–5, 107

Haidu, Peter, 23–24, 204–6
Hanning, Robert W., 209–10
Harrison, Robert Pogue, 211–12, 217
Heidegger, Martin, 20, 205, 211
hermeneutic circle, 55
Hill, John M., 217
historia, 8–12, 45, 62, 143, 151, 153
Howard, Donald R., 217–18
Huchet, Jean-Charles, 201, 206
Huot, Sylvia, 210, 215, 217

Il Novellino ("Novella LXIV"), 71–81, 103
individualism, 1–4, 12, 52, 59, 71, 87, 130
Jaufré Rudel, 111
Jean de Meung, 214
Jean Renart (*Le Roman de la Rose ou de Guillaume de Dole*), 10–11, 38, 134–36
Jofre de Foixà (*Regles de trobar*), 15
John of Gaunt, 176–77, 192, 197, 218
jongleur, 62–65, 167–68, 180, 186, 191, 194
Joufroi de Poitiers, 134–42

Kendrick, Laura, 211
Koehler, Erich, 205

La Châtelaine de Vergi, 80, 213
La Donna del Vergiù, 80–81
Lacan, Jacques, 205–06
Lai d'Aristote, 34–42, 47, 207
Lai de l'oiselet, 44–57
Lai d'Ignauré, 101, 109–33
Langholm, Odd, 208
langue, 14–15, 20, 70, 73, 86; vs. *parole*, 13, 16–18, 25, 45, 67, 83, 108, 119, 136, 140–41, 143
Le Sort des Dames, 111
Lejeune, Rita, 215
Leupin, Alexandre, 214
Liborio, Mariantonia, 213
Limentani, Alberto, 212
losengiers (*lauzengers*), 6, 21, 24–25, 30, 59, 74, 83, 86, 106, 113–14, 123, 146, 150, 205
lyric, 8–11
lyrico-narrative, 59, 71, 182–83, 209–10

Mandel, Jerome, 219
Map, Walter, 207
Marcabru, 136

Marie de France, 213; *Le Chaitivel* or *Les Quatre Deuls*, 82–96, 103, 114, 117, 120, 131
Marx, Karl, 20
Mazzotta, Giuseppe, 105, 214
Minnis, A. J., 200, 213

narrative, 8–9, 70, 92–93, 140–41, 143, 149, 182; subjectivity in, 58–60
Nietzsche, Friedrich, 4, 20

Ovid, 154–58, 165
oxymoron, 28, 145, 169, 186, 196–97

Palmer, John N., 217
Patterson, Lee, 199
Peire Rogier, 26–29
Peire Vidal, *vida* of, 66–70, 73, 109
Petrarch, 1, 10
Plato, 1
Poe, Elizabeth Wilson, 202
Prior, Sandra Pierson, 218
Priscian, 7, 43
pronoun, as *pro-nomen*, 7–8, 11, 85
Pythagoras, 148

Raimbaut d'Aurenga, 112–13, 121, 131, 215
Raimbaut de Vaqueiras, 29–32, 79, 115
Raimon de Miraval, 211
Raimon Vidal (*Las razos de trobar*), 14–20, 65
razos, 8–9, 59–71, 73, 92–93, 101–4, 108, 114–15, 128, 134, 136, 152–53, 211
Renaissance, idea of, 1–4, 11
Renaus de Beaujeu, 109, 131–32
rhyme, 16–17
Richart de Barbezill, *razo* of, 71, 79
Roman de la Rose. See Jean Renart
rondeau, 38
Ross, Diane M., 218

Saussure, Ferdinand de, 20, 203
senhal, 68, 94–95, 107, 110–14, 191
Simmel, Georg, 199
singing subject, 7–12, 13–14, 18, 20–21, 23, 26–27, 32, 39, 60, 76–79, 94, 103, 111, 139, 156, 164
song, 19, 42, 47–48, 54–57, 62; as origin of desire, 35–37, 46–48, 65, 137
Song of Songs (Solomon), 7–8
Spearing, A. C., 217
specularity, 29, 33–34, 36–40, 98, 154–55

Stillinger, Thomas, 210, 217
subject/object, undifferentiation of, 24, 27, 31, 33–34, 36–40, 65, 131, 164

Terramignino da Pisa (*Doctrina d'Acort*), 15
Thurot, C., 199
Thomas Aquinas, Saint, 100
troubadour, death of, 11–12, 44, 103

Uc de Saint-Circ, 211

Vance, Eugene, 58, 201, 206, 209–10, 217
Vattimo, Gianni, 208
vidas, 8–9, 59–60, 66–71, 101–4, 136
Vitz, E. B., 212

Wallensköld, Axel, 205
Wasserman, Julian N., 219
Wimsatt, James I., 217

Zink, Michel, 215
Zumthor, Paul, 201–02, 211, 213